BYRON AND JOYCE THROUGH HOMER

BYRON AND JOYCE THROUGH HOMER

Don Juan and *Ulysses*

Hermione de Almeida

Columbia University Press
New York   1981

Library of Congress Cataloging in Publication Data

De Almeida, Hermione, 1950—
  Byron and Joyce through Homer.

  Includes bibliographical references and index.
  1. English literature — History and criticism.
2. English literature — Greek influences. 3. Byron,
George Gordon Nöel Byron, Baron, 1788—1824. Don Juan.
4. Joyce, James, 1882—1941. Ulysses. 5. Homerus.
Odyssea. 6. Homerus—Influence. I. Title.
PR127.D4 1981   820'.9   80—19980
ISBN 0—231—05092—5

For two good men:
Carl Woodring and Lionel Trilling

Contents

Oh Love! O Glory! what are ye? who fly
    Around us ever, rarely to alight;
There's not a meteor in the polar sky
    Of such transcendent and more fleeting flight.
Chill, and chained to cold earth, we lift on high
    Our eyes in search of either lovely light;
A thousand and a thousand colours they
Assume, then leave us on our freezing way.

And such as they are, such my present tale is,
    A non-descript and ever varying rhyme,
A versified Aurora Borealis,
    Which flashes o'er a waste and icy clime.

(VII, 1)

My eyes are tired. For over half a century they have gazed into nullity, where they have found a lovely nothing.

(Joyce to Giorgio, 1935)

Acknowledgments

I wish to thank Random House, Inc. (New York) and the Bodley Head (London) for permission to quote from James Joyce's *Ulysses* (copyright 1914, 1918 by Margaret Anderson, renewed 1942, 1946 by Nora Joyce, 1961 by George and Lucia Joyce); Viking Penguin Inc. (New York), Jonathan Cape Ltd (London) and the Society of Authors for permission to quote from Joyce's *A Portrait of the Artist as a Young Man* (copyright 1916 by B. W. Heubsch, 1944 by Nora Joyce), and *Finnegans Wake* (copyright 1939 by James Joyce, renewed 1967 by George and Lucia Joyce); Faber and Faber Ltd (London) and Viking Penguin Inc. (New York) for permission to quote from *The Letters of James Joyce*, edited by Stuart Gilbert and Richard Ellmann (copyright 1957, 1966 by the Viking Press); Harcourt Brace Jovanovich, Inc. (New York) and Faber and Faber Ltd (London) for permission to quote from T. S. Eliot's *Collected Poems 1909–1962* (copyright 1936 by Harcourt Brace Jovanovich, Inc., renewed 1943, 1963, 1964, by T. S. Eliot, 1971 by Esme Valerie Eliot); New Directions Publishing Corp. (New York) and Faber and Faber Ltd (London) for permission to quote from Ezra Pound's *Personae* (copyright 1926 by Ezra Pound). I rely on the 1971 revised Variorum Edition of *Don Juan* (University of Texas Press) and on the 1961 Random House edition of *Ulysses* for my quotations from the poem and novel.

I am grateful to Columbia University for continued fellowship support while I was a student there; to Frances Steloff for endowing a fellowship in honor of William York Tindall which I received; to the staff of the libraries of Columbia University and the University of Miami; to William Bernhardt; to Donald Reiman for advice that was always cheerful and astute; to my colleagues in the English Department at Miami, especially William Babula and George Gilpin, for their good-humored support and encouragement.

I must also name here four individuals in whose debt I shall remain without hope of making recompense. Olivia Estella de Sodder, Felix Joseph de Almeida and Lionel Trilling passed on while this book was being drafted, and can only be acknowledged in memory as the subjects of countless impossible wishes. Carl Woodring, an incomparable teacher for so many of his students, will always be my ideal of intellectual and personal goodness.

Coral Gables, Florida   H. A.

Introduction

    — And who do you think is the greatest poet? asked Boland, nudging his neighbour.

    — Byron of course, answered Stephen.

Heron gave the lead and all three joined in a scornful laugh.

    — What are you laughing at? asked Stephen.

    — You, said Heron. Byron the greatest poet! He's only a poet for uneducated people.

    — You may keep your mouth shut, said Stephen, turning on him boldly.

    — In any case Byron was a heretic and immoral too.

    — I don't care what he was, cried Stephen hotly.[1]

Flayed by the boy's canes, his flesh torn by barbed wire, Stephen Dedalus, like any good martyr, would rather be persecuted for his beliefs than admit the poet was 'no good'. Dedalus's experience is one Joyce had as an adolescent; his estimate of Byron, Ellmann tells us, was his creator's, one Joyce held to in later life.[2] The opinion is certainly in character for melancholic, self-centered young artists. We presume that the mature Joyce, by showing his youthful persona's affinity with Byron, declared his own aversion to the poet and egocentric Byronism.

    It would be difficult to find two more antipathetic writers than Byron and Joyce. The former, a man of action, wrote verse because it was 'in fashion'. The latter, a man of introspection, wrote prose because it was most fitting to the breadth and high intention of his art. The first was a worldly nobleman, a parliamentarian, philanderer, philanthropist and collector — of, according to Shelley's count, ten horses, eight dogs, five cats, five peacocks, three monkeys, two guinea hens, an eagle, crow, falcon and Egyptian crane, plus an indeterminate number of bears, women, Greek turtles, retainers, bastards and, albeit unwillingly, Yahoos (the little Hunts); he was a man who exulted in his reputation as the unfaithful, unprincipled roué who had murdered his mistress and made her skull into a drinking cup, who had conjoined saintly Annabella Milbanke with the devil for one long year, who was known to favor all political novelties, and who, a true courtier, tossed off idle verse without remuneration and published only at his friends' request. The second was a family man, unacceptably poor and lower-class, bookish, withdrawn, a near-priest whose only collections were a brood of starving, quarrelling siblings, a series of domestic crises, and a set of anti-social legends — by his own account, he was known to be a crafty, cynical, selfish, dissimulating Ulysses-type, a jejune Jesuit, a dour Aberdeen minister, a spy in Switzerland, a cocaine addict in Trieste, a dying man in New York, a crazy who carried four watches and always asked the time, a kind of Dick Swiveller, and a good-for-nothing;[3] he espoused no politics, loved but one woman and, a consecrated artist, sacrificed motherland, mother Church, and Mother Joyce to his calling, and made much of his ability to live, and sometimes starve, on the profits of his art. One lent his name to the mood that was a hallmark of the Romantic age; the other's name became synonymous with the spirit of nihilistic modernism, with chaos, alienation and futility.

The antipathies in temperament carry over to Byron's and Joyce's primary works. *Don Juan* and *Ulysses* seem to be quite inimical. The poem is a merry, random, careless, digressionary sail through the sophisticated world and its inheritance, apparently indifferent to the literary flotsam that surfaces in the passage. Undisciplined, subjective, reading like the public chatter of a gossip column, it tells of a young boy's adventures; some would say it is written for the uneducated eye and ear, that it is surface poetry holding no secrets from the mind, the product of a crude ear. The novel, on the other hand, is a web of scrupulous organization, precision and literary competence. Patterned and highly objective, reading like a compendium of abstruse learning for the select, it tells of Ulysses in a modern Ithaca; most would agree that its cross-references and symbolic minutiae make it profound, secretive literature, that it is a private myth, the product of a refined mind.

Frank Kermode has said that the major modern novel 'is a poem'.[4] John Galt, a novelist and Byron's friend, called *Don Juan* 'a poetical novel'; critics since have noted that Byron's poem belongs not so much to English poetry as to the history of the Victorian novel.[5] This tenuous connection in mode between poem and novel must be countered by the fact that Joyce, in *Ulysses*, wrote against the nineteenth-century novel tradition that Flaubert and James closed. It must also be supported by the realization that if Joyce conceived of his work as a monumental criticism of his century and its antecedents, a counter that would send the Romantics and his contemporary Dubliners spinning into the Abyss, so also did Byron proffer a counter-voice on his century in *Don Juan*, a highly critical, 'satirical perspective on the vatic stance of his Romantic contemporaries'.[6]

Robert Durling, in his study of the poet in Renaissance epic, makes an unexpected but prescient concluding statement. Asserting that Spenser and Ariosto represent two of the most significant literary traditions we have inherited from the Renaissance, he says: 'Spenser looks forward to Milton and ultimately to Wordsworth and Yeats. Ariosto looks forward to Montaigne, Byron, and Joyce'.[7] My inquiry will examine whether Byron's and Joyce's writing does indeed belong in one literary line as Durling implies it does: whether *Don Juan* and *Ulysses* might come close to being epic equivalents, each functioning for the post-Kantian era in much the same way as Homer's epics did for early Greek civilization; whether, despite all the odds, antipathies and inimicalities, *Don Juan* and *Ulysses* might prove to be about the same tasks and, with like manners, productive of near identical effects.

Any attempt to place Byron and Joyce within one tradition must also take into account the ambivalence toward literary tradition and the cultural heritage that *Don Juan* and *Ulysses* manifest. In these works the authors intentionally take the *Odyssey* as their first pattern, as Chapter 1 will document; they deliberately address themselves to its criterion. They also wilfully depart from the *Odyssey*'s epic formulae by absorbing and criticizing other major works and directions in the Western tradition, and by highlighting the differences between early Greek culture and its achievements and post-Enlightenment culture and its problems.

Any attempt to address Homeric precedent necessitates a consideration of epic tradition and its mock-heroic, picaresque, and comic epic mutants. Nor can the discussion cease at these, for the innovative *Ulysses* and the novelistic *Don Juan* face forward and invoke their times. Any attempt to recall the early Greek manual for noble action and civil behavior within the *polis* as a foil for present conduct requires that one reflect, also, on not only the unlikely prospect of distinctive action in a democratic milieu, but on the inevitable mutations in human behavior that have contributed to the state of the polity of Europe's decadent courts and Dublin's slums. All these subjects, in turn, must be subsumed by the preconceptions on writing of the skeptical, self-concerned, post-Kantian consciousness.

Homer is an obvious starting-point, and Byron and Joyce thought so too. Their poem and novel provide us with the pattern for our inquiry. They could not stop at Homer any more than we can. Through Homer they reach, and we perceive, a very different end. Acknowledging their necessary dependence on Homeric example and the literary-cum-cultural tradition since Homer, Byron and Joyce accomplish a most subversive assumption of literary precedent and a highly traditional abuse of the Western heritage. Endorsing Saintsbury's premise that 'Ancient without Modern is a stumbling block, Modern without Ancient is foolishness utter and irremediable', they yet achieve radical novelty. Revolutionary and inner-directed, but displaying precedents everywhere and insisting on their epic status, *Don Juan* and *Ulysses* are their creators' declarations of independence,[8] their manifestos for the future.

1 Odysseus and the Realm of Gold

'We are all Greeks – our laws, our literature, our religion, our arts have their root in Greece. But for Greece, Rome, the instructor, the conquerer, or the metropolis of our ancestors would have spread no illumination with her arms, and we might still have been savages and idolaters.' Shelley, the most Romantic poet of them all, was also the most Greek. Because of Shelley's sheer classicism Joyce, when he was not affirming Byron as the greatest English poet, would award the palms to this poet of Hellas. In tribute to the truth of the assertion in the Preface to *Hellas* with which I have begun, Joyce and Byron made their epic stories *Ulysses* and *Don Juan* turn on the story of Odysseus and its traditions.

However singular their individual responses to the classical tradition and to Homer, Byron and Joyce partake in common of Western man's ineluctable return to Greece. For, as Werner Jaeger says, our history begins with the Greeks, and we always return to Greece. The return presupposes the timeless influence and authority of Greece, but the variety possible in our response denies blind, rote imitation: on the contrary, 'we always return to Greece because it fulfills some need of our own life, although that need may be very different at different epochs'.[1] Jaeger's clarification is important. The needs of Byron's and Joyce's epochs were different; classical example was hardly an unchallenged authority for either of them, and their responses mirror all the distinctions and corruptions that time and space have wrought for each one. Yet, Byron and Joyce 'return to Greece' – by way of the Age of Revolution.

The romantic nineteenth century was infinitely more classical, and specifically more Greek, than its reputation. As an age that produced Keats's 'Ode on a Grecian Urn', Shelley's *Prometheus Unbound*, Goethe's *Roman Elegies*, Chateaubriand's *The Martyrs* and Alfieri's tragedies – with a Shelley who knew more Greek than Pope, a Goethe who knew more Greek than Klopstock, an August Wilhelm

Schlegel known as one of the strictest metricians in German literature, a rigorous ethical philosopher named Fichte, and classical scholars Leopardi, Hölderlin and Chenier among its elect[2] – the revolutionary era belies its old reputation for permissiveness, emotion and excess. The Romantic age was not anti-classical but anti-classicist and, where late eighteenth-century dicta of tasteful composition colored this, anti-Latin.

The difference between it and preceding centuries was essentially one of emphasis. The classics were read for those aspects of particular significance to the age's values. A romantic charm was found in the *Odyssey*, in Sappho, even in Virgil; the tragic joy in Euripides and Aeschylus received special praise; Greek literature for its purity and spontaneity was exalted over Latin literature; and Homer, the supposed composer of heroic ballads, took precedence over Virgil, the court-poet and his literary epic. Highet notes that the Renaissance and Romantic eras represent complementary stages in the exploration of antiquity. The former marked the assimilation of Latin. The latter meant a closer approach to Greek. Renaissance men like Montaigne would speak of 'the ancients' but in pratice think of the Romans; they would quote Homer sparsely but fifth-rate Latin poets like Silius Italicus freely. Goethe and Shelley, in their dramas, sought to emulate not Seneca but Aeschylus and Euripides; during their turbulent times the rococo garlands and cupids copied from Latin adaptations of late Greek art disappeared – to make way for the Elgin Marbles.[3] Gibbon and the Baroque marked the end of the Age of Rome in modern Europe. Thereafter came the Age of Greece.[4]

In and of this age, chronicled for both its revolutionary nature and its reverence for the ancient Greek spirit, Byron lived and wrote. To this age, James Joyce was heir. One must acknowledge, Lionel Trilling says, how entirely Joyce was a man of the century in which he was born, how thoroughgoing his commitment was 'to its concerns and sentiments, how deeply rooted he was in its ethos and its mythos',[5] for Joyce was heir not only to the nineteenth century's presentiment for originality, but also to its primary values, which exalted the natural over the civilized, pagan over Christian, man over God, Greek over Roman, and Homer over Virgil.

Because of their ages' inclinations, despite their ages' reputations, Byron and Joyce chose 'Homer and his unchristian heart'. Their decisions to have *Don Juan* and *Ulysses* turn on Homer's *Odyssey* (the specifics of which we will discuss shortly) are certainly part of that potent modern reaction against Christian doctrine and morality which found its apotheosis in the century that nurtured Shelley's juvenile pamphlet 'The Necessity for Atheism'. Greek ideas of God and morality were deemed better, more real, more positive, less austere and misanthropic, more human.[6] Homer, the 'blind illiterate minstrel', became for the nineteenth century (with its interest in folklore, Märchen, ballads and 'original' epics) the pre-eminent example of the pagan, the primitive, the spontaneous, the natural, the human. For the twentieth century, which has fostered a naturalism more excessive than Zola's, Pound – Eliot mythopoetry, and Mann, Homer was all this and, most of all, author of Western man's first myth.

The two centuries are hardly unique in their reverence for The Poet. He is the force Western tradition has always had to come to terms with. Virgil based his story of Aeneas on the time and location of the *Iliad* and *Odyssey*; Aristotle based his standards in the *Poetics* on Homer's example; Dante welcomed Homer by way of Virgil; Petrarch and Boccaccio placed Homer within the Renaissance; Chaucer put 'grete Oomere' in his Hall of Fame; Spenser permeated his *Faerie Queene* with Greek mythology; Shakespeare wrote his *Troilus and Cressida*; Milton wrote of paradises lost and gained, and of Comus, son of Circe; Chapman, Dryden and Pope did their translations and their mock-epics; and Swift attempted to settle the problem of Homeric criticism once and for all in *Gulliver's Travels*. In recent times we have, among others, Keats's sonnet on reading Homer, *Hyperion*, Tennyson's *Idylls* and *Ulysses*, Arnold's *On Translating Homer*, Ruskin's envisioning of Homer as a standard of literary excellence, *Don Juan*, and *Ulysses*. Like the needs of the eras, the responses are diverse. But Homer remains the touchstone against which character, human behavior, civilization and, above all, the writing of literature is tested. No longer a body of work of about the mid-eighth century, Homer is a tradition. Every acknowledgment of Homer responds to other such acknowledgments since Homer. Even when these responses take a parodic cast, as they do with Byron and Joyce (and as they did with Rabelais and Cervantes, Pope and Fielding), a genuine sense of the precedent prevails.

For those who would make an epical response to the task of writing literature, 'The Epic is Homer'.[7] Homer did not invent the epic himself;[8] a long line of precursors must have felt their way ever nearer to the perfect form until, at last, The Poet came and achieved it. But once the form was incarnate, it was not possible or right to go beyond it.[9] Any later poet seeking to narrate a heroic story, be he writing a millennium after, had yet to reckon with the Homeric manner: the meter, the diction, the machinery. One might revivify and update the form, as Brian Wilkie discusses in his study of the Romantics and epic tradition, [10] but one cannot dispense with its conditioning. This truth applies directly to Milton and those of his time who felt Homer and Virgil were the irreproachable models of style and primary sources of poetic material, but it includes, no less, the Byron and the Joyce who address epic pattern and declare epic intention in *Don Juan* and *Ulysses*. This was the situation under which they, also, wrote. Homeric organization was historic, impeccable, and inexorable. In using Homer they accepted the tradition with full ramifications, for better and for worse.

Joyce and Byron saw themselves as distinctly *within* classical tradition. They were writing at the end of a long line of literary endeavor that had begun with The Poet; however novel and combative or rejective of its parts they might be, they were still *ipso facto* part of it. Whatever their reason or purpose, whatever fate they intended for Homer, whatever they might do in the end, by invoking the pattern they wilfully placed themselves in the tradition.

One is surprised at the paradoxical significance of their action. For as the *Iliad* and the *Odyssey* were themselves, despite their place at the start of Western tradition, cumulative and culminative works, perfected forms of earlier heroic ballads and aspirations to epic form [11] — so, too, were *Don Juan* and *Ulysses* to be cumulative works and end-products. The novel and poem were situated at the end of the process that began with Homer, but they were to serve also as summaries of Western literature and culminations to Western civilization. As Byron and Joyce inherited the older myths and tales that went into making the *Odyssey*, so also did they inherit the patterns, conventions and variations that had become part of the epic machinery since Homer.

When speaking of how Homer represents a culminating pinnacle and summary of the early Greek experience, Hermann Fränkel says that the Greeks themselves, retroactively, constructed a theory according to which all Greek literature, indeed Greek education and civilization as a whole, had its origin and end in Homer. [12] The story of Odysseus has become for us, even more so than for the Greeks, a multiple myth; its author is the basis of our literature also. [13] By declaring their affinity with Homer, by appropriating the pattern of the *Odyssey* for *Don Juan* and *Ulysses*, by absorbing and criticizing Homer at once, Byron and Joyce assume responsibility for recording and criticizing not only the developments and variations on Homer's myth, but the departures — whether comic parodies or serious substitutes — from the epic tradition this myth (and the *Iliad*) spawned. They share totally with Homer his culminative task, his purpose of representing, at its end, the ways and manners of a long and diverse literary tradition.

Precedent piles on precedent to create new precedent; diverse directions in literature are superimposed upon each other for cumulative representation. The credentials for the poet's and the novelist's unusual use of Homer in *Don Juan* and *Ulysses* become impeccable. Byron and Joyce begin with Homer so that, summarizing all that has preceded them like Homer also, they might best end the tradition he began.

I

One should be aware of the ambivalence underlying these two writers' response to Homer before one considers the precise use and function, in and after creation, to which Odyssean pattern is put in *Don Juan* and *Ulysses*. This ambivalence is echoed in, and partly caused by, their attitudes to Greece and classical learning.

Greece was a symbolic place for Byron (as his 'Isles of Greece' suggests). Its liberation from the Turks would be an assertion of the virtues of classical civilization over the vices and tyrannies of the modern world. It was the place where he came of age, emotionally and politically.[14] Greece had Turks, Giaours, bandits, bearded priests, black-eyed virgins, Ithaca, and a passionate, compelling history: 'I was happier in Greece than I have ever been before — or since, and if I have ever written [well?] (as the world says I have — but which they will pardon my doubting) — it was in Greece — or off [of] Greece'.[15] Contemporary Greeks, beaten, divided and insecure, did not always live up to the poet's ideal. Nevertheless, cursing Greek inefficiency, stupidity and greed, he died for Greece.

The classics received yet more qualified support from Byron. Classical erudition was 'antequarian twaddle' perpetrated by 'emasculated fogies'. In young Juan's education:

His classic studies made a little puzzle,
    Because of filthy loves of gods and godesses,
Who
    — . . . never put on pantaloons or bodices;

His reverend tutors had at times a tussle,
    And for their Aeneids, Iliads, and Odysseys,
Were forced to make an odd sort of apology
For Donna Inez dreaded the mythology.[16]

The wry story of how the Spaniard read only the unexpurgated
appendices of his textbooks masks 'a sickening memory' Byron had
of being tutored in the classics. Rote-memorization was 'the daily
drug', and poetry was approached through the drudgery of Latin
grammar and vocabulary 'forced down word by word' (*Childe
Harold*, IV, 75).

Despite a repugnance for the methods, Byron remembered his
lessons. He never denied the artistic and intellectual pre-eminence of
the ancients; he found contemporary writers vulgar by comparison —
like slums or Gothic castles when compared with the Parthenon; he
studded his poetry with allusions; he composed 'Hints from Horace'
and so recognized the classics' right to school us in good writing; he
maintained a fascination for the myths of Prometheus and Odysseus.
This paradox in the poet's attitude to classical learning and Greece was
perhaps first noticed by Goethe, who made Euphorion,[17] that child
of opposites who soared and fell like Icarus, bear in death the visage of
the poet's well-known form.

For Joyce, Greece had none of the immediate associations and
attractions that it had for Byron. He neither spoke Greek, nor visited
Greece. As a young man, he described Hellenism as 'European
appendicitis'[18] and remarked to Padraic Colum that the Greek epics
were before Europe, and outside European culture. Dante's *Divine
Comedy*, he claimed, was Europe's epic. Yet he was to connect Ireland,
which he had once dubbed 'an afterthought of Europe', with
Greece.[19]

Joyce's early opinion of classical Greece was undoubtedly aided by
a Catholic school system not unlike young Juan's, which fed him
large doses of a dead language (to produce the 'pig-Latin' for which
Dedalus is famous), and even larger doses of orthodoxy and Jesuitic
scholarship. The irony of what resulted was inherent from the start.

Unlike Byron who saw the corruption of learning and the like
corruption of his learning, and infinitely more egotistical, Joyce, the
scholar, the young man at University College, wished passionately to
be direct heir to those ancient arbiters of literature whom he could not
always read in the original. His pride as a man of letters willed him to
be the castigator, coach, and molder of taste for his generation; his

aspiration to be the artistic giant of all ages led him to revere literary tradition. From here it was but a short step before he came to see himself as Homer's best interpreter and worthiest heir, though self-appointed; the man best able to continue Odysseus's story, make it the blueprint for modern living, and so reintegrate the myth into Western civilization.

The story of how Joyce 'discovered' the myth as an adolescent, how he planned a story, 'Ulysses', to be included in *Dubliners*, is a familiar one. What is significant is the ambiguity from which this discovery sprang, the paradox of the novelist's early attitudes and his subsequent assumption of classical tradition.

In education, milieu, and personality Byron and Joyce were different. But both shared, at different times and to varying degrees, an ambivalence toward the Greek influence, an equivocation which they seemed to deny and disavow by the classical themes of their works, but which continued to underlie their double-minded treatment of Greece through Homer.

When Byron describes Juan and Haidée as 'a group that's quite antique,/Half-naked, loving, natural, and Greek' (II, 194), and when Joyce has Mulligan say of Bloom (as he ogles the nude statues in the Museum) 'He's greeker than the Greeks', they are clearly speaking in fun, of sexual liberty (in Juan and Haidée), and homosexuality (in Bloom), and echoing the common inclination to read into the thin draperies and nude statuary of Greek art an intimation of sexual excess. But behind the comic irreverence poet and novelist also wish to ascribe a very serious 'Greekness' (beauty, nobility, naturalness, simplicity) to Haidée, Juan, and Bloom. Precisely this mixture of reverence and irreverence informs their treatment of Homer throughout *Don Juan* and *Ulysses*.

That Byron and Joyce chose Odysseus's story as their criterion, over that of wrathful Achilles, is itself indicative of their centuries' related perceptions, and the paradoxical mentality they share. Byron knew of Odysseus from Chapman (among others), the translator of 'divine Homer' who idolized Ulysses 'the much-sustaining, patient, heavenly man'.[20] He may not have known Vico, but he was cognizant of Goethe's unfinished *Ulysses in Phaecia* (1786), where Ulysses and Nausicaa were to represent pure, natural, unspoiled humanity (*Urmenschen*). Joyce knew of Odysseus not only from the archetype but as portrayed by Hauptmann, d'Annunzio, Phillips, Tennyson, Fénelon, and Racine, and as interpreted by Vico, Bérard, and Samuel Butler. His first encounter with the story came through the 1808 work[21] of a contemporary of Byron, Charles Lamb. 'I was twelve years old when I studied the Trojan War' he says, 'Ulysses alone remained in my recollection. It was the mysticism that pleased me'.[22] Thunder, lightning, and ghostly stories of the wrath of gods thrilled the adolescent, Catholic Joyce. He was led to read more sophisticated interpretations of the myth, until he finally came to appropriate it as his primary symbolic pattern for the 1906 short story, *Dubliners*,[23] and *Ulysses*.

To ask why these two writers found the story of Odysseus particularly congenial elicits countless possible explanations. Some post-Homeric writers, like Tennyson, have presented Ulysses as a primitive Byronic figure filled with melancholic wanderlust. This variant of the myth would have appealed to those Dedalian aspects of the young Joyce – betrayed, full of defiant postures and Manfredian assertions of '*Non serviam*', the artist-in-exile, defector from religion and society, and writer of an eight-hundred page *Stephen Hero* based on a Childe Harold – Juanesque travelog entitled *Turpin Hero*. Other post-Homeric writers have portrayed Odysseus as a primitive Don Juan, one who formed suspect and adulterous liaisons with shady ladies (Circe, Calypso), and have speculated on his subsequent journeys, and his fidelity to Penelope. This interpretation of the myth would have appealed to the roué in the older Byron, and matched his free-loving young Juan. The comic possibilities within this variation would have appealed to poet and novelist alike.

That the myth had a special place in Byron's thought, over and above his reverence for Greece and any enthusiasm he may have caught from Chapman and Lamb, can be seen from scores of episodes in the poet's life. When in Cephalonia, he visited nearby Ithaca for its Homeric associations. On learning that a nearby cave might be the place where Odysseus spent the night of his return, Byron insisted on sleeping the night there. That the myth was uppermost in his mind as he composed *Don Juan* is clear from the poem's repeated Homeric echoes, apparent even in the plan of the unwritten cantos. These latter were to be in the manner of a disorganized, unepic picaresque based on the life of Anacharsis Cloots. Yet this Frenchman had taken his name from Anarcharsis, the philosopher of ancient Greece who, like Odysseus, visited and observed the customs and governments of countries in the Eastern Mediterranean.[24]

Unlike Byron Joyce, ever-concerned for his reputation with posterity, left ample records of how and why the story of Odysseus served him so well. His observations, in retrospect, also provide insight into the poet's intentions. 'It embodies everything,' Joyce told a friend, adding 'I am almost afraid to treat such a theme'. For him the *Odyssey* possessed 'the most beautiful, all-embracing theme' of Western literature, one 'greater, more human than that of *Hamlet*, Don Quixote, Dante and Faust'. The situation of Odysseus was the most human one in world literature: 'After Troy there is no further talk of Achilles, Menelaus, Agamemnon. Only one man is not done with; his heroic career has hardly begun: Odysseus'.[25] Like several artists before him not the least of whom was Byron, Joyce realized that Achilles and the *Iliad* formed a closed book of martial success. The real potential for development, for Homer as for modern times, lay with the human story of Odysseus. The motif of wandering, of return, of Ulysses as musical artist willing to risk his life rather than renounce his interest in the Sirens' song, and the 'splendid parable' of Scylla and Charybdis, Joyce marked as particularly significant to his purpose.

There is no modernist use of symbolism in *Don Juan*, as there is in *Ulysses*.[26] Homeric plot nevertheless serves as a symbolic or allegorical model for Byron's poem almost as much as it does for Joyce's novel. Byron may have referred to Homer as that 'blind old man of Scio's rocky isle' beguiled by dreams ('The Bride of Abydos', II, 2), and he may have chided the Greek poet for his tall tale of the memory of Odysseus's dog.[27] He may have been too self-conscious to overtly call attention to the thicket of Homeric parallels in his poem. But his signals are clear. We cannot fall prey to the poet's ambivalence toward the Greek's legendary influence and so miss his intention to use Homer's wandering tale as his pattern for *Don Juan*. Nor can we let the poet's parodic echoes of epic convention blind us to the serious, intended, Odyssean parallels in his poem. These latter, which will be shortly listed in detail, signal distinctly enough Byron's epic intent in *Don Juan* – and his chosen model.

II

Almost a century before Joyce created his 'jewgreek' Bloom as the lost hero of a wasted modern metropolis, Byron had noted the symbolic link between the figures of the wandering Jew and the wandering Greek, and between a persecuted, subjugated people and the modern condition of man. In 1811 the poet said the Greeks 'like the Catholics of Ireland and the Jews throughout the world . . . suffer all the moral and physical ills that can afflict humanity'.[28] His

Hebrew Melodies focused on the Semites as a symbol of the desolate condition of modern humanity and emphasized the artistic significance of their tragedy:

> Tribes of the wandering foot and weary breast,
> How shall ye flee away and be at rest?
> The wild-dove hath her nest, the fox his cave,
> Mankind their country – Israel but the grave!

> Thou [Saul], thy race, lie pale and low,
> Pierced by shafts of many a bow;
> And the falchion by thy side
> To thy heart thy hand shall guide:
> Crownless, breathless, headless fall,
> Son and sire, the house of Saul.[29]

Joyce, we know, was influenced by Victor Bérard's theory of the Semitic-Phoenecian origins of the *Odyssey*, by the old Irish chroniclers' belief in the Grecian origins of the Celts, and by the tendency of Irish political rhetoric to draw parallels between persecuted Irishmen and dispossessed Israelites. But his creation of Bloom, the Jewish Odysseus, and Stephen, the Greek-Irishman, who together would 'Hellenise' Dublin, is owed more to an artistic sense, akin to Byron's, of the pervasive and tragic connection between myths of wandering, persecution, bondage, and the general human condition. Judaism as a religion was of as little interest to Joyce as to Byron; the Jews' historical place, their tradition, their antiquity, their symbolic tragedy, was of the highest aesthetic value to both as they sought to create epics of their times.

'The *Odyssey* serves me as ground-plan', Joyce said, and Byron might have so claimed. Following the tripartite structure of Homer's epic, he divided *Ulysses* into a 'Telemachia' of Stephen Dedalus, an 'Odyssey' of Leopold Bloom's passage through Dublin, and a 'Nostos' where the two protagonists come home. *Don Juan*, more loosely, follows the same Homeric structure. Cantos I through III are of the young Telemachus-Juan, Cantos IV through XI follow Odysseus-Juan through his adventures abroad, and Cantos XII through XVII bring the Spanish Don 'home' to England.

Beyond his formal, and essentially superficial, structure Joyce meant the blueprint of his *Ulysses* to function geographically, socially, and symbolically, as the Homeric poems do. He said he wished to give a picture so complete of his Ithaca-Dublin that 'if the city one day disappeared from the earth it could be reconstructed' solely from his book. As the Homeric poems are vital to the reconstruction of the Aegean civilization — as the embodiment and expression of early Greek *paideia* and extant source for its history — so also would Joyce's *Ulysses* be essential to the reconstruction of Dublin and its cosmos by future historians.

Never this meticulous, Byron yet shared Joyce's purpose. He, also, wished *Don Juan* to be a map of Europe in his time, especially of its social mores. He intended to create a composite picture of European society as he knew it, as complete a presentation of upper-class behavior as Homer's own. As The Poet had linked the decorum of the courts at Sparta, Phaeacia and Ithaca so, too, would he imply the fatal connection in manners of upper-class Spain, Turkey, Russia, and England. In this he would be meticulous and unsparing, scrupulously mean; and, though he might generalize as Homer had, his documentary poem would stand as a social and cultural map of 'Regency' Europe for future generations.

From this perspective the parallels with the *Odyssey* follow effortlessly, necessarily. The poet of *Don Juan* proposes to tell the story of a versatile young hero, prudent for his age, who is fated to journey to distant climes. There is shipwreck and horror at sea, and rescue on a Greek isle by a Nausicaa (Haidée). As Homer loved sea-raid formulae[30] so also are we given a piratical 'sea-solicitor' named Lambro who momentarily changes places with his *de facto* son-in-law to become another Odysseus, unexpectedly returning home. Coleridge praised the episode of Lambro's return for its classical air, calling it the 'best', 'most individual thing' in Byron's work.[31] The scene certainly mirrors Homer's original minutely, down to the mixed mood of joy (at his return) and sadness-apprehension Lambro feels (at what awaits him) when 'He enter'd in the house no more his own', to witness joy and merrymaking in his house (on *his* goods), feel the insults of the revellers, and find an usurper in the royal bed.

Odysseus's visit to Hades finds parallel enough in Juan's internment in the belly of the slave-ship, and in Haidée's ghastly visions and death. As Juan's ordeal continues, a mercenary named Johnson serves well as the shade of Achilles, even 'though his name . . . sounds less harmonious' (VIII, 39). While Lambro, in his mood of blind anger and fond madness, which results in the destruction of Haidée and her unborn, is 'like the Cyclops, mad with blindness' (III, vii).[32] Gulbayez, Sultana of a Turkish town, functions well as the sensual, alien Circe; and the frozen Lady Adeline, who would detain young

Juan for a secret purpose she does not yet know, fulfils the role of the golden nymph Calypso.

The poet makes certain that he portrays the massacre of the innocents at Ismail as an outrage fit to match the slaughter of the Sun-King's sacred kine. His Duchess Fitz-Fulke makes an irresistible Siren, even if she cannot sing. Finally the Spanish Don, as concubine in the seraglio, 'Love's Artillery-man' for Catherine, and ambassador to the Court of St James, is a sufficiently disguised Ulysses returning (to the poet's) home.

It would be impossible to deny the intention, indeed the deliberation, behind these Odyssean echoes in *Don Juan*. The poem is truly Byron's Odyssey-equivalent: his acknowledgment of his enduring fascination with The Poet and Western man's first myth, and his response to the traditions it spawned. These parallels, casual and surreptitious though they seem, prove to be Byron's wilful, positive finishing touch to his career and all that nurtured it. He casts them, at once, in the face of his own dual attitude toward things Homeric and Greek, and in the face of the epic tradition he criticizes. The parallels must constitute the foundation of any critical attempt to elicit the poet's intentions in *Don Juan* and to judge their effects.

Joyce was far more scrupulous in his parallelings with Homer than Byron, far more arrogant, and far less self-conscious. From the Homeric links in episode, instance and character as institutionalized in the Gilbert—Linati schema, to Gerty MacDowell's spanking clean knickers with blue bows (fit counterparts to the Phaeacian's legendary white linen), the compulsive organizer in Joyce never forgot his epic blueprint.

Since *Ulysses*'s Odyssean pattern is common knowledge, we shall pass over this in quick review. There is a chapter for each of Homer's episodes; a peripatetic and prudent Bloom wields his cigar much as Odysseus did his burning olive-stave; a displaced Telemachus wanders through Dublin searching for his 'true' father, doubting his paternity and suspecting his mother (literal and figurative). There is a family bed; and a Penelope ensconced, whenever we see her, in this bed. She may do no weaving, but she does knit lamb's-wool jackets and she is pursued by a host of suitors, all suitably bold, callow, and horsey.

A gabbling schoolmaster serves as Nestor in Joyce's novel; a windbag editor plays Aeolus. Nausicaa is a young, Dublin virgin; Calypso is a nymph-daughter Milly; Circe takes the form of a powerful, fearful Madam. The visit to this Madam's house and an earlier visit to a cemetery, together, parallel Odysseus's visit to the Underworld, complete with fear, sacrifice, the snub of Ajax-Menton, ghostly visions of women, Elpenor the avatar, and promises of doom and salvation.

A return home, and a somewhat extenuated reunion of Odysseus, son and wife, to the accompaniment of domestic rituals, is also furnished in *Ulysses*, in close parallel to the Homeric model. There are Sirens, whirlpools, rocks, sacrificial organs, gormandized potted-meat (to stand for the mindless gorging in the house of Odysseus), cannibals, Cyclopes, *et hoc genus omne*. Even Homeric discrepancies prevail, and Paddy Dignam, whom someone takes 'the liberty of burying', is both dead and alive.

'I think that we will learn again', Yeats wrote, 'how to describe at great length an old man wandering among enchanted islands, his return home at last, his slowly gathering vengeance, a flitting shape of a goddess, and a flight of arrows, and yet to make all these so different things . . . the signature or symbol of a mood of the divine imagination'.[33] Like others before him, Yeats found Homer's tale of the wandering Achaean appropriate to his own age; he disagreed with Mallarmé's contention that the lyric would be the primary medium of the modern era and argued instead for the writing of a new *Odyssey*.

Yeats's belief underlies Joyce's use of the *Odyssey* as framework for his grand response to literary tradition and the problem of writing literature in his time. Though Byron had none of the modern studies of myth to support him, his intuition served him well. He shrewdly perceived that he could use Homer's story to write *Don Juan* as his Odyssean counter; as a response to Homer that would also counter his own shallow age and a too-old epic tradition, and as a counter to any criticism that his poem was not epic enough and hardly an equivalent.

If the story of Odysseus proved most adaptable to Byron's and Joyce's intents, the versatile character of Odysseus (in Homer, and in the tradition since Homer) was primary guide for Juan and Bloom. Something in the prudent, pragmatic, thoughtful, curious, essentially peace-loving, 'man of many turns' appealed directly to Byron and Joyce. They felt a kinship with Odysseus, even if this was a half-humorous one which fully acknowledged their shrunken proportions. Joyce used a host of models for his Ulysses (John Joyce, a Mr Hunter of Dublin, a Murray uncle) but, most of all, himself. Byron felt a like identification, ironic though it was, as an anniversary verse of 1821 entitled 'Epigram on My Wedding Day – To Penelope' implies.

('This day, of all our days has done/The worse for me and you: − /'Tis six years since we were one,/And five since we were two.') His Odyssean counterpart, Juan, is as he himself would have wished to be. Bloom and the young Don possess most of those characteristics for which the mythic Achaean is known: they are prudent, considerate, peaceloving, experienced (the boy is experienced for his age, over and above any sexual connotation of the word), curious, thoughtful and human; they serve as ambassadors, as Odysseus did; they seek a faraway home as the lost Greek did (Bloom, a Promised Land, Juan, a home to replace that from which his mother cast him), and the understanding of like-minded individuals. The transition from Greek hero to eighteenth-century Spanish stripling and Edwardian Dubliner takes place, as we will observe in a later chapter, by way of Pantagruel, Don Quixote, Candide, Joseph Andrews, Tom Jones, Tristram Shandy, and other post-Homeric variants of the epic character. But Juan and Bloom remain, in essence, Odyssean figures.

The *Odyssey* has been one of the most adaptable of Western myths owing, largely, to the ambiguity inherent in the first Odysseus: not only was he the most complex in character and exploit of all the Homeric heroes, he was also a more equivocal personality than any other figure in Greek mythology until Archiloclus.[34] The pliancy of the archetype encouraged subsequent variations of the myth to interpret and ascribe qualities to the character at will. For example, the first Odysseus was known for his intelligence, but intelligence, as 'myriad-minded' Homer indicated, is a neutral quality. 'It may take the form of low and selfish cunning, or of exalted, altruistic wisdom.' Between these two poles, firmly established in the archetype, Odysseus's character has vacillated through the whole tradition.[35]

Homer's hero was also known to be an adaptable man. This versatility, a character-trait, is of particular significance to Joyce's and Byron's artistic intents. The changing modern environment portrayed in *Don Juan* and *Ulysses* demands versatility. Juan must grow up overnight in exile, survive a shipwreck, adjust to life as slave-concubine in a harem, play dutiful lover to Catherine the Great, and act as roving ambassador to English society. Bloom must navigate the hostile Dublin streets, playing dutiful husband, friendly mourner, surreptitious would-be-lover, advertising man, peeping Tom, Christ, Samaritan, dissipated hallucinator, and father. The two protagonists change roles in exacerbated versions of what the first Odysseus once did when he adjusted to the varied conditions of the Cyclops' cave, the shady nymph's island, the wily sorceress's citadel, the fickle hospitality of windy Aeolus's clime and the fair court of Phaeacia.

With Homer's help, the paradox is complete. Juan and Bloom have their origin, organizing principle, and foundation set in an ancient myth. Yet they are allowed an unusual versatility of character, that they might adapt to their modern world and its multiple challenges.

Consequently, *Don Juan* and *Ulysses* have connections with Homer that go beyond those of a shared mythic configuration. At times, these correspondences take the larger form of a parallel in essential character or situation; but at other times they are literary and symbiotic, and we receive them in the form of 'a hint, a nuance, a grotesque, a parodic reminiscence, a phrase repeated in a dream, a poignant echo'.[36] In both varieties of parallel, it is important to recognize the true emphasis, and the quality and manner in which this emphasis is tendered. The central fact about the correspondences, between the *Odyssey* and *Ulysses*, whether of structure, event, or dramatis personae, 'is that Joyce's emphasis was always on deriving the essential quality from his model rather than on literal, easy, or even ingenious, parallels.'[37] Vivienne Koch's comment is no less applicable to *Don Juan*. The Cyclops, Lambro, and the Citizen at Kiernan's Tavern seem to have little in common. Yet Lambro, blinded enough by anger and revenge to bring about the death of his own daughter, and the prejudice-blinded, ignorant talker at Kiernan's, do share with Polyphemus a basic quality of monocularity-bordering-on-sightlessness.

The parallels between Gerty MacDowell, the innocent, virginal Dublin girl, Haidee, the innocent, virginal Greek maid, and Nausicaa, the innocent, virginal Phaeacian damsel, are, in the last analysis, only the most superficial of correspondences. But a deeper and infinitely more vital connection relates the girls across 3,000 odd years: the quality of their response to the strangers, Odysseus, Juan, and Bloom. They instinctively recognize the men as 'different' despite their innocence of worldly things; they impulsively accept the strangers and treat them compassionately because of their innocence; they intuitively sense that these battered voyagers are superior, special because alien, to other men they have known.[38]

Likewise, there do not seem to be any parallels between joking dirtily in a maternity hospital (*Ulysses*), the butchering of a few hundred Turks (*Don Juan*), and the original killing of the Sun-God's sacred kine by Odysseus's men. Yet Joyce did read his episode as one concerning a 'crime against fecundity', just as Byron did see his incident as a crime against human life. These readings connect, directly and profoundly, with Homer's suggestion that the action of Odysseus's men was a sacrilege, a violation of sacred life.

III

Byron's and Joyce's response to Homer remains essentially paradoxical. They are pervasive versions of the archetypal response to the naive poet outlined by Friedrich Schiller: 'A feeling in which joyous mockery, respect, and melancholy are compounded'.[39] As part of their ambivalent feeling for Greece and the classics, and their ingrained, near-Shakespearean respect for tradition and history which increases the tension and enjoyment of their eventual revolt, they would respect Homer for his childlike naiveté, and mock him for his childish simplicity.

In *Don Juan* as in *Ulysses*, if Homer is touchstone he is also punching-bag, if he is point of direction he is also point of divergence, if he is authority he is also reason for rebellion; and, if Homeric plot is used for organization, its final purpose is to show up what is not organized, and what is organized counter to it.

Homeric plot and tradition serve Joyce and Byron as plot served Sterne in *Tristram Shandy*. They emphasize change, difference, the functionlessness of plot and the failings of tradition. As Byron and Joyce well knew, massive mutation, disturbance, change, in life as in literature, separate them from Homer and early Greece. One primary intent behind their use of Homeric plot and tradition must therefore be to show up, by indirection, the parallels that are not there, and the sentiments and conditions that have changed so radically since the tradition's inception.

As a result, correspondences with Homer that do not exist in *Don Juan* and *Ulysses*, and the manner in which these books depart from Homeric form, are, paradoxically, as important as the parallels themselves. Koch says of *Ulysses*:

> It seems that the qualitative aspect of *Ulysses* in relation to its three thousand year old model can best be suggested in terms of their *differences*. By *differences* I mean not merely the obvious facts of language and content . . . but rather those shifts in value which occur because of conscious planning or unconsciously executed divergences from the prototype. For example, it is not the *order* of events as it bears on the *Odyssey* which is important in *Ulysses*, but

rather the *kind* of relationship suggested either through likeness or difference.[40]

We might carry the point yet further. It is precisely the differences, the shifts, the divergences and contrasts, all made (consciously or unconsciously) in the face of having set up Homer as a model and having inherited a diverse tradition, that are of ultimate significance in *Don Juan* and *Ulysses*.

These differences serve as a kind of unvoiced commentary on Homer, on the tradition, on the two diametrically opposed worlds, on the writers' own accomplishments because of and in spite of Homer, the tradition, the two worlds, and on the irony of any attempt to write in parallel and in tradition.

Byron and Joyce write in full knowledge of Homer's world: an aristocratic world like Shakespeare's, and like Tolstoy's in *War and Peace*; a world with unique views of hospitality, whose gods are more like men than gods have ever been; a world exclusively of warriors and kings, where few things count except riches, prowess and honor.[41] They write in full knowledge of the literary tradition this world established. The inevitable disparities that result serve as an editorial on whatever parallels they may have set up in their poem and novel, and on any tradition in which they may write. Even as we acknowledge the truth of a Homeric parallel in either of the two works, we acknowledge the immense distinctions that preclude and include this parallel.

Homeric precedent in *Don Juan* and *Ulysses* becomes, paradoxically, most important in and as they depart from its example. Parallels and traditions set forth serve only to heighten the writers' departures from these in their books, and the manner in which these departures take place. Even as Byron and Joyce invoke Odyssean patterns, evoke Greek ideals, match Homer's perceptions and address the literary criterion of his two epics, they acknowledge the immense variations and corruptions that have occurred in literature and in the times since Homer.

'[We] are [Homer's] literary brethren, and if we would read his lines intelligently we must also read between them', Butler says.[42] Through *Don Juan* and *Ulysses* Byron and Joyce read, intelligently, through the myth of Odysseus. They read between Homer's lines with a mixture of mockery and respect. They read, also, between Homer and themselves — which is to say, they study the distinctions and accept the responsibility for being aware of all the existential differences and literary departures that separate Western man's first myth and the modern story.

The *Odyssey* and the *Iliad*, together with the *Aeneid*, form a complex massive in its authority. Myths, they gave rise to an epic tradition that swelled over the years not only with true successors but, in alarming fecundity, with pretenders to epic, parodies of epic, and solemn substitutes to epic. Paralleling, absorbing, mocking and challenging Homer in *Don Juan* and *Ulysses*, Byron and Joyce realize they must do no less for everything literate that Homer has fostered.

We are all Greeks. As the early Hellenes had always maintained, all things literate have their origin in Homer. To begin with The Poet, with the beginning, ensures one of an enormous task and a very complex end. This is Byron's and Joyce's discovery and, with it, they pass through Homer. The inherent paradoxicality underlying their perceptions in *Don Juan* and *Ulysses*, hence, is not confined to their response to Homer alone. It belongs with their attitude toward myth and tradition. It is itself subsumed by the modern apprehension of myth.

2 Myth and Tradition

'We ought to be glad' Keats said, noting Dante's addition to the Odyssean story, to have 'more news of Ulysses than we looked for'.[1] And so we should. Byron and Joyce, like numerous writers before them not the least of whom was Dante,[2] have continued the story of Odysseus. Through mythic organization in *Don Juan* and *Ulysses*, the authors declare their right to wander in those 'realms of gold'. They write for their times, facing forward, varying an old story as never before done. Yet their action presupposes the same step backward of which Thomas Mann spoke:

> The Spanish scholar Ortega y Gasset puts it that the man of antiquity, before he did anything, took a step backwards, like the bullfighter who leaps back to deliver the mortal thrust. He searched the past for a pattern into which he might slip as into a diving-bell, and being thus at once disguised and protected might rush upon his present problem. Thus his life was in a sense a reanimation, an archaizing attitude. But it is just this life as reanimation that is the life as myth.[3]

In *Don Juan* and *Ulysses* Byron and Joyce harken back to myth (especially Homeric myth), finding there pattern, protection and disguise — from whence they rush upon present problems. They strike an archaizing attitude, they reanimate myths and plunder traditions, in order to create revolutionary new stories for their times.

Goethe, Schiller, and the Schlegel brothers were the first to note the significance of myth to the modern artistic effort. Wordsworth was the first Englishman to assign to myth its specific, contemporary importance. Book Four of his *Excursion* says myths are fictions in form but tremendous truths in substance, that they are vital symbols of the religious imagination.[4] Then Mycenae, Egypt, and Crete were excavated, Tylor, Frazer, and Malinowski published on primitive culture, and soon Eliot was proclaiming the twentieth century as the age for which myth made art possible.

Yeats with his Cuchulain cycles, Lawrence with his Mexican tales, Dylan Thomas with his Biblical patterns, and Mann himself joined Graves, Sartre, O'Neill, Gide, Durrell, and Fry in forming the modern apprehension of myth. *Don Juan* and *Ulysses* place Byron and Joyce within this movement. But their perception of myth, myth-telling, and literate tradition distinguishes itself by its ambivalence; by its massive and often ironic inclusion of mythic and literary pattern; by its repeated critical reflections on past and present conditions. Mythology, Kerényi says, lays a foundation. More source than reason, it 'does not answer the question "why?" but "whence?"' The telling of myth, like its enactment in ritual, is a return to the first principle, 'a spontaneous regression to the "ground"'.[5] For primitive man this regression was vital because his objects, acts and thoughts became real only insofar as they imitated mythic archetypes; far from enacting fictions, mythic rituals ascertained reality. For modern and archaic, the recounting of myth serves as a defense against the novelties and irreversibility of historic time; it provides images of permanence and continuity through return and repetition.[6]

With Homer as with modern writers, myths are perceived as being awesomely larger than a particular time or place, apparently external, and of a perpetually receding tradition that is always available to new interpretation:

> The stuff of mythology is composed of something that is greater than the storyteller and than all human beings — 'as they are now' said Homer — but always as something visible, perceptible or, at least, capable of being expressed in images. . . . These images are the stuff of mythology, just as tones are the stuff of music: 'such stuff as dreams are made on', to quote Shakespeare; an entirely human stuff, which presented itself to the man who gave it shape, to the myth teller, as something objective, something pouring, as it were, from a supra-individual source; and it also presents itself to the audience — despite the new shape that the narrator has given it, despite the new 'variation' — not as the narrator's subjective creation, but again as something objective.[7]

For the self-centering modern consciousness, the ability of myth to seem objective, visible, tangible, external, was of first significance; its ability to provide infinite variation within the pattern for the individual whims of this consciousness was the unexpected bonanza. Sigmund Freud said myths were the dreams of the race, its psychical attitudes, instincts, wishes, as dream was the myth of the individual. Carl Jung said myths were the patterns in which the soul of every man develops because of the humanity he shares with other men. Eric Fromm said myths were messages from ourselves to ourselves, delivered by treating inner event as if outer event. Thomas Mann said myths were the foundation of life, the timeless religious formulae to which life shapes itself.

Whether myths are to be considered archetypes of human emotions and urges, or archetypes of human situations of tension and problem-confronting; whether Helen, Oedipus, Samson, and David are more wish-projections than individuals, or whether the experiences of Odysseus are more prototypes of *uomo universale* facing the worst possible imaginings of humanity's psyche than actual incidents – none of these requires distinction here. The essential functions behind all these interpretations remain the same, and it is these that are vital to modern mythopoeic.

Myths are images of truth, not merely truth in fact – events that actually occurred – but what could or possibly should happen within a set of circumstances. As Joyce says in *Finnegans Wake*, 'utterly impossible as are all these events they are probably as like those which may have taken place as any others which never took person at all are ever likely to be' (*Finnegans Wake*, p. 110). Myths are universal patterns for life which the modern consciousness can use as a pattern for its art. They are, most of all, of infinite utility. They 'contain from the moment of their inception all the meanings which can be extracted from them',[8] they cannot be misused or misinterpreted, and every rewriting of a myth is powerful and true.

Byron and Joyce assume all this when they write of Odyssean Juan and Ulysses in Dublin. Kerényi calls the tales and formulae that form the body of human mythology *mythologem*, and he defines mythology as 'the *movement* of this material: it is something solid and yet mobile, substantial and yet not static, capable of transformation'.[9] In *Don Juan* and *Ulysses* the authors move the 'mythologem' they have inherited from over 3000 years with the intent of not only adapting these to their own plans, but of questioning all such past intents, especially as they relate to the modern world-picture. With Homer's aid, they make the modern mythical, give permanence to the impermanent, value and meaning to the trivial, and to the trivial the intensity of dream.[10]

While the essential mythic method may remain the same, and while a human society without myth has never been known, there is a crucial difference in awareness between the mythmaking of the archaic mind and that of the modern artistic consciousness. To the former, mythmaking was a surety against disturbing novelty, and an expression of integration. To the latter, mythmaking is the primary means whereby the individual may temporarily maneuver his own reintegration with a world of his own making.

'One measure of man's advance from his most primitive beginnings to something we call civilization is the way in which he controls his myths, his ability to distinguish between the areas of behavior'. Homer, Finley adds, 'occupies the first stage in the history of Greek control over its myths'.[11] The Homeric poems do show a genius for ordering their world, but it is important to remember that Homer, as that unspecified person, collective, or corporation, represents the archaic mind, pre-philosophic, synthetic, 'whose content is myths, symbols, and paradigms'.[12] For the ancient Greeks and their poets, their mythical world had a reality and objectivity of its own which merely awaited a mythical poet to disclose its patterns, giving utterance to what was already in existence, more powerfully if more so inspired. Homer, hence, was both mythical poet and objective expression of this world. As Vico put it simply, Homer was the whole Greek people and there was no sense of any distinction between poet, mythic world, and culture.

For the modern world and its artist, the situation is quite different. The waking mind of primitive man has become the unconscious mind of modern man[13] and the conscious pattern of the modern artist. Mann called his attainment of the mythic typical viewpoint an epoch in his evolution as a writer, one which 'signified a singular intensification of his artistic mood'.[14] In the life of the human race the mythical is an early and primitive stage, but in the individual artist it is late and mature. Provided with novel refreshment to his perceiving and shaping powers, the modern mythmaker gains

> an insight into the higher truth depicted in the actual; a smiling knowledge of the eternal, the ever-being and authentic; a knowledge of the schema in which and according to which the supposed individual lives, unaware, in his naive belief in himself as unique in space and time, of the extent to which his life is but formula and repetition and his path marked out for him by those who trod it before him.[15]

Campbell has traced parallels between the courses of Mann's and

Joyce's writing careers. He calls *Ulysses* and *The Magic Mountain* 'mythic mysteries' in which the myths refer not to supernatural beings and miraculous occasions as in archaic times, but 'symbolically, to the root and seed potentials, structuring laws and forces, interior to the earthly being that is man'.[16] In the modern apprehension of myth, mythic symbols reflect inward, they explain the self, order its experiences, and communicate both through signs. Romanticism, Northrop Frye said, marks the beginning of an 'open' attitude to mythology which is seen as 'a structure of the imagination, out of which beliefs come . . .'.[17] The perception comes full circle and the modern artist discovers, with Wilde, that his own particular imagination is 'concentrated race experience'.

In myth Joyce and Byron found the prototype of a simple, dramatic communication; they found also a sophisticated set of symbols that reflected inward as well as outward: the enduring significance of what myth had come to represent over a long psychical and literary history. No longer, as with primitive man, a pattern of order to which existence could refer for validation, myth now justifies from within and, external in its symbols, is the source of order.

Ulysses, Levin said, 'outdid the naturalists at their own game by treating a slice of life so broad and banal that only myth could lend it shape or meaning'.[18] This point of myth providing organization was first made by Eliot, when he said Joyce's mythic method was 'simply a way of controlling, or ordering, of giving shape and significance to the immense panorama of futility and anarchy which is contemporary history', and by Pound, when he said myth in *Ulysses* was essentially 'a scaffold taken from Homer, and the remains of a medieval allegorical culture [which] matters little, [and] is a question of cooking . . . a means of regulating the form'.[19] The point is valid, for Byron as for Joyce; it is also altogether too simple.

The mythic method, for both men, was more than just a means of organizing contemporaneity with parallel and prototype. It had the much larger purpose of allowing for echoing or retelling. Myth would provide links with past history (and literature) to suggest a recurringly real condition of humanity — echoes between a Seige of Troy and a seige of Ismail, a pain-blinded Cyclops and a bigoted drunk — but it would also provide another kind of echoing.

'In mythology, to *tell* is to justify'. In order to be communicated in its true nature, myth 'must be translated back into its medium, the medium in which it [is] still inwardly and outwardly "resounded"'.

The Greek *mythologia* contains the sense not only of 'stories' (*mythoi*), but also of 'telling' (*legein*) or narration that is 'echo-awaking', in that it forces an awareness that the story personally concerns narrator and audience alike. Fragments of mythology handed down to us, to be restored from 'dead matter' to their 'live selves' must therefore be 'translated back into the medium of such narration and such participation by the audience'.[20] This translation must occur through, and despite, the various archeological and literary layers.

Byron and Joyce 'justify' the myths they employ in *Don Juan* and *Ulysses*; they not only use them to parallel, structure and echo, they perform the dynamic action of 'telling', of making the myths contemporary, personal, part of one live tradition. They affirm the old myths in their previous forms even as they enliven them and make them anew. They also, explicitly, criticize them. What results is a complex of contrast and multiple perspective. Ages and conditions, patterns and traditions, mythic or literary, are layered together like the layers of Troy, and a mechanism for critical contrast and creative reflection through all of Western tradition is established.

Justifying mythic tradition in *Don Juan* and *Ulysses*, Byron and Joyce find themselves justifying literary tradition – and reckoning with epic law – also. The transition from the one to the other is not so strange. Myth has always been the direct ancestor of literature. Epic has always been the primary tradition. Myth has always nourished a form of history ('Troy owes to Homer what whist owes to Hoyle' III, 90), with oral poetry preserving record before the advent of the historian: Mnemosyne, goddess of myth, soon became goddess of memory and record. Hence literary, specifically epic, tradition can be read as a history of myth's attempts to record history and culture.

The form of Greek epic was inaugurated when a new social order set out to revalue its heritage by removing the barbarities of its recent conquest from the record, expurgating the folk-memory, and transforming 'old stories, as "nasty and brutish" as they were short . . . into myths and legends of a new order'.[21] Myth, civilized, became epic; and Virgil received the tradition, formal, conventioned and historied, in its completed form.

Virgil's heirs were Dante and Milton, and Byron and Joyce. These latter, too, would 'civilize' myth and reckon with epic example. They, too, would write their national epics for Ireland and Europe. Although, unlike Virgil, their intent would be not to build up the national ego but to deflate it. Their response to myth, their reflections on its implications for past and present times, hence, subsumes their response to the literary tradition to which myth gave rise.

I

In *Don Juan* and *Ulysses* the authors treat myth with an ironic comprehensiveness that is the inevitable product of their self-conscious comparison of mythic and modern worlds, and their reflection on the task of writing literature in each era. They follow Schiller's perception of the difference between mythic and modern milieus, and of the artistic ramifications of this distinction. The heroic world was simple, natural, direct, unified and concrete. It was unable to visualize any achievement except in concrete terms: gods were anthropomorphized, emotions were located in specific organs of the body, the soul was materialized; every quality or state was translated into some specific symbol, honor into a trophy, friendship into treasure, marriage into gifts of cattle. Indeed, the whole structure of its social life 'was founded on perceptions, not on a contrivance of art'; their theology was itself 'the child of a joyous imaginative power'. Their heroic poet, not having lost nature in his humanity

> could not be surprised by her outside it either and thus feel a pressing need for objects in which he might find her again. At one with himself and happy in the sense of his humanity he was obliged to remain with it as his maximum and assimilate all else to it . . .[22]

Homer wrote simply, naturally, mimetically of nature because he could afford to be simple. His art was nature, and his ideal was real.

The modern world, on the contrary, sees nature opposed to art, and the ideal opposed to actuality. Where Homer was naive, we are sentimental. Where the ancients felt an external, finite harmony, and their oneness with this proportion, the moderns feel an internal discord. For the modern artist his art and its concepts have no concrete frame of reference, his world is not imitable and, worse, may not even be out there. There exists, only, the artistic ego, with its ideals and aspirations that cannot be fulfilled, and its disillusions that accrete with any attempt to fulfill. The sense of being out of joint with the world is coupled with a knowledge that the world is out of joint with an ideal of the mind. The modern does not feel naturally, as Homer did; he feels only the loss of the natural and a pressing need to find objects or myths where he might locate traces of the original naiveté. He uses these, once found, to contrast and heighten his perception of the corruption, disunity, and artificiality of his world.

The dichotomy, and the awareness of dichotomy, began with Virgil, the civilized poet who wrote of idylls and past times, and August Schlegel places it directly in the percepts that nurtured Christianity. Unlike the heroic age's satisfaction with finite perfection, in the Christian consciousness

> everything finite and mortal is lost in the contemplation of infinity; life has become shadow and darkness, and the first day of our real existence dawns in the world beyond the grave. . . . Hence the poetry of the ancients was the poetry of enjoyment, and ours is that of desire: the former has its foundation in the scene which is present, while the latter hovers betwixt recollection and hope.[23]

Discord, despair, self-consciousness, the aspiration unfulfilled follow, as Eric Auerbach sees, in Dante, and since Dante. The distance separating Byron and Joyce from Dante may seem as great as that between ancient and modern world, but their perception of the disparity between past idyll and present situation is of the same order, although far more exacerbated; their artistic awareness of what this means is more acute.

Byron provides the metaphor for the immense difference between the two worlds. Child of nature Dudu is 'kind and gentle as The Age of Gold', an age unlike our own

>   . . . whose metal
> The devil may decompose but never settle;
>
> I think it may be of 'Corinthian Brass',
>   Which is a Mixture of all Metals, but
> The Brazen uppermost.   (VI, 55−6)

Brazen, prone to decomposition, untrustworthy, of uncertain value, such is the mettle of the age in which Juan and Bloom wander. Corruption and complexity envelope all. Whereas in the *Odyssey* the idyll with Nausicaa occurs at the end of the story, before the journey home, in *Don Juan* it is the first and only idyll of the tale; Juan's subsequent encounters with women are progressively less innocent and less idyllic. In *Ulysses* the episode is placed near the middle; but, immediately preceded by adultery and immediately succeeded by whoring and sacrilege, it is undermined by the farce and shame of auto-eroticism.

We find ourselves a long way from the clear-cut individual roles of the Homeric figures, or even the categorized clarity of epics like the *Chanson de Roland* (where Charlemagne and his advisors are all whitely good, with the Saracens black-faced and black-garbed). Juan must be both Odysseus and Telemachus, perversely young and old at the same time, playing father (to Leila) even as he is child himself. Dedalus is allowed three fathers and three mothers, and he resolves at the end to do without paternity or, better, to be his own father (to his art).

This blurring of distinctions continues with the lesser characters: Catherine the Great could be Calypso, tarrying with her young lover for seven years, but she shares some characteristics with Circe.[24] Gulbayez is Circe, yet as mistress of a large household and favorite wife, she owns something of Penelope's place; her position as first wife among a hundred concubines, moreover, is exemplary of the crowded loneliness of the modern condition. Odyssean Lambro, demanding *his* rights of household, is further usurped of his other role as the Cyclops by the tyrannical Sultana, demanding *her* rites of love. Molly is both seductive-nymph Calypso (a role she shares with her daughter, Milly) and a thoroughly adulterous Penelope. Even Nestor, Homer's 'sweet-speaking', wise, tactful, pious if somewhat garrulous old man, suffers drastic change in the contemporary world. A composite of ineffective mentors in *Don Juan*, Nestor becomes a bumbling old fool in *Ulysses*, condemned by his own prejudices. Nestor-Deasy and Pedrillo are fellow with the batch of impotent, high-voiced old men of Troy who chattered like cicadas, all portraits of what aged wisdom evolves into in corrupt times, and fit reason for the rebellion against family, father-figures and prevailing mores.

II

The writing of literature in such times must be the more difficult task: more complex, more doomed to failure, but also more spectacular where it succeeds in becoming art. If Homer's simple world made his art easy, his manner was likewise simply mimetic. His stories were a static pattern, formed by the interweaving of a large number of familiar elements which recurred through the poems. At no time did Homer seek words for an idea never before expressed; poetry in his day was composed 'only by putting together old verses and old parts of verses in old ways'.[25] The attempt to make new (or find new expression for the recognizable) in a sophisticated world that affords no imitable unity, is fraught with danger and potential. Homer's poetry, while intuitive, harmonious, and capable of achieving perfect form, is limited in its content; whereas modern literature, self-conscious and discordant as it is, and incapable of perfection, is 'unlimited in its scope and, though inferior in beauty, superior in sublimity'.[26]

The perspectives underlying the creation of the arts of ancient and modern times also differ. With the former art, characterized by its lack of self-consciousness and its existence as a natural object without any purpose beyond itself, the artist composes with a conviction of the irrelevance of criticism to his work. In the case of the latter art, the artist's feelings are filtered by intellect and scrutinized for validity and propriety. The modern artist is mistrustful of inspiration; the critic in him looks over his shoulder as he writes, controlling, correcting, assuring the conceptual consistency of what is said, gauging its didactic impact, and calculating all effects in terms of some antecedently determined purpose.[27]

Byron and Joyce write critically in *Don Juan* and *Ulysses*, at the end of a long myth-epic tradition, and at the end of a long mock-epic or critical tradition, in a critical age. The critical ability of their intellects is the primary thing they trust, over and above any inspiration, precedent, or literary tradition, and they employ these only as the former permits. Not only can they not afford to be simple, they do not wish to be simple. Their purpose is complex, critical, charted to their heritage and world.

Schiller said the sentimental poet responds in one of three ways on seeing that his world falls short of an ideal: if repelled by actuality he is satirical; if mournful of an ideal lost he is elegiac; if inclined to treat the ideal as present he is idyllic. Byron and Joyce assume a composite form of all three modes: they are satirical of their times; they mourn, implicitly, an innocence that cannot be rewritten; they attempt to form a new ideal that might function for their corrupt times. Criticism and complexity, products of a problem world, become its means and its virtues.

Despite its artistic simplicity, the *Odyssey*, certainly, can be seen as a compiled, multiple story. Fénelon said it was '*un tas de contes de vieilles*' and so it is: a mass of old wives' tales or Märchen, with emblems that look back to theriomorphic cults, folktale motifs, Boeotian catalogue patterns, elements from Phoenician, Ugaritic, Hittite, Hurrian,

Sumerian, and Egyptian myth, as well as borrowings from a primitive common source that gave rise to it, the epic of Gilgamesh, and the *Ramayana*.[28] Its impression, however, is not that of a myth made up of a host of disparate sub-mythic elements and individual myths. There is no overt sense of variance or multiplicity. Themes are related, and historical roots are shared, because the mythic world-picture is the same.

Old myths of the annual loss and return of the earth's vitality and old rites of the death and recovery of gods pass, effortlessly, to become myths of quest and the story of Odysseus's search for home. The Greek's journey home includes all themes of passage: through life, the pilgrim's progress to eternity, passages of *Nekyia*, and the westward journey of the sun. As Odysseus's scar, memento of his encounter with a wild-boar on Parnassus, recalls the myth of Adonis without any violation of the story's progress, so, too, do the various elements that form the *Odyssey* mesh together, without startling discrepancies, to form a unity sufficient in itself.

In the world of *Don Juan* and *Ulysses* such a single myth, composed of like elements and a common history, is not enough, cannot function alone, cannot be. Scores of ancillary myths, disparate in theme, origin, and story, are required to complement the primary myth of Odysseus and, together, symbolize the modern condition. Myths of the fall of Satan and of man layer the myths of Phaeton and Icarus (and the legends of Faust and Don Juan) to symbolize the ascending and falling fortunes of Juan, Stephen, and Bloom. Dedalus's assumption of the fate of both his namesake and Icarus and his concept of 'diabolic pride' in the artist which he shares with Byron ('For oftentimes, when Pegasus seems winning/The race, he sprains a wing, and down we tend,/Like Lucifer when hurl'd from Heaven for sinning;/Our sin the same, and hard as his to mend,/Being pride . . . ' IV, I) combine to find further mythic symbol in Pegasus, source of earthly, accidental poetic genius.

Bloom as Odysseus is also 'Christus Bloomus', and Stephen as Telemachus is also the holy ghostly artist. Juan shows Christian compassion in saving infidels and, though a type of mythic pagan, like the legendary Don, refuses to chew a corpse (Pedro) much as Dedalus shunned the un-Christian 'corpse-chewing' rites of his church. Molly is Penelope the weaver, but she encompasses the myth of Gaea-Tellus, Rhea, Anima-Matrix, Hera, la belle dame sans merci, Aphrodite and – most curious – the Virgin Mary.

The Oedipal myth, albeit in warped form, is present in both stories:

in Juan's throttling of his mother's lover (Alphonso), and in his maternal loves, Gulbayez and Catherine; in Stephen who remembers the day his mother stopped kissing him, worries about incest, and believes Mulligan's accusation that he killed his parent. A hart pursued by the treacherous arrows of friends, Stephen raises Sigfried's battle-cry 'Nothung!' at a crucial moment. Shades of the Orpheus story surface when a group of opera singers sing impotently to a Juan-Eurydice imprisoned in the pit of the slave-ship. Stephen, as Telemachus, thinks of Athene when he sees the birds at the end of 'Scylla and Charybdis', but he thinks also of Thoth, Egyptian God of Birds, and Aengus the Celtic bird-god; and the three myths, together, serve as muse to his Daedalian art. There are traces of various primal waters myths in both works, and in *Ulysses* there are aspects of Celtic myth (oaks, ashplants, Fergus, Aengus, Mananaan), and references to Buddhist-Hindu mythology.

However appropriate these allusions seem in particular situations, they do not form a unity as do the elements of the *Odyssey*. They are entities yoked by violence together; each true but not always related and often contradictory, they represent in their disparity and disconnectedness the random, fragmented modern situation. Where the mythic components of the *Odyssey* cleave together, channeling toward each other to form one impression, the mythic components of *Don Juan* and *Ulysses* tense and pull in multiple directions of meaning (or mystery) without resolution.

Hence, even as they use Homer's story of Odysseus as their model, Byron and Joyce declare the inadequacy of this myth as sufficient archetype for the infinitely more complex contemporary world-picture. And, even as they employ disparate ancillary myths to complete the inadequacy of the *Odyssey*, they declare, by their actions, the insufficiency of myth itself.

III

Byron's and Joyce's assumption of myth here, like their response to epic pattern which we will soon discuss, is fully paradoxical. As they would employ myth to parallel and highlight the corruptions of their world, they would also diminish myth and question its ideal environment. Byron's response to Shelleyan visions of a golden age (based on Homer's descriptions and Plato's ideals) best sums up this equivocal mood:

O Mirth and Innocence! Oh, Milk and Water!
Ye happy mixtures of more happy days!
   In these sad centuries of sin and slaughter,
   Abominable Man no more allays
His thirst with such pure beverage. No matter,
   I love you both, and both shall have my praise:
Oh, for old Saturn's reign of sugar-candy! —
Meantime I drink to your return in brandy.   ('Beppo', LXXX)

The golden days of the mythic past are past. Any attempt to revive
them presupposes a quixotic absurdity. The very revival of mythic
pattern is presumptuous; it requires stern modern evaluation to
prevent the use of milk, water, and Saturn's reign of sugar-candy to
soothe contemporary ills. Poet and novelist know the charges they
must level against myth and its literary successor. They know their
response to myth must be critical, whimsical, ironic, with praise for
both the old patterns and the modern world's ability to avoid such
sugar-candy perfection, and parody for the excesses of each.

    Myth, since Homer's story of the Wrath of Achilles, gave the
words, pictures and personification to war as the expression of honor:
'Oh blood and thunder! and oh blood and wounds! These are but
vulgar oaths . . . shocking sounds: . . . yet thus is Glory's dream
Unriddled . . . call them Mars, Bellona, what you will — they mean
but wars' (VIII, 1). The incorporation of Mars, Bellona, Kali-durga,
Ares and Odin as rightful deities in an ideal environment is
unpardonable. Robert Emmet's bombast (at the end of 'Sirens' in
Ulysses) is but one offshoot of the mythic muse's unforgivable
equivocation of bloodshed and honor in the human mind for all
future generations. For its shallow, criminal rhetoric, this muse
deserves to be damned by its own echoes.

    Buck Mulligan's invocations of the Great Mother, Father, and
other first principles, and Stephen's profane use of his religious and
classical training, are of the same reductive order as *Don Juan*'s
facetious reverberations. The long-boat has 'a curious crew as well as
cargo,/Like the first old Greek privateer, the Argo' (II, 66), and
Donna Julia's charms are as natural 'As sweetness to the flower, or salt
to the ocean,/ Her zone to Venus, or his bow to Cupid' (I, 55). An
absence of beef in the 'oxless isles' of Greece quickly sinks the fable of
the Minotaur to the proposition that Pasiphae, whatever her taste,
'promoted breeding cattle,/To make the Cretans bloodier in battle'
(II, 155). Poet and novelist ridicule mythic fondness for the threefold

goddess or trinity of women;[29] Juan's fate in the Great House will be decided by three women, and Bloom's (in 'Circe') by three prostitutes or Molly, Mrs. Virag-Bloom and Martha. Both writers mock, in particular, the Christian myths.[30]

Don Juan could be read as a satire of the myth of Parzival, with Juan the innocent wanderer, narming others unintentionally if he does, curious but without a question, ending his passage in a court of many ladies, virile where the Fisher-king was sterile. Lambro is a fisher of men 'like Peter the Apostle', and he fishes 'for wandering merchant vessels' (II, 126). The poem's ten commandments read impudently:

> Thou shalt believe in Milton, Dryden, Pope;
>   Thou shalt not set up Wordsworth, Coleridge, Southey;
> Because the first is crazed beyond all hope,
>   The second drunk, the third so quaint and mouthy:
> . . .
> Thou shalt not steal from Samuel Rogers, nor
> Commit — flirtation with the muse of Moore.

> Thou shalt not covet Mr. Sotheby's Muse,
>   His Pegasus, nor any thing that's his;
> Thou shalt not bear false witness like 'the Blues' —
>   (There's *one*, at least, is very fond of this);
> Thou shalt not write, in short, but what I choose;
>   This is true criticism, and you may kiss —
> Exactly as you please, or not, — the rod;
> But if you don't, I'll lay it on, by G–d! (I, 205–6)

This is blasphemy. It is also serious use of sacred ordinance for something Byron feels is of equal importance: the tenets by which writers must write.

Mulligan celebrates his bowl of shaving-lather with 'This is the genuine Christine, body and soul and blood and ouns'; Stephen sees profane connections in the religious instruction he has received: 'A.E., Arval, the Name Ineffable. . . . The Christ with the bride-sister, moisture of light, born of an ensould virgin, repentant sophia, departed to the plane of buddhi',[31] — and he tells of how Mary, confronted with the fact of her pregnancy, responded 'C'est le pigeon, Joseph'. These too are sacrilege; profane uses of sacred myth by Joyce. But when Bloom says 'This is my body' at the end of 'Lotus-Eaters', and Stephen says 'God is a cry in the street' in 'Nestor', the intent is also solemn. For the artist, that cry in the street does call upon him to bear witness to its existence; and Bloom's declaration, like Molly's stained, orange-keyed chalice, celebrates human life as the first invocation did immortal life.

In their encyclopedic absorption of myth for massively ironic effects Byron and Joyce recall Rabelais. *Gargantua and Pantagruel* tells of the birth of cyclopean Gargantua: 'climbing through the diaphragm . . . he took the left fork and came out of the left ear' of his mother, saying 'Drink! Drink! Drink!' Much mythic erudition justifies this peculiar birth:

> Was not Bacchus begotten by Jupiter's thigh? Was not Rocquetail-lade born from his mother's heel, and Crocquemouche from his nurse's slipper? Was not Minerva born from Jupiter's brain by way of his ear, and Adonis from the bark of a myrrh-tree, and Castor and Pollux from the shell of an egg laid and hatched by Leda? But you would be even more flabbergasted if I were now to expound to you the whole chapter of Pliny in which he speaks of strange and unnatural births; and, anyhow, I am not such a barefaced liar as he was.[32]

Myths justify and parallel the story, the learning is impeccable, an honesty greater than Pliny's supports all, but the results are not what we expect. Six pilgrims, eaten in a badly-washed salad, pass through Gargantua's alimentary canal in imitation of Jonah and Odysseus. Pantagruel's descendancy from a grab-bag collection of ancient 'Who's Who', from Atlas, Goliath, Titus, Polyphemus and Briareus to Sisyphus, Hercules, Morgan, Galahad, and Bruyer, meanwhile, mimics the ordination of Biblical genealogy and the pedigree of mythological ancestry.

Like Rabelais, Byron and Joyce show their awareness that the mythic tradition is too long, too self-indulgent, too vulnerable to reduction through massive juxtaposition. But unlike Rabelais (as we shall see in a later section of this chapter) their ridicule of the mythological heritage forms part of a serious attempt to tell vital myths for their time. The paradox of their ultimate intention to write true myth feeds their ambivalence toward tradition. It further resolves them in their destruction (necessary before they can create anew) of all decadent patterns and fictional stories. 'One system eats another up. . . . Much as old Saturn ate his progeny' (XIV, I), Byron says, and we wonder whether his mythic system in *Don Juan* will not gobble up all earlier systems. In a Rabelaisian mood, just after he has wished 'Womankind had but one rosy Mouth', that he might kiss them all, from North to South, he peremptorily summons forth his fictive inheritance:

> Oh, enviable Briareus! with thy hands
> And heads, if thou hadst all things multiplied
> In such proportion! – But my Muse withstands
> The giant thought of being a Titan's bride,
> Or travelling in Patagonian lands;
> So let us back to Lilliput. . . .   (VI, 28)

Stephen Dedalus's mythic allusions, encyclopedic and laden with innuendo, accomplish the same purpose: 'Antisthenes, pupil of Gorgias, Stephen said, took the palm of beauty from Kyrios Menelaus' brooddam, Argive Helen, the wooden mare of Troy in whom a score of heroes slept, and handed it to poor Penelope' (p. 201). And in 'Circe' Joyce provides the shocking picture, as learned as it is inclusive, of Mananaan, God of Winds, as Mananaan McLir rising from a coal-scuttle, complete with druid mantle, eels and elvers writhing about his head, and a crust of weeds and shells. He holds a bicycle-pump in his right hand, a huge crayfish in his left and, in blanket evocation of Hindu, Buddhist, Celtic, and Theosophic mythology, spouts 'Shakti, Shiva, Dark Hidden Father . . . Aum! Baum! Pyjaum! I am the light of the homestead, I am the dreamery creamery butter' (p. 510).

Each new venture in writing, Eliot says in 'East Coker', is a new 'raid on the inarticulate'. If we may take myth to be one form of this inarticulate, as wordless paradigm of human instinct, then every artist's attempt to employ myth becomes another such raid on the inarticulate. For the writers of *Don Juan* and *Ulysses*, this raid takes the form of a great chain robbery spanning hundreds of centuries, a comprehensive romp through the mythic and literary past of Western civilization.

History is the devil's scripture, Byron says; it is, as Stephen says, the nightmare from which he is trying to awake. History includes myth, as it does literary tradition.[33] The purpose, for Byron as for Joyce, is to give that past – grown to a monstrous, unwieldly nightmare – a good, head-clearing shake. Their critical, inclusive, plundering romp will pass, not only through the past inarticulate of myth (as we have seen), but through the past articulate of epic tradition and its offspring.

IV

'True critics are not the sterile judges, the phrase makers. The efficient critic is the artist who comes after, in order to kill, or to inherit; to surpass, to augment, or to diminish and bury a form'.[34] Efficient critics Byron and Joyce prove true heirs to that literary form we call epic. Epic has been defined as a formal composition which has drawn into itself the poetry of past ages through many levels (mythical, legendary, historical) of cultural experience. It boasts among its characteristics lucidity of language, little subordination of thought, swiftly balanced movement, the music of the hexameter verse, a constant heroic world, and characters who function in epic purity.[35] Virgil took possession of this form and gave it its exalted, 'beautiful style' (as Dante describes it). Horace, whose verses form that 'pattern of Latin thrift',[36] institutionalized the pattern for all times. To this tradition *Ulysses* and *Don Juan* address themselves. And, since many centuries and much literary effort in epic's name separate them from the first masters, it is epic tradition as they inherit it – with its offspring legitimate and illegitimate, in verse and in prose – that they absorb and reflect on. They are literary responses to literary conventions.

To Edgar Allen Poe, epic was 'the art of being dull in verse'. Byron and Joyce would agree, for they write epics which castigate the conventions of being dull in verse. Following other writers who also responded critically to the art, they yet preserve epic intent in their works and so save the art from itself. Byron clearly thought of *Don Juan* in the light of the epic tradition; the remarkably frequent epic echoes in the poem carry distinct, serious intention behind their obvious parodic effects.[37] It is also clear that Joyce planned and executed *Ulysses* as a modern epic; as one which, despite its ridicule of epic solemnity, would be a fair alternative to its legendary models – and possibly more true to its time.

To accept Byron's repeated epic claims (which are at such odds with the poem's unheroic content, its colloquial voice, its careless composition, its attempts to destroy all fictive ideality to the point of undermining its own credibility) requires one to conclude (as Trilling and others did)[38] that it is an epic poem mocking the very idea of epic poetry. Joyce's epic parody forces the same response. But an acknowledgment of the paradox little explains their situation. In poem and novel the mockery is two-fold. As with their reflections on myth, the writers play past and present against each other, 'denying there has been greatness in the past, yet also evoking an illusory idea of greatness as a judgment on [their] own uninspired age'.[39] If they come to judge the diminished statures of modern Europe and Dublin in the light of heroic ideality, they also question the sincerity of the early masters and ponder the fraudulence of their literary premises. If, as McHugh says in 'Aeolus', 'The masters of the Mediterranean are fellaheen today' (p. 144), then the point of disparity raised reflects as much on contemporary corruption as it does on the epic writers who made golden claims for their Achaean sailors and Roman raiders. 'Very pretty poems Messrs. Homer and Virgil', as Byron would say, 'but you must not call them truth'.

V

Determined to make true epics of *Don Juan* and *Ulysses*, but questioning as much the sincerity of the epic masters as the epicality of their own times, Byron and Joyce launch themselves into a pattern of ironic reversals. As epic manner soothes and inflates, they, in their epics, mock, incite, and deflate. Their vision of unheroic Juan and even more unheroic Bloom in heroic posture is Swiftian, cutting three ways, to past and present times, and to epic-writing in each age, and Homer, 'like Gulliver's giant, pigmy, or horse, becomes an instrument for man's dissection'.[40]

The mock-heroic tradition is an old one. It may well be the tribute that satire pays to the heroic, since people tend to parody what they like, not what they dislike. The *Batrachomyomachia* (of around 700 B.C.) is our oldest example. Hexametered, with traditional epithets and bardic turns, the poem tells of frogs and mice in the grand Homeric manner: of heroes with noble compound names (Cheesescooper, Saucepan-invader, Lord Lickplatter), whose fates are marked by the intervention of gods. The poem's primary difference from Homer would appear to be that of scale. Ever since, the writing of mock-heroic has been an exercise in scaling down.

When *Don Juan* and *Ulysses* reduce the heroic and parody its manners they are hardly unique. But they are not simply mockheroic. As works that reckon with epic tradition and make a major departure on its example, they have specific kinship with those prose works preceding them which also took epic as their point of departure and fashioned themselves in critical response to its tenets. We call *Ulysses*, despite its vein of lyricism and its parodic links with a number of other genres, a novel. The novelistic character of *Don Juan* has been noted by most critics since Boyd.[41] Hence as novelistic, critical reactions to epic tradition, *Don Juan* and *Ulysses* must belong in a group of works which includes those by Rabelais, Cervantes, Fielding, and Sterne — works which themselves recall the picaresque mode and the example of Petronius.

The following paragraphs will review these writers in turn as they may anticipate Byron and Joyce. It should be noted however that none of these writers' works, nor even the picaresque tradition, forms more than partial precedent for the ultimate effects of *Don Juan* or *Ulysses*. Departing from Homer and epic tradition in their search for a truly epic medium, Byron and Joyce depart from other departures like theirs, also. They acknowledge the techniques of earlier criticisms of epic — only to reject these for not being critical enough. They absorb earlier literary directions that had sought to reform epic tradition by writing at a level lower than the epic milieu — only to go beyond even these by writing at yet lower levels.

Petronius's *Satyricon*, with its mixture of prose and verse, its teeming succession of events and subjects, its concern with bourgeois notions of life, its shocking realism, its broadly satiric intents and cumulative effects, makes a certain ancestor of the two works. Thompson sees it as a possible progenitor of the novel, if only through its influence on Rabelais, Cervantes, and key eighteenth-century figures (like Fielding, Sterne, and Smollett) who shaped the genre. He calls it 'a satiric *Odyssey* in prose', the first of this kind, bearing a resemblance in this 'to *Joseph Andrews*, and *Humphry Clinker*, more [yet] perhaps to the *Ulysses* of James Joyce'.[42] Traces of talkative Trimalchio, vulgar but touchingly vulnerable, grotesque but human, surface in Leopold Bloom. Byron, as we know, found the *Satyricon* a rare source for quotation,[43] and his narrator in *Don Juan* can often be as lewdly loquacious as Trimalchio.

The poem and Rabelais's comedy (especially the exploits of Gargantua and Pantagruel, which are borrowed from Luigi Pulci's *Morgante Maggiore*) share common source in the Italian jocose epics and their art of *improvisazione*. Joyce, who had a copy of Rabelais in his Trieste library, was delighted when Valery Larbaud said *Ulysses* was as 'great and comprehensive and human as Rabelais', and reported with pride to Harriet Weaver that Larbaud had placed the book in the sphere of Rabelais as a *comédie humaine*.[44]

Written after the Enlightenment, the French Revolution, Waterloo and (in Joyce's case) the First World War, *Don Juan* and *Ulysses* do not exhibit the exuberant energy and sweeping good humor of Rabelais's work. One occasion where *Gargantua and Pantagruel* remains their best model should be noted: its catalogue of the mythic heroes' lowered circumstances in Book Two (pp. 266–7). Revived by Panurge, Epistemon tells of his visit to the Underworld, where he found the epic heroes' 'way of life most strangely altered'. Achilles, a hay-trusser, had ringworm. Ulysses was a mower, Agamemnon was licking dishes, Aeneas was a miller, and Nestor a snatch-thief. Priam sold rags, Hector was a sauce-taster, and Paris a ragged fellow. Helen was a placer of chambermaids, Archiloclus a chimneysweep, and Pyrrhus a kitchen scullion.

Among other literary principals in Rabelais's underworld, we find Alexander the Great darning breeches, Xerxes hawking mustard, and Cleopatra peddling onions. Cicero is a blacksmith's bellows-man, Arthur of Brittany a cap-cleaner, Morgan a brewer of beer, and Lancelot, most appropriate of all, a flayer of dead horses. Odysseus wandering Europe as a libertine, or Dublin as an ad-man; Penelope, singing operetta in Dublin music-halls and reading novels by Paul de Kock; Circe, starving for love in a harem, or as 'madam' of a brothel; and Parzival and Christ taking the unlikely forms of Juan and Bloom, are all situations that directly follow Rabelais's reductive example.

The *Odyssey*, as an epic of travel which observes diverse civilizations, with a hero who must often survive by his wits, shares elements with one of its mock-heroic offshoots: the epic of the road. Petronius's *Satyricon* also can be seen as a picaresque tale, a parody of the romance of love, travel, and adventure, telling in the first person of the adventures of three scoundrels travelling through certain Mediterranean cities.[45] By default, *Don Juan* and *Ulysses* become heirs of the picaresque mode.[46] They are written after a long and various tradition that began with Apuleius's *Golden Ass* and Lucian, filtered through satiric prose tales like Rabelais's, and became the specific seventeenth-century genre by way of *Don Quixote*.

Byron freely acknowledges the example of Cervantes in *Don Juan*, and Joyce (the self-appointed heir of all the literary ages) had to be aware of the latter's novel achievement. A mad hidalgo sets forth to realize the ideal of the *caballero andante* in seventeenth-century Spain. Imposing the values of one age on to very different realities of another thus, Cervantes made limitless his subject's potential for artistic play. When they transported Odysseus to range over nineteenth-century Europe and twentieth-century Dublin, Byron and Joyce were attracted by the same possibilities for layered, montaged perspective that the transposition from one age to another would afford. As a novel of the dilemma of a fifty-year-old man who has read too many books, fashioned as a burlesque of epic, pastoral, and romance, *Don Quixote* criticized literature as a whole. In this also it is clear precedent for the Byron and the Joyce who would address the entire literary heritage in *Don Juan* and *Ulysses*.

'The otterer it is, the igherer he flies', Byron said, in Finnegans-Wakian language, of Fielding's manner which he admired so much. Gaffer and Gammer Andrews become epical parents of us all in *Finnegans Wake* ('Gammer and Gaffer we're all their gangsters', p. 215), and Kettle has astutely noted that the description of *Joseph Andrews* as 'a comic-epic poem in prose' better fits *Ulysses*.[47] Fielding's thoughts in the Preface to the novel are key to any study of attempts to write new epic, and we will return to these in a later section of this chapter. It should suffice for now to say that *Don Juan* and *Ulysses* follow Fielding's example also when viewing the low, basic reality of their times *de haut en bas*.

Laurence Sterne, whose *Tristram Shandy* freed the English novel so early, even as it was yet being formed, and who declared his affinity for Rabelais and Cervantes, provides the closest precedent of mocked epic and scorned tradition for Joyce and Byron. Sterne was an Irishman. (Joyce felt Sterne and Swift, to best describe their work, should have exchanged names.)[48] In *Finnegans Wake* he lists both in an elite catalogue of elect yogibogeys: 'This is Steal, this is Barke, this is Starn, this is Swhipt, this is Wiles, this is Pshaw, this is Doubbllinnbbay-yates' (p. 313). Byron undoubtedly knew Sterne; and critics have often called *Don Juan* a 'Tristram Shandy in rhyme.'[49] The poet and Joyce have none of Sterne's high-strung nervousness and sentimentality, and they are serious in their epic claims as Sterne could not have been. But the Shandean manner (of Chinese-box digressions, multiple narrative levels, imaginary conversations, wilful soundings-off, abrupt asides, disruptions of sequence, coy pauses on the verge of naughtiness) and, most of all, its mushrooming attack on the conventions of literature, prove to be remarkable anticipations of the effects of *Don Juan* and *Ulysses*.

Byron and Joyce are certainly precedented to a high degree in their mockery of epic manners. What is unusual about them is that they succeed in writing epic while spurning the idea of epic rule, reversing its effects, and scorning every convention that has established epic's

place in literature. They each say truly as Tristram once said
facetiously, 'in writing what I have set about, I shall confine myself
neither to [Horace's] rules, nor to any man's rules that ever lived'.

Invocation, the epic convention formed of pre-epic prayer
and mythic apostrophe, unavoidable since Milton's famous one to
Light, becomes in *Don Juan* 'Hail Muse! *et cetera* – we left Juan
sleeping,/Pillow'd upon a fair and happy breast' (III, I) – and in
Ulysses, 'Agonizing Christ, wouldn't it give you a heartburn . . . etc.'
Not Wisdom or Beauty but aging, adulterous Molly is invoked:
'Pride of Calphe's rocky mount, the raven-haired daughter of
Tweedy', (p. 319). As Fame was invoked for the making of money in
Tom Jones, as the Bright Goddess was asked to not be too busy to look
after Tristram, Byron and Joyce intone 'Oh ye! who teach the
ingenuous youth of nations . . . I pray ye flog them upon all
occasions' (II, 2) and 'Send us, bright one, light one, Horhorn,
quickening and wombfruit' (p. 383). The reversal of sacred invocation is complete when 'Byrnes!' (a Dublin pub) becomes the
magic word of light that ends an episode, disperses the seers of
medicine, and heralds the message of salvation from a pidgin preacher
selling quack cures.

Epic songs fare no better. Eve's morning song in *Paradise Lost*
reverses in Byron's chant from a recollection of how sweet is the
evening star, the night winds, the rainbow, the lark, falling waters,
the voice of girls, the songs of birds, the lisp of children, to

> Sweet to the miser are his glittering heaps,
> . . .
> Sweet is revenge – especially to women,
> Pillage to soldiers, prize-money to seamen.
>
> Sweet is a legacy, and passing sweet
>   The unexpected death of some old lady
> Or gentleman of seventy years complete,
>   Who've made 'us youth' wait too – too long already
> For an estate, or cash, or country seat. . . .   (I, 122–5)

Joyce, in turn, provides the panegyric to the hero who has
accomplished a great deed: the addition of a fourteenth child to a
starving Dublin family:

> The air without is impregnated with raindew moisture, life essence
> celestial, glittering on Dublin stone there under starshiny *coelum*.

God's air, the All-father's air, scintillant circumambient cessile air. Breath it deep into thee. By heaven, Theodore Purefoy, thou hast done a doughty deed and no botch! Thou art, I vow, the remarkablest progenitor barring none in this chaffering all-including most farraginous chronicle. (p. 423)

Catalogues in the early epics and in Homer served the vital purpose of transferring necessary cultural information to the audience. Here Byron and Joyce use catalogue to summarize cultural follies and to destroy the convention retroactively. The poet provides catalogues on the Turkish town, on the places, the sites, and the natural resources of England, until the poet begins to wonder if Dan Phoebus takes him for an auctioneer and, arriving at Norman Abbey, begs off from the inevitable duty: 'But a mere modern must be moderate — I spare you then the furniture and the plate' (XIII, 74). Byron's list, by sound association, of the unutterable Russian names is worthy of Rabelais's and Joyce's best effects: 'Strongenoff and Strokonoff . . . Tschitsshakoff, and Roguenoff, and Chokenoff . . . . Scherematoff and Chrematoff, Koklophti, Koclobski, Kourakin, and Mouskin Pouskin' (VII, 15 – 17).

Ulysses, meanwhile, exhibits a Rabelaisian fixation for catalogues. We recall the learned monk's preposterous catalogue of books in the library of St Victor (The Codpiece of the Law, the Poor-Wretch's Worm-Powder, the Leeches' Lattice, and so on). We are reminded of the curious list of implements five-year-old Gargantua uses to keep himself 'good and clean' (a lady's velvet mask, ear-flaps with spangles on them, a feathered page's bonnet, a March-born cat, spinach leaves, nettles, hay, straw, litter, cow's hair, wool, a hare, a cook, and so on) which Rabelais terminates in a fully heroic — and Joycean — manner:

But to conclude, I say and maintain that there is no arse-wiper like a well-downed gosling, if you hold her neck between your legs. . . . Do not imagine that the felicity of the heroes and demigods in the Elysian Fields arises from their asphodel, their ambrosia, or their nectar, as those ancients say. It comes, in my opinion, from their wiping their arses with the neck of a gosling, and that is the opinion of Master Duns Scotus too.   (Bk I, ch. xiii; pp. 64 – 9)

After both Homer and Rabelais, sundry items spawn forth in catalogues from the pages of *Ulysses* to reach gargantuan proportions.

A list of Irish heroes reads gigantically from Cuchulin through to Captain Moonlight, Jack the Giantkiller, Lady Godiva, and the Queen of Sheba (p. 296). A catalogue of foreign dignitaries, convening by nationality and name at a viceregal house-party, evolves cosmically:

> The delegation, present in full force, consisted of Commendatore Bacibaci Beninobenone (the semi-paralysed *doyen* of the party who had to be assisted to his seat by the aid of a powerful steam crane), Monsieur Pierrepaul Petitepatant, the Grandjoker Vladinmire Pokethankertscheff, the Archjoker Leopold Rudolph von Schwanzenbad-Hodenthaler, Countess Marha Virága Kisaszony Putrapesthi, Hiram Y. Bomboost, Count Athanatos Kara-melopulos. Ali Baba Backsheesh Rahat Lokum Effendi, Señor Hidalgo Caballero Don Pecadillo y Palabras y Paternoster de la Malora de la Malaria, Hokopoko Harakiri, High Hung Chang, Olaf Kobberkeddelsen, Mynheer Trik van Trumps, Pan Poleaxe Paddyrisky, Goosepond Prhklstr Kratchinabritchistich, Herr Hurhausdirecktorpräsident Hans Chuechli-Steuerli, Nationalgymnasiummuseumsanitoriumandsuspensoriumsordinary-privatedocentgeneralhistoryspecialprofessordoctor Kriegfried Ueberallgemein. (p. 307).

A Conradian knitting-machine, the epic convention of cataloguing has gone mad in *Ulysses*. Including all things into its unreal self, ravening until all has been consumed, feeding on itself, it annuls itself. The cumulative effect of these writers' efforts on behalf of the convention extends it beyond its limits. The explosion that must follow is immense, silent, complete, witnessed only by a grinning Muse (released at last from brooding over Milton's vast Abyss).

Byron and Joyce assume the techniques of their mock-heroic predecessors with vengeance, to obliterate each of the conventions (from similes and funeral games to boasts and digressions) in turn. Canto v of *Don Juan* demures epically, and rests:

> Thus far our chronicle; and now we pause
> Though not for want of matter; but 'tis time,
> According to the ancient epic laws,
>   To slacken sail, and anchor with our rhyme.
> Let this fifth canto meet with due applause,
>   The sixth shall have a touch of the sublime;

> Meanwhile, as Homer sometimes sleeps, perhaps
> You'll pardon to my muse a few short naps.

So, too, in *Ulysses*, the Muse will pause to make private jokes, to eat, to pick its nose, to eavesdrop on a visit to the jakes, to speculate scatologically, and to worry about hoof-and-mouth disease. Theirs is an enveloping denial of the very organization of epic: its choice of 'fit subject', its elliptic inclusion of only the most significant of events, its steady, clear progression to a point of goodness and resolution. 'Most epic poets plunge "*in medias res*"' but the poet's way is 'to begin with the beginning'. In this he joins forces with Sterne, who felt any true history of a hero should begin at his conception, and with Joyce who, a century later, began his one-day odyssey with the first movements of awakening: breakfast, bath (or non-bath, for Stephen), and visit to the outhouse.

In the face of traditional epic pithiness *Don Juan* and *Ulysses* cast wilfully accretive digression. The poem's digressions amass and increase until we reach the defiant, mocking eleventh Canto, which is over seventy-five percent digression. *Ulysses* increased by a full third in galley-proofs, and we have Joyce's letters to his Aunt Josephine — requesting stories, gossip, incidents, place-names, and 'any damn junk you can think of' — to tell us where the additional material came from, and of its significance. Clearly, the modern epic can have its own bastard eloquences; the modern Muse can express its own form of loquaciousness; and the modern author's *Willkur* [caprice], as Friedrich Schlegel informs us, will be subject to no rule.

'I have prated/Just now enough; but by and bye I'll prattle/Like Roland's horn in Roncevalles' battle', Byron says to us in Canto x. His simile is particularly apt for what he and Joyce wish to intimate about epic and their function with respect to its traditions. Unlike their mock-heroic forbears, Joyce and Byron do not wish to pay a back-handed compliment to the heroic. Far more distant than Rabelais, Cervantes, Fielding, and Sterne, their response is drastic; their criticism goes deeper to annul the form: they are anti-heroic and anti-epic. Not only is epic too little and too late, like that blast of Roland's horn, mock-epic is also too little, too late. The literary and historical balloon must be punctured. Mere mocking will not do. Epic talk has become mere prattle, and prattle too late, like Roland's horn sounding distantly from the lungs of a dying man. Poem and novel will use the very epic horn to forcefully burst the epic vein.

'All the classical genres are now ridiculous in their rigorous purity'.[50] The point, for Byron as for Joyce, is that even those writers who have recognized the truth of this statement, have yet failed to ridicule the genres adequately. As they see it, they fulfill a need — a need to destroy before anything new and truly epic can be written.

Don Juan and *Ulysses* exceed the mock-heroic, the comic epic, and the epic-of-the-road traditions in their destructive parody of that first literary tradition. By absorbing these directions and, ultimately, finding them wanting in zeal, they criticize them also. The poem and the novel surpass all their precursors (which had also sought to reform and supplant epic) by their intents: by their creators' attempts to write true epics for modern times through parody. As Geoffrey Hartman says, parody has become the new — possibly the only — genre of our times: personal experience has become the sole authority and source of conviction, and the poet a new intermediary. His real mediation

> is to accept and live the lack of mediation. . . . not acknowledging a sacred text, the poet is also coming to refuse the concept of literary authority so firmly accepted by continental classicism and with continuing influence even to the present day. The poet in our day who wishes to use traditional themes and marks of style is forced to write in what is becoming an entirely new genre, that of parody.[51]

Since Kant, as Schiller has shown, the artist finds he must write in parody. Through Homer, Byron and Joyce pass through the other literary directions since Homer.

VI

The articulated past which Byron and Joyce descend upon, to romp through, plunder, and raid, is not just the historical epic and its bastard progeny but the entire European tradition of letters. *Don Juan* and *Ulysses* show their authors to be the chroniclers of their cultural heritage. By parody, irreverent allusion, or outright ridicule, each provides a critical anthology of the high-points of Western civilization. The best writing of our contemporaries is not an act of creation but an act of evocation, Harry Levin said. But in Joyce's and Byron's case the evocations take a critical, inclusive, encyclic, saturated form. Their encyclopedic treatment of myth and epic evolves into an encyclopedic critique of the literate tradition itself.

Flaubert said he read fifteen hundred books in preparation for writing *Bouvard and Pécuchet*. It was to be an intellectual satire that took into account the whole intellectual life of France, and he subtitled it 'Encyclopedia in the form of farce'. Rabelais conceived of *Gargantua and Pantagruel* as a mad, farcical compendium of what the sixteenth century knew and thought about, from literary style to philosophy, science, architecture, geography, etymology, warfare, evangelism, jurisprudence, gastronomy, and meteorology.[52] When speaking of *Ulysses*'s inclusive attack on its heritage, Ezra Pound notes the similarity in Joyce's effects to those of these two Frenchmen. 'Cervantes parodied but a single literary folly, the chivalric folly', he says. 'Only Rabelais and Flaubert [and Joyce] attacked a whole century, setting themselves against a whole idiotic encyclopedia – in the form of fiction'. But Byron also parodied, cumulatively, his literary and learned inheritance in *Don Juan*. Trilling alone has perceived that the poem belongs on Pound's list:

> Burlesque is usually directed against a particular literary work or kind of work, with the intention of showing that it is false or foolish. But it may also be directed against the whole enterprise of literature, which it represents as an institution licensed to traduce reality. Parts of Flaubert's *Bouvard and Pécuchet* take this direction, as do parts of that great modern instance of burlesque, Joyce's *Ulysses*. And this is true also of *Don Juan*.[53]

We will discuss Byron's and Joyce's parody of specific literary genres and figures (of courtly romance, lyric, epic, of Ovid, Dante, Shakespeare, Milton) elsewhere. It is enough to note that this forms part of a comprehensive anatomy of erudition which is specifically reminiscent of Rabelais, Burton – and to a lesser extent Sterne.

Like Joyce, Rabelais was intoxicated by every sort of learning and information. Both mockers of the Church, their minds were marked by the priestly tutors of their youth, and they came to share a jeering compulsion to erudition. Hardly a compulsive scholar, Byron nevertheless read far more than he would have posterity know, and he learned Rabelais and Burton well. Rabelais's inspiration was literary. For his characters' actions, stories, and the endless treatises that string these together, he resorted to books – quoting, assembling, contrasting, parodying and mocking authors great and small, famous and obscure.[54] Ceaseless successions of allusions to literature, myth, history, learning, general information, and contemporary events clog Rabelais's sentences and disintegrate his story.

So, also, do Joyce and Byron conceive of things in terms of their literate past, amid a wealth of knowledge and information to which they are heirs by default. Theirs is an environment of plethoric scholarship, literary pattern and erudite precedent that they cannot – and have no real wish to – escape. They use literature in *Don Juan* and *Ulysses* to discredit literature and learning to abuse learning.

> Ovid's a rake, as half his verses show him,
>   Anacreon's morals are a still worse sample,
> Catullus scarcely has a decent poem,
>   I don't think Sappho's Ode a good example,
> Although Longinus tells us there is no hymn
>   Where the sublime soars forth on wings more ample;
> But Virgil's songs are pure, except that horrid one
> Beginning with '*Formosum Pastor Corydon*'.   (I, 42)

Defiantly, in the face of his massive, rigid inheritance, Byron vows

>   I shall enrich
> My text with many things that no one knows,
>   And carry precept to the highest pitch:
> I'll call the work 'Longinus o'er a Bottle',
> Or, 'Every Poet his *own* Aristotle',   (I, 204)

as Rabelais might have, mixing encyclopedic knowledge with comprehensive irreverence. The poet is as allusive as Rabelais and as offhand in his appropriations as Sterne. Recall how Sterne lists with learned abandon precedents for crying over loss:

> 'Tis either *Plato*, or *Plutarch*, or *Seneca*, or *Xenophon*, or *Epictetus*, or *Theophrastus*, or *Lucian* – or some one perhaps of later date – either *Cardan*, or *Budaeus*, or *Petrarch*, or *Stella* – or possibly it may be some divine or father of the church, St *Austin*, or St *Cyprian*, or *Barnard*, who affirms that it is an irresistible and natural passion to weep for the loss of our friends or children. . . . And accordingly we find that *David* wept for his son *Absalom* – *Adrian* for his *Antinous* – *Niobe* for her children, and that *Apollodorus* and *Crito* both shed tears for *Socrates* before his death.   (Bk V, ch. iii)

The haphazard manner of allusion of these examples, the appropriation for comic ends, the exhibition of uncontrolled erudition, the overall impression of an intellectual whirlpool, are of the same order as that found in Burton's *Anatomy of Melancholy* and through the pages of *Ulysses*.

Auerbach has spoken of the irreverently encyclopedic manner of *Ulysses* 'with its mocking *odi-et-amo* hodge-podge of the European tradition'.[55]

> Spouse and helpmate of Adam Kadmon: Heva, naked Eve. She had no navel. Gaze. Belly without blemish, bulging big, a buckler of taut vellum, no, whiteheaped corn, orient and immortal, standing from everlasting to everlasting. Womb of sin. Wombed in sin darkness I was too, made not begotten. . . . Where is poor dear Arius to try conclusions? Warring his life long on the contransmagnificandjewbangtantiality. Ill-starred heresiarch. In a Greek water-closet he breathed his last: euthanasia. (p. 38)

Passages lifted from almost anywhere in Dedalus's monologue provide illustrations of this 'hodge-podge' appropriation from the Western heritage. The Burtonesque play with erudition, mixing metaphysics and high comedy, which Boyd placed in *Don Juan* (in the Democritus Junior tones of some of Byron's digressions) sports through *Ulysses* also, especially where Joyce ridicules his persona's pedantic training and compulsively-alluding mind. The question of what poet and novelist achieve through their encyclical ridicule of Western tradition, whether they have any aim at all beyond negation, becomes an urgent one.

VII

'We bear the burden of our fathers, just as we have inherited their goods, and we actually live in the past and the future and are nowhere less at home than in the present,' Novalis said.[56] Byron and Joyce feel, acutely, this palpable, inexorable past bearing down upon an impalpable present. Hence the fate of tradition — mythic, epic, literary and scholastic — in *Don Juan* and *Ulysses*. With the lancet of their art, poet and novelist will awake from the nightmare of the past that Stephen Dedalus fears so much. Their intentions, as always, are twofold and paradoxical. If they would purge tradition, they would also rescue some portion of it. If they would awaken and put the nightmare to rest, once the dust settles and images fade, they would also wish to examine these images by daylight to see what positive might remain for their world and its art. If they would diminish (myth, heroic forms, modern life), they would commend the same; if they would destroy, they would also recreate. They write modern epics — through necessary, destructive parody. Burying, they intend to resurrect tradition; burdened by inadequate myth, they will attempt to form new myth; anti-epic, they will write epically of non-epic times; ridiculing learning, they will be the most literate, learned (and last learned) men of their ignorant ages. They will make the present palpable despite — yet through — the past.

Their apparent negation of the past is the means for an attempted definition of what may be epic in the present. Byron and Joyce ask the same questions Matthew Arnold asked of epic — its place and function in the modern world, of how it may be adapted, and what might constitute epic behavior in our time. They ask, also, what the content of any new epic could be and what the method of the modern myth-maker should be.

Such questions are not easily answered. The modern world is unheroic; its characters are rarely strong, aggressive, successful; its society is hardly noble; and its poets and muses have a difficult time distinguishing fit from not-so-fit subject in a landscape fast becoming a landslide of mediocrity, ignorance and hopelessness. To be learned in such a time only further exacerbates the problems.

Don Juan and *Ulysses* were intended to be epics of their age, as Virgil's and Dante's were. But the era subverted the act of writing to make them satires born of a nulling anti-epic sentiment. Hence, when writing them, the authors' primary problem was to control the subversion without denying its source or the validity of its critique: the works had to be unepically epic, 'true' and 'real' where past epic was not, ordered where their world was not.

Cervantes faced a similar problem which he overcame through paradox. Of the Spanish writer's accomplishment in that 'too true tale' Byron says:

> Cervantes smiled Spain's Chivalry away;
>   A single laugh demolish'd the right arm
> Of his own country; — seldom since that day
>   Has Spain had heroes.

> Of all tales 'tis the saddest — and more sad,
>   Because it makes us smile: his hero's right,
> And still pursues the right; — to curb the bad,

His only object, and 'gainst odds to fight,
His guerdon: 'tis his virtue makes him mad!
But his adventures form a sorry sight; —
A sorrier still is the great moral taught
By that real Epic unto all who have thought.   (XIII, 11, 9)

Like Cervantes, poet and novelist must find heroes where there are none. They must create 'real' epics that define what is good and true in and for their world.

It grieves him, Quixote says, 'to have undertaken the exercise of knight-errant in this detestable age' — but he must, much as Byron and Joyce must define heroism in their age. Quixote explains (to the curate) how he finds the old ideals more true than his passing existence:

> Why then, I find by my accounts that the enchanted and senseless man is yourself, seeing you have bent yourself to speak so many blasphemies against a thing [knight-errantry] so true, so current, and of such request in the world, as he that should deny it, as you do, merits the same punishment which as you say you gave to those books when the reading thereof offends you . . .[57]

The mad knight's problem in distinguishing the real and the true is one Byron and Joyce also face. They know that if the heroic ideal can make their age seem grotesque, the real world can also make the heroic seem absurdly dysfunctional. They know that if ancient learning was designed to elicit and teach the good, learning has not fulfilled this purpose for the contemporary world. Reality and goodness have become two fine and evanescent lines in the post-Enlightenment world.

If these writers solve their problem by adopting a method of ironic superimposition as Cervantes once did, the superimposition in *Don Juan* and *Ulysses* is yet distinct from the Cervantean model. They do not introduce a single set of past ideal values into a contemporary format of reality. Rather, they impose their contemporary world upon an entire epic, mythic, and literary tradition. Theirs is, in effect, a secular form of exegesis by type, or revisional interpretation, as employed by Biblical scholars and as immortalized by Milton in *Paradise Lost*. The past — all of it — is approached through the present, not vice versa.

Byron and Joyce take a host of related and disparate myths and superimpose one upon the next – and the unmythic modern atop them all – in an attempt to see what patterns might remain beyond the levelling and the contradictory criticism. Likewise, they take epic types (from Odysseus, Aeneas, Icarus, and Satan to Quixote, Candide, and Tom Jones), and epic manner, and superimpose the lot with the modern non-hero and his artless world – to see what value and method might thus survive.

Gleaning whatever prevails through these superimpositions, and learning from the multiple reflections they allow, these two writers find the wherewithal for their new order. The results may not be edifyingly pure when compared with earlier types. Nor might they always make clear the line between travesty and sincerity. But they have unchallengeable historical precedent and, significantly, are most 'true' in type and direction for the modern artistic effort. The paradox prevails. Providing the common denominator, such an exegetical method points, ultimately, the way to divergence and difference – to newness in the contemporary myths of *Don Juan* and *Ulysses*.

VIII

Old myths and old stories are turned on their head and reused with radical creativity to form the new order (or disorder), to make the present palpable. 'Writers move upon other writers not as genial successors but as violent expropriators, knocking down established boundaries to seize by force of youth, or of age, what they require. They do not borrow, they override.'[58] And the point here, specifically, is that Joyce and Byron override in order to borrow. In acts that are as presumptuous (and precocious) as they are violent, they make new myth. Remaking more radically than any of their forebears, Byron and Joyce wilfully obliterate their own mythic patterns in *Ulysses* and *Don Juan*. They fulfil the myth-making dictum of 'justifying' to its full extent: they echo, integrate, override, turning dead *mythologem* into live order. Conditions in their world do not support their action (hence the singularity of their myths among older ones), but they are two of Schiller's sentimental poets upon whom has been conferred the power, or lively impulse, to restore out of themselves 'that unity that has been disrupted by abstraction, to complete the humanity within [themselves] and from a limited condition to pass over into an infinite one'.[59] This achievement must employ paradox.

To suit the contemporary world-picture Ulysses must be, in one myth, a stripling repeatedly seduced and, in the other myth, a middle-aged canvasser of dubious parentage and more dubious religion. Their adventures must present more the image of 'the man on the run' of contemporary society (fleeing from Inez, Gulbayez, Catherine; Church, anti-Semitism, erotic shame), than that of wandering Achaean in search of knowledge and home. Penelope is a faithless adulteress by invincible law, the same law that decrees Juan will find no marital counterpart. Magical, alluring Circe has to metamorphose into sex-starved Sultana or whore-madam by a similar law of exacerbation. As such, modern Circes change men into women, not swine (Juan, the newest concubine in the seraglio, Bloom, in 'Circe', the 'virgo intacta . . . about to have a baby') and, seriously psychological as these changes may be, the modern magic can also turn out to be – with Wildean appropriateness – no more than a set of hallucinations (for Bloom) and a change of clothes (for Juan).

Seventeen episodes of an original form eighteen episodes in *Ulysses* because this suits the modern schema better, and Byron promises a hundred cantos should his milieu so deserve. Appropriate companions on the visit to Hades are, not benevolent muse and singing poet, but six Dublin bums, a group of bad opera singers, and an evanescent dog of changing breed. Misses Douce and Kennedy are apt Sirens for a mundane world: giggling, exchanging sly glances with patrons, twanging garter-straps, they are irresistible to the unhappily domesticated, alcohol-fogged Dubliners.

To follow the trend, Bloom has a cat instead of the faithful Argos; and Juan is forced to eat his spaniel as his odyssey starts. Odysseus's bed, meanwhile, built on a steadfast, rooted tree, must be represented in the modern world by Bloom's four-poster, wriggling and jingling on its quoits for all the land to hear; and by Juan's 'musical' bed, which changes regularly beneath him like that game of chairs, each time with a more succulent (but also more crafty and less eligible) female within its confines.

We cannot be dismayed by such components of the new myth. Nor can we say, simply, that they portray the mock-epic dimensions of *Don Juan* and *Ulysses*. They do emblem the modern condition: they are true types and situations for its milieu. They are part of a serious attempt to emulate and rival the old patterns, now discredited, to form contemporary myths which, like the world, are humorous, human, genuine, genuinely confused, and paradoxical.

The possible precedent of Fénelon's work suggests itself here. *Les*

Aventures de Télémaque (1696) was to be a reworking and continuation of the *Odyssey*. Composed of eighteen episodes and incorporating elements from tragedy, pastoral, romance and other genres, it was meant to be, at once, a rival to the *Aeneid* and the *Divine Comedy*, a summary of past tradition, and a modern myth of diminution, inconclusion, and unfulfillment. Highet called the work 'an unconscious ancestor of Joyce's *Ulysses*' when, in actual fact, it was one of Joyce's models.[60] As a contemporized version of the *Odyssey* turned *Bildungsroman*, it could serve as an ancestor of *Don Juan* also.

Samuel Butler's paradoxical treatment of Homer and the *Odyssey* provides a closer example of the attitude underlying Byron's and Joyce's recomposition of the myth. 'The Humour of Homer' appeared in 1892, closely followed by *The Authoress of the Odyssey* (1897). Butler discussed whether Homer may have been criticizing the pettiness of gods and women in the *Iliad* and whether the *Odyssey*, critical of men and heroism, might not have been an answer to this by a woman. His appraisal of the two myths, and his tone which refused high seriousness at all times, accomplished two ends. It posed the possibility of humor and paradox in the epics; it also succeeded in humanizing them, breaking their frame of convention and permitting them to be viewed as ancestors of the modern novel.

Joyce learned Butler's paradoxical tone. It was a greater precedent to his efforts than *The Way of All Flesh*. There is paradox of manner and tone in *Don Juan*. Byron could not have known Butler but he did know the style of *Don Quixote*, and he did write in the same age as William Blake. The poet, Butler, and Joyce all come to ask: cannot the more humorous implications of myth and existence be given rein? and cannot Homer and human tradition be truly humanized?

Fielding, of course (whom Byron called 'the *prose* Homer of human nature'[61]), anticipated all three: in his part-humorous perception of Homer, and in his attempt to write a 'prosai-comic-epic'. 'I wish,' he says, in a Butlerian tone of serio-comedy, 'that *Homer* could have known the Rule prescribed by *Horace*, to introduce supernatural agents as seldom as possible. We should not then have seen his Gods coming on trivial Errands . . . to become Objects of Scorn and Derision'. Indeed, he has been inclined to suspect that Homer 'had an Intent to burlesque the superstitious Faith of his own Age and Country' (*Tom Jones*, Bk VIII, ch. 1). Before them Fielding thought of taking the heroics out of the epic, of humanizing it to the level of ordinary life. Fielding, moreover, was serious in his intent to write epic. In the Preface to *Joseph Andrews* he said his work was not romance or burlesque but comic epic, more various but of highest literary value, counterpart to Homer's epics and prose successor to the lost Greek original, *Margites*.

In many ways *Tom Jones*, with its conscious epic overtones, is closer to the Homeric narrative and its noble wanderer than to the picaresque tales and their vagabonds. Like Odysseus (and like Joseph Andrews), Tom is sent out on a journey in order that he may ultimately come home.[62] So, too, are Juan and Bloom each sent out on journeys that they might ultimately come home. Howard Mumford Jones, in his introduction to the Modern Library edition of Fielding's novel, has remarked on how 'after two centuries of the English novel . . . *Ulysses* should recur to a theory of fiction which is outlined in the Preface to *Joseph Andrews*'.[63] *Don Juan*, a story without the heroic trimmings, is no less a comic 'successor to epic grandeur'.[64] The poet notes that there is but one difference between him and his epic brethren – his poem is true and therefore moral – and he means his claim, 'My poem's epic', as seriously as Fielding did his, and as seriously as Joyce did his historic echoings in the 'wine-dark sea' of Ireland.

Brian Wilkie makes the assertion that *Don Juan* and *Ulysses* are 'in the true epic tradition' in a way that Fielding's novels are not, and that Fielding's assertions for a new epic better fit certain Romantic works than Fielding's own. *Joseph Andrews* and *Tom Jones*, Wilkie says, assert their epicality on technical grounds, briefly, whimsically. Fielding errs, he adds, in claiming a new genre should replace traditional epic for the simple reason that epic is a tradition, not a genre. It is a tradition 'rooted in the past [which] typically rejects the past as well', one in which 'the partial repudiation of earlier epic tradition is itself traditional'. It is, in effect, a tradition distinguished by its paradoxical relation to tradition, by its intentions, and by its effects.[65]

In their thorough critical revaluation of epic tradition *Don Juan* and *Ulysses* follow Wilkie's thesis and fulfil Fielding's vision. Fielding sensed correctly that the force of the epic spirit could appropriately (and perhaps more effectively) be channelled into the modern novel – but it was left to Fielding's successors to write the novelistic epics he had wished to write. Byron and Joyce are numbered among these successors. They successfully meet the challenge of evoking the true epic spirit, they mark epic as an ongoing tradition that requires renewal to maintain pertinence, they make *Don Juan* and *Ulysses* fit epics for their world.

IX

If they fulfil the conditions of modern epic where previous attempts did not, what perspectives distinguish *Don Juan* and *Ulysses* as such? At the heart of their creation is a determination to evolve something no less significant than past heroics but infinitely more valid — because it is human. To Murray's urging that he write some 'great work' the poet replied, citing *Childe Harold*, 'you have so many *"divine"* poems — is it nothing to have written a Human one? without any of your worn machinery?' In a later conversation he affirmed: 'If you must have an epic, there's *Don Juan* for you . . . it is an epic as much in the spirit of our day as the *Iliad* was in Homer's'.[66] The poem is human, with minor heroics and fleeting triumphs over life in a mundane world. *Ulysses* is epic also precisely because it is human.[67]

Joyce and Byron take Coleridge's advice — that an epic poem must be either national or mundane — deciding with Milton on the side of the mundane. But what they espouse is of a totally different order: it is that other, rarely mentioned side of human life, made up of ordinary acts and petty shames. As Byron says of Don José: 'A better cavalier ne'er mounted horse,/Or, being mounted, e'er got down again' (I, 9). It is this side of human life they will represent: the places where traditional epic would pause or pass over (trust exchanged over mutual imprisonment in a harem or chocolate in a kitchen and urination under the stars); the unusual perspectives (of Leila wondering why God would build such a splendid temple — St Paul's — in a heathen land: 'A mosque so noble, flung like pearls to swine' X, 75) that traditional stories would not think to notice. They shun heroics preferring, instead, to highlight little heroisms: of an old Pascha at Ismail ('Am I/Describing Priam's, Peleus', or Jove's son?/Neither — but a good, plain, old, temperate man,/Who fought with his five children in the van,' VIII, 105); of Juan and Bloom surviving or rising above absurd situations; or of Stephen, triumphing over his ghastly visions.

Their characters are heroic because they are not, because of their humanity not despite it; it is the epic thing about them. Certainly, this is a paradoxical use of humanity in the epic (along the order of old Quixote, who is heroic despite his acts and most noble when he is most mad), with petty absurdity seen as human and therefore good, and humanness seen as epic and therefore sublime. The fault (or justification) for this lies with the world of *Don Juan* and *Ulysses*.

Where, in Homer's world, hell was an underworld Odysseus

visited during a spell of bad luck (from whence the Achaean returned to the safety of Ithaca), in these epics hell is everywhere and inescapable. Dublin City and the courts of England, Russia, and Turkey in Juan's time are places where desperate spirits abide. Here there can be no behavior in emulation of the gods. The gods are displaced, dispersed in the 'miasmic mist', and humanity alone survives raggedly rather than reigns.

Where Odysseus was god-fearing, god-resembling and god-beloved, Juan is too simple and too beset by problems of survival to concern himself with metaphysical questions. Bloom, meanwhile, is an agnostic by default (a Jew with one Protestant and two Catholic baptisms to his record), an epitome of religious history and its end in his time.

Religion and the gods may have passed by the world of the modern epic but the human problems of the sexual urge, guilt, and evil have not. Human threat (to human survival) now replaces divine punishment. Juan must survive in societies not planning for nor concerned with his survival. Bloom must weather a more hostile environment, tolerating where there is no toleration, loving where love is not wanted. Survival, in such an environment, is heroic by default. The individual acts of this survival: compassion for an infidel child, understanding an adulterous wife, acknowledgment of an artistic calling doomed to come to nought, are what make these characters distinct, mythic standards for their world.

Time and again the writers distinguish their stories from others by building upon intimations in the Homeric stories ignored by later tradition, upon twists to the stories brought about by their fallen perspectives. 'In all of Penelope's devotion to her husband' Butler says, 'there is an ever-present sense that the lady doth protest too much'.[68] Using this perspective, making of it allowance and precedent for human failure, Byron writes of faithless wives Inez and Gulbayez (as he did, in *Beppo*, of a lady who protested too much), and Joyce of titanic Molly Bloom of the (purported) thirty-three lovers. Homer seemed on occasion to deplore the destructiveness of heroic passion, and he used the Athene-Odysseus relationship to express his more humane instincts.[69] Poet and novelist now seize his example to write pacifistic epics. They show heroism without bloodshed, valor without cruelty, conquest without force. The accomplishment is as subtly precedented as it is contradictory to standard practice; and Odysseus, the only Achaean with a mind and some human charm, directly presages Bloom, who triumphs mentally through tolerance and equanimity, and Juan, who conquers through curiosity and natural charm.

With Hardy, Byron and Joyce believe 'the business of the poet is to show the sorriness of the grandest things, and the grandeur of the sorriest things'; they feel entitled to include in their defiantly human myths all the acts of existing, loving, denying, and affirming: the afflictions of the body (tears, vomiting, defecation, micturition, menstruation), random thought, and meaningless event. These may not seem epic contents by any standards, but they are true. They form part of the attempt to reconcile (instead of ignoring) the animal and spiritual aspects of man in the face of a knowledge (shared with Sterne[70]) that life is pathetic, bumbling, ludicrous, and an enormously tragic exercise.

Joyce, who never forgot Blake's proclamation that Eternity was in love with the products of time, owes something of his method to the latter's exemplary accomplishment. Blake enlarged the epical vision until extremes met: the largest of things were contained in the smallest, and concentration on the Minute produced Eternity — heaven in a wildflower, the world in a grain of sand.[71] Joyce and Byron likewise settle their gaze on the commonest things. When *Ulysses* begins 'Introibo ad altare Dei' it is, despite the blasphemy, quite serious. The corruptible trivia forming the content of the book (and the poem) *is* the altar of the gods, for the gods celebrated are the humble and the ordinary: scrutiny of these leads to the same plane of divine profundity as did the myths of old.

'If there is any difficulty in what I write it is because of the material I use,' Joyce once remarked. 'The thought is always simple,'[72] he added, pointing to a further internal paradox in his (and Byron's) myth-making. Having affirmed vulgar minutia and formlessness as the hallmarks of their new myths' milieu, he and Byron (to a lesser extent) turn the tables to become more obsessed with organization than the ancients. Their art becomes *the* integrating principle for their chaotic world, its only order.

Mythic parallel, hour, art, color, organ, and technique interweave *Ulysses* with mind-boggling exactitude. The principle of artistic expression as an ordering and integrator surfaces in curious form in *Don Juan*: in its digressions. More than Homeric and mythic parallel, more than any narrative line, Byron's digressions organize his poem. Insistent, they grow more relevant to the work with each extension, until they become the work and fulfill Hazlitt's comment about *Don Juan* being written about itself.

Organized, but with an ease and a prevailing open-endedness that accommodates the varieties and recurrences of contemporary experience, *Don Juan* and *Ulysses* fulfill their modernity. The former has a vitality that is never spent; it is an impulse that may never stop — over twelve cantos, a hundred cantos, a thousand cantos. The latter's impression of ceaselessness led Pound to ask Joyce if *Ulysses* had twenty four books. Unlike Byron, Joyce finished and charted his book. But, like Pound, we know no more of Bloom's future today than we do of Juan's who, like Woolf's Orlando, was to pass through more than one lifetime and a score of lives. Unfinished, *Don Juan* is never finished; and Molly's soliloquy sends us back to life, to another day and the endless process that gave reason to Joyce's book.

Speaking of myth, epic, literary tradition, learning, the arts, and all of Western civilization, *Don Juan* and *Ulysses* fulfill Eliot's utterance on the simultaneity of literature in 'Tradition and the Individual Talent' in a way he would not have predicted. They do not simply modify the ideal order of existing monuments of the art. New, radical myths for their world, they jostle and question older myths and older traditions, working in tandem with them and with one another. The poem and the novel are commentaries on one another — on their individual eras and shared modernity. They are re-commentaries on the *Odyssey*, the mythic realms and every conceivable expression of Western civilization these might have spawned up to their creators' own times.

3 The Hero and his *Areté*

I want a hero: an uncommon want
  When every new year and month sends forth a new one,
Till after cloying the gazettes with cant
  The age discovers he is not the true one,

Byron begins, observing the dearth of true heroes in his age and the dilemma of his need. He would agree with Joyce's rhetorical question: 'Do you not think the search for heroics damn vulgar — and yet how are we to describe Ibsen?'[1] and with the problem the question poses. 'Heroics' in the modern world cannot be justified; the search for heroes is not only difficult but invalid, for 'probably in life and certainly in literature, the democratic idea has put an end to the heroic hero'.[2] Nevertheless, both writers must find principals for their epics; they must define virtue, goodness, distinction, in an age that voids all moral classification.

What is a hero? The question has been addressed by thinkers from Homer and Virgil through Arnold (each according to his era); and, according to succeeding generations, unsatisfactorily answered. Byron and Joyce take this question, unanswered in the epic tradition by their perception, as *the* dilemma of their mundane world. The poet (in *Don Juan*) was one of the first writers to make profound examination of the possibility of heroic action in a democratic milieu. His conclusions were those Joyce also reached: that mere humans cannot perfect their lives[3] and that heroism as an ideal constant state cannot exist. *Ulysses* reversed the search for heroics and showed the imperfectibility of life in contemporary Dublin. *Finnegans Wake*, meanwhile, applied the levelling process of its unprivileged age to past notions of heroism: killed in the prime of his heroic life, the hero is resurrected that he might outlive his heroism to achieve old age and ignominy.[4]

When they choose protagonists for *Don Juan* and *Ulysses* and isolate certain qualities in them (as we shall see in this chapter), Byron and Joyce follow their Greek model and criticize its tradition of behavior at once. The paradox results partly from their ambivalence toward Homer, partly from their tendency to declare themselves against the *Iliad* and on the side of the *Odyssey*,[5] and partly from the ambiguity inherent in the Odyssean prototype. Poet and novelist continue the paradox (as we shall also see), to assert 'little, nameless, unremembered [attributes and] acts of kindness and of love' in the modern world as more prevalent, more distinct and more heroic than the epic values these replace.

'I am sure however that the whole structure of heroism is, and always was, a damned lie, and that there cannot be any substitute for the individual passion as the motive power for everything – art and philosophy included'.[6] Joyce's statement on the real foundation of heroism provides the best preface to his and Byron's choice of their protagonists. Individual passion, a neutral but passionate form of selfishness or sense of self, is the dominant and reliable source of contemporary virtue. A man is worth the sum of himself and his best urges; heroism, if it exists in this world, is personal, isolated, self-centered.

This is a far cry from the mythic (and subsequent literary) concept of the heroic norm: the *chevalier sans peur et sans reproche* who could exist only on the field of battle, with military victory as the meaning of his life and the honor code his only guide; the man who, out of a sense of distant honor and high zeal, unselfishly sacrificed himself for the common weal of his society. But the ideal was limited from its inception – by the very code, to the outlook of the hero's class and time. And the hero's selflessness, when it took the form of a ravening honor, of an Achilles who would wrest 'honor from Zeus', of a Roland who would lead a vanguard to slaughter for an honorable whim, was not so selfless and, in fact, far more reprehensible than the apparent selfishness of the modern hero. Knowing that selfish honor can mask as chivalric heroism, and that their societies are not worth the heroic sacrifice, Joyce and Byron choose Juan and Bloom.

Heroic equivalents in the poet's day include Vernon, the butcher Cumberland, Bonaparte, Mirabeau, Danton, Marat, and other members of 'the military set'. Given such candidates, and the dismal state of epic virtue in his society, Byron cynically settles on a legendary figure of passion and selfishness:

> I'll therefore take our ancient friend Don Juan,
> We all have seen him in the Pantomime
> Sent to the devil, somewhat ere his time.

Such an unlikely prospect, he declares, is one most 'fit for my poem';
such an anathema he will prove, wilfully, to be heroic and good.
Joyce spent three chapters of *Ulysses* in critical inspection of
Stephen Dedalus's heroic potential. Dedalus has combative courage,
Satanic pride, Achillean wrath; he is bereaved, Hamletesque, flawed
in character and, like Ajax (and Julien Sorel[7]) he never forgets a slight.
Yet he rejected Stephen with his daydreams and nightmares as too
serious; he rejected the angry young man's book-learned heroism as
intractable and ultimately petty. Instead, ordinary Leopold Bloom is
the exemplary principal of his age; with the man's self-centered
consciousness as the medium of its epic.

Formed of a passionate urge where the heroes of old were selfless,
of generally unlikely epic material, Juan and Bloom are also comic.
Aristotle said heroes could exist only in a tragic genre for tragedy
shows men as better than they are, nobler, more dignified, more
elevated. Comedy voids the existence of a hero since it shows men as
less than they are, ignoble, undignified and silly. However serious
their intents, *Don Juan* and *Ulysses* are comic works. But their heroes,
however funny and absurd, are also conceived as following in the
tradition of the tragic heroes.

We cannot be certain whether these writers are going against
tradition to define a new kind of heroism, or whether they are acting
within tradition and merely returning to a more original truth.
Homer after all, long before Aristotle codified and Virgil institutionalized the genre's virtues, modelled the epic hero. His
Odysseus is fully heroic – and consistently comic: his creator laughs
at the hero's tendency to look short when he stands up and tall when
he is sitting down;[8] at his eating of three enormous meals in quick
succession; and, during a night of anxiety, compares him to a bag of
guts roasting over a fire (xx, 25).[9] The very concept of heroic nobility
may well have arisen out of a prior perception of human absurdity.
We presume that the comic is a response to the tragic, that it is in
essence an adverse comment on the heroic. But is it not just as possible
that the germ of the heroic idea is to be found in the comic itself?

> that at the moment at which men think of themselves as funny they
> have conceived the idea of their dignity. As soon as they joke about
> their natural functions, about the absurdity of defecation and
> copulation and the oddness of the shapes their bodies grow into,
> they are on the way to contrive to appear nobler than they really
> are. How else do men recognize their ignobility than by imagining

their potential nobility? — a state of being which in time will come
to burden and bore them and arouse their mockery.[10]

As heroes who make us laugh, Juan and Bloom fulfill this
suggestion and follow Homer's example. Homeric precedent and an
older maxim than Aristotle's allow Juan to be shown as innocent of
any code, ridiculous in harem pants, seduced by platonic love, and
inclined to seasickness where he should have been more sublime or, if
not, then more self-controlled. Bloom, also, is justified in being too
deferential to his natural functions, ridden by sexual guilt, and too
nervously attuned to his wife's 'Poldy!' to perform at the climax
('Circe') of his epic venture.

Through paradox and parody, Byron and Joyce distinguish
goodness in the modern world. Surveying what might constitute
heroic behavior in an egalitarian age, they come to assign certain
qualities to their principals. These qualities manifest a Greek, and
specifically Odyssean, source (as the body of this chapter will discuss)
even as they isolate Juan and Bloom and show them as modern
creations formed in opposition to traditional concepts of heroism.
Along with other qualities that are neither Greek nor precedented in
epic and other literary directions (as a late section of this chapter will
note) these shared attributes of Juan and Bloom make them the true
heroes of their world and allow them to surpass, at once, not only
their earlier epic anti-types but also their prototype, Odysseus.

Poet and novelist reveal their protagonists as good men because
they are, first, funny men; they make them models of modernity with
the aid of ancient example; and they prove them as most heroic
among all past literary heroes precisely because they are not heroic in
any traditional sense — through their mundaneness not despite it.

I

Don Juan and *Ulysses*, as we have said, override tradition in order to
borrow from it. Setting themselves directly against the Homeric
model of virtue (as represented in the *Iliad*), scorning its subsequent
variations, Byron and Joyce sift through a spatialized tradition and
the timeless traits of the first Odysseus seeking support. They seek out
the hallowed characteristics of the Homeric hero against which they
might pit the urges of contemporary Juan and Bloom. But they also
seek out the essential qualities, hints, nuances, and even grotesqueries
in that original Achaean upon which they might build to illustrate

worth in their own protagonists. Their divergences from the Homeric model can be as important as their parallels, as Chapter I has shown, especially where these departures serve to highlight vital connections with the first *Odyssey*. Contemporary heroes because they are not heroic in the old epic sense, Bloom and Juan will prove to be remarkably, traditionally, Odyssean in spite of their modernity.

'How like you to be so wary! And that is why I cannot desert you in your misfortunes: you are so civilized [*epētes*], so intelligent [*anchinoos*], so self-possessed [*echephron*]', Athene exclaims, when Odysseus doubts her word on his return to Ithaca (XIII). Civility, intelligence, and self-possession form the basis of Odysseus's worth, they are the foundation of all that is admirable and individual in his character. They are also the essential qualities of Juan and Bloom.

'*Epētes*', as Stanford glosses the term, 'implies personal attentiveness, kindness, and gentleness, in contrast with boorishness and selfish indifference to other people's feelings – a quality closely akin to that philosophic gentleness which Plato praises in his *Republic*'.[11] We recognize this aspect in Juan, who protects his tutor, responds to a Sultana's tears and saves an enemy child from ravaging Cossacks; and in Bloom, who deals kindly with Paddy Dignam's bereft children and gently with a suffering Mrs Purefoy and a vulnerable Stephen.

'*Anchinoos*' means 'a kind of skill in hitting the mark, which is quick in action and not dependent on logical thought. . . . It implies a quality approximating to what is called feminine intuition . . . instantaneous insight into the essence of a complex matter . . .'.[12] Juan and Bloom are intuitive at least partly because of that basic passionate urge they own. The latter senses, correctly, that Molly will tire of Boylan's boorishness, he knows the secret yearnings of crippled Gerty, and he sees at once the pathetic side of Dennis Breen's behavior. Juan, less overtly intuitive, nevertheless acts on intuition: he 'happens' upon a host of astute moves throughout his adventures, and knows the tact of silence and inaction.

'*Echephron*' implies an ability to exert mental control where necessary, without allowing 'impulses and thoughts to lead to wrong words or actions'. It is 'the highest form of self-control', a form of keeping one's own counsel.[13] Motivated by 'individual passion', Juan and Bloom yet keep their self-possession. The former remains calm during shipwreck and is the only one on board with the presence of mind to prevent the people from drinking themselves into helplessness. Bloom, amid an undercurrent of innuendo and hostility in 'Hades' keeps his counsel even more than his legendary counterpart did. (Indeed, it is this quality that leads the Dubliners to vilify the Jew as a suspicious 'codseye'.) 'Goodness' in the mythic archetype and in the diminished new hero coincides. Beyond any superficial correspondences of fate or pattern, and superseding the parodic contrasts, these qualities point to that deeper connection *Don Juan* and *Ulysses* have with their three-thousand-year-old prototype, and with one another. By concentrating intensely on underlying and essential relations, Byron and Joyce are able to criticize an ancient model, justify their right to begin anew and define a truer form of virtue, and affirm a vital connection of meaning with the past.

'*Chaque homme porte la forme entière de l'humaine condition,*' Montaigne said. Odysseus and the two men may have begun at different points, the former yearning toward that hypothetical ideal man of Greek 'humanism',[14] while Juan and Bloom are ever on the way to appearing more diminutive, singular and splintered. Yet all three cease at the same point, as emblems of Everyman. Everyman may imply static eternal type, but Juan and Bloom deny all limits to experience and assert their right to change with the occasion. The Dubliner, is 'allrounded Bloom', who eats with relish 'thick giblet soup, nutty gizzards, a stuffed roast heart, liver slices fried with crustcrumbs, fried hencod's roes . . . [and] grilled kidneys . . .' (p. 55). He will try anything at least once; he will taste anything, smell anything, talk about anything, and speculate on such diverse subjects as the sensation of turning into worms — or of giving birth. The Spaniard, also, is 'all things unto people of all sorts' (xiv, 31); with an easy vulnerability to experience he sets off from Cadiz, prospects on a Greek isle, goes to a Turkish harem 'for lunch', and to England for freedom (presented, unfortunately, in the form of two highwaymen) and the ladies.

The first Odysseus was also 'much-experiencing' — to the point of risking the Sirens' fatal magic, as Joyce once noted. Dante interpreted this quality in the archetype as an Eve-like vice, an obsession for forbidden knowledge, and his Ulysses asserts with the hunger of a dying flame: 'Neither fondness for my son, nor reverence for my aged father, nor the due love that should have cheered Penelope, could conquer in me the ardour that I have to gain experience of the world, and of human vice and worth' (*Inferno*, xxvi). Coming full circle, Joyce and Byron (like Tennyson) ignore Dante's forbidding suggestion and make of the archetypal urge for experience a modern virtue.

Given their worlds, the quality in Bloom and Juan may be as much virtue as requirement for survival. Again the precedent of the archetype suggests itself. Odysseus has a facility for adapting to the unusual situation: as the 'man of many turns', he moves with circumspection, feeling his ground and playing roles appropriate to the uneasy environments he visits. Nineteenth-century Dublin and eighteenth-century Europe are at least as varied, demanding and alien as the places the Greek is forced to visit; they also require a versatility for roles: Bloom ('always imitating everybody', p. 771) must switch rapidly from sensualist to mourner, gay blade, peeping Tom, woman, and domestic man; and Juan must play at being dutiful son, platonic lover, concubine, 'Love's Artilleryman', Russian ambassador, and eligible bachelor on the English scene. To adapt is to know variety but it is also to survive, as Byron advises his young creation:

> Tomorrow sees another race as gay
> And transient, and devoured by the same harpy.
>   'Life's a poor player,' – then 'play out the play,
> Ye villians!' and above all keep a sharp eye
>   Much less on what you do than what you say:
> Be hypocritical, be cautious, be
> Not what you *seem*, but always what you *see*.   (XI, 86)

Spaniard and Dubliner are prudent and pliant as much by instinct and mythic example – as from necessity.

This fourth Odyssean quality, moreover, provides the bridge between ancient epic trait and modern means. We have already noted connections between the *Odyssey* and the picaresque novel; with the protean facility of their heroes the two come closest. The picaro serves many masters and plays various roles with an inconstancy that is his essential characteristic in the face of an inconstant world.[15] Juan and Bloom have no masters but themselves; nor are they ultimately inconstant. But they are sometimes overcome by fate and chance and, in this, they mirror their inconstant world to join forces of survival with the picaro of all ages. Stuart Miller says the picaro assumes whatever appearance the world forces on him, that his a–personality is typical of the picaresque world where appearance and reality repeatedly intermingle.[16] The evanescence of Joyce's Circean visions, and Byron's advice to Juan to always be what he sees, reiterate the same necessity to mirror changing forces and shifting realities in the modern environment. But even here a paradox prevails. By accommodating change and mirroring flux the modern hero, like the picaro, [17] is also more free — from any responsibility to the fixed and stable social order, and to assume responsibility for his own existence. Juan and Bloom are freer than the men of their environments: free to identify their own values, not their societies', and free to comment on the societies that might otherwise limit them.

II

As critics of their societies, the unlikely Don and Jewish advertising-man (as the next chapter will discuss) perform the picaro's primary function of satiric outsider. ('I cannot enter the social order except as a vagabond', the young Joyce remarked. Byron, also, cultivated his image as rogue-roué on the periphery of his society.) Nevertheless, in one important aspect, the two protagonists do not conform to the character of the picaro, or the first Odysseus. Juan and Bloom are not crafty: they are not embittered 'victims of enmity' full of vengeful tricks and devices like that son of Sisyphus and grandson of Autolycus; [18] nor do they, like the standard rogue, bide their time until they can abuse a system that has long abused them, tricking society as it has tricked them. They may be wry (Juan) or jaded (Bloom) on occasion, but they are not deceiving; however indifferent the external world may be to them, they still help and love unasked. They do not learn society's cynicism, its crooked ways: they remain men apart from the system, open and natural.

The former is a Rousseauistic innocent, the latter a Zolaesque creature without the disgust. We recognize them as naturals from the moment we see Juan fleeing naked into the Spanish night and Bloom floating in his Turkish bath. Byron found 'ironic force in reversing his protagonist's traditional character (the corrupting rake) and making him an innocent creature of circumstance with a well-meaning naiveté akin to that of Candide'. [19] Joyce planted Bloom's feet firmly in the clay: the man may be too preoccupied with the workings of his body, but he also affirms, with sacrilegious literalness, 'This is my body' (p. 86). The precedent, again, is Greek: the central Greek principle, freedom of thought, 'is based upon the belief that man's nature is, in itself, capable of the best'. [20] Poet and novelist do not espouse the natural ethic without qualification. Juan, certainly, is victimized in the Julia episode as much by social relationships as by his sexual urges.[21] It is also true that Bloom's problems arise as much from the fact that he is a Jew in a Catholic society as from his own (and his wife's) sexual needs. The natural aspect of Juan and Bloom nevertheless provides the means for a series of vital, positive contrasts with their environments. Each has a certain immunity to society; their instincts are always true to nature and to self. They are men conceived in direct opposition to that perfect being of epic literature – Aeneas – who had had to be a paragon (to justify Roman imperium) and dared not be a man. They fulfil Fielding's thesis that all heroes:

> notwithstanding the high Ideas, which by the Means of Flatterers they may entertain of themselves, or the World may conceive of them, have certainly more of Mortal than Divine about them. However elevated their Minds may be, their Bodies at least (which is much the major Part of most) are liable to the worst Infirmities and subject to the vilest Offices of Human nature (*Tom Jones*, Bk IX, ch. 5).

We recall the 'chilling heaviness of heart, Or rather stomach' that Juan feels on the ship, and several similar bodily functions in Bloom's story. These are Fieldingesque and Rabelaisian examples of the descent of the hero to human (and absurd) levels. But, like the unusual attention paid to food not only by these two protagonists but by the first Odysseus,[22] they point to a far more significant assertion their creators wish to make. 'Since Eve ate apples, much depends on dinner' (XIII, 99), Byron says and, learning from Homer's Achaean of the importance of 'dinner', he and Joyce make the gratification of appetites a human virtue.

Coleridge's comment in his critique of Shadwell's *Libertine* (which analyzes the character of the legendary Don Juan) is to the point: 'Obedience to nature is the only virtue: the gratification of the passions and appetites her only dictate'. For the natural man the only sin is to act contrary to his own nature.[23] By following their nature and refusing to act contrary to it, by appearing passionate, selfish and even absurd, by unselfconciously indulging their appetites and failing to notice their societies' forbidding disapproval, Juan and Bloom are true to their selves and truer than their milieus. What Auerbach says of Rabelais's naturalism in *Gargantua and Pantagruel* is equally true of *Don Juan* and *Ulysses*:

Rabelais takes a stand, and it is a stand which is basically anti-Christian; for him the man who follows his nature is good, and natural life, be it of men or things, is good. . . . his creatural treatment of mankind no longer has for its keynote, as does the corresponding realism of the declining Middle Ages, the wretchedness and perishableness of the body and of earthly things in general; in Rabelais, creatural realism has acquired a new meaning, . . . that of the vitalistic dynamic triumph of the physical body and its functions. . . . It is triumphant earthly life which calls forth his realistic and super-realistic mimesis. [24]

Not to deplore the physical for the other worldly, not to reduce humanity to its mock-heroic dimensions, nor yet to wallow in the swill with Zola, natural life in poem as in novel is singularly vital in an artificial society.

Like the early Greeks, as Schiller says, those of a natural or childlike temperament 'often act and think naively in the midst of the artificial circumstances of fashionable society; they forget in their own beautiful humanity that they have to do with a depraved world, and comport themselves even at the courts of kings with the same ingenuousness and innocence that one would find only in a pastoral society'. [25] To complement their guilelessness Juan and Bloom display an ingenuousness quite at odds with their environments; they can assert that the emperor has no clothes even if this shows them to be the only outsiders – or the only ones with true vision. Spontaneous, playful, Juan is 'quite "a broth of boy",/A thing of impulse and a child of song . . . always without malice', if he wars or loves it is with the best intention (VIII, 24–5). Juan's innocence (despite the irony of the last line) is a positive in his milieu. Bloom is hardly innocent, but he shares with the boy a lack of malice, a spontaneity for the physical world, and an ability to enjoy limited circumstances. He impulsively befriends strangers, volunteers assistance, tells the truth unasked, and is not above enjoying the incidental pleasures of bar-room sob-songs or bats at twilight. His fetal position in sleep at the end of *Ulysses* attests to the same point.

The two protagonists' childlike aspect can often disrupt society (as we shall see in the next chapter), but it is a constant that does not change. They may grow more wise or wary from their encounters with society, they might even assume the decadence of their surroundings on occasion, but they are not fatally tainted. They share with Alter's picaro and the mythic primordial child the equivocal situation of being at once orphaned outsiders and children of the gods:[26] vulnerable to the hostility of the environment yet protected by their own instincts.

The heroic world was a world of men and masculine action, for 'hero' had no feminine gender in the age of heroes.[27] In the human epic, Bloom and Juan must be complete representatives of humanity to the point of being not only childlike but feminine. At the height of the siege of Ismail, when Juan is in the thick of traditional blood-letting, Byron describes the boy as 'a generous creature,/As warm in heart as feminine in feature' (VIII, 52). There is a certain softness to Juan, an artistic grace, as there is to Bloom – 'There's a touch of the artist about old Bloom', someone says in 'Rocks'. Joyce described Bloom as 'womanly' and, at his trial in 'Circe', Dr Dixon attests that 'Professor Bloom is a finished example of the new womanly man' (p. 493). The two men's femininity places them beyond the heroic standard. But it recalls a quality in the *Odyssey* and its protagonist which Butler once identified as a fascinating sweetness, 'the charm of a woman, not a man'.[28] It supports, also, an obvious truth that nature is two-fold and goodness (or genius) androgynous. Juan's soft features and charm and Bloom's 'firm full masculine feminine passive active hand' (p. 674) are of the same paradoxical specialness in their worlds as the hermaphroditean Image Shelley's *Witch of Atlas* forms:

> A sexless thing it was, and in its growth
> It seemed to have developed no defect
> Of either sex, yet all the grace of both.

Intuition, tactfulness, compassion, tolerance, grace, artistic sensi-tivity – if these are all qualities commonly isolated as unmanly, then one more should be added to the list that sets Juan and Bloom outside the heroic norm: passivity.

III

There are no overt acts, in the old heroic sense, for Bloom and Juan to perform. Given the condition of the world of *Don Juan* and *Ulysses*, human action is not significant. As evidenced by the empty heroism of Dedalus and the gory honor of Suwarrow, such action is almost always absurd. Instead, and in corollary, the modern environment acts upon Juan and Bloom.

'I believe him to be more sinned against than sinning', Mulligan says in 'Circe' of the strangely Christlike guilt-ridden Jew (p. 493). The statement comes at the end of a story throughout which Bloom has refused opportunities to strike the heroic stance: avoiding conflicts, urging moderation in political quarrels, fleeing encounters with his cuckolding enemy. Juan, despite his namesake, is more pursued than pursuing. He is sinned against by everyone from his mother and tutors to Lambro and the societies of Europe. Even at Ismail, presumably *the* place of heroic action in the poem, the Don is passive; noticed accidentally by the wrong side at the right time, he stumbles 'backward into a medal for heroism'.[29]

No longer the man of vigorous action of the old epics, the modern hero prevails as an observer: acute, perceptive, curious, with a thoroughly active mind. He is one of Henry James's sensitive souls on whom nothing is lost. Juan passes through Europe passive but alert in mind, keenly attuned to the shifting winds of the societies he visits. Bloom's journey through Dublin, devoted to the seeking and giving of understanding, is essentially a passage of observation. Their triumphs, when they occur, are mental triumphs, victories of perception and sympathy.

Like Wordsworth, Byron and Joyce believe that the inner life of the imagination is the field of true heroism. Against the epic example of honor gleaned through physical force they assert the powers of human understanding. This assertion may be a modern peversity but it, also, has the precedent of the first Odysseus. We recall how Odysseus won Achilles's arms because of his strength *and* his intelligence; how it was he who conceived of the Trojan horse;[30] how he is known for his level-headed diplomacy at Troy. He is consistently portrayed as the most intelligent of the heroes, one given to philosophic, abstract language, with an unusually developed awareness of the human lot.[31]

Spaniard and Dubliner are in prudent company. On occasion their mental exertions take the form of Odyssean '*curiositas*' and work against them (as Juan's curiosity over the Black Friar does at Norman Abbey, as Bloom's speculation at Kiernan's Tavern earns him the scornful nickname 'Mister Knowall'). But most of the time their powers of mind go beyond the Odyssean variety of pragmatic intelligence to become an acuity of perception that works toward salvation (theirs or others). Hence they are always able to perceive and execute the good response for a bad moment: to will a recovery from the depression of slavery or save a Leila from rampaging Russians, to avoid intruding on a young girl's fantasy and protect a young man whose friends have deserted him. Bloom, in particular, owns a power to extract mental triumph out of physical defeat. No matter how much he represents the brutish body to Dedalus's soaring spirit, he is a man of mental heroism. 'Hades' describes him as 'a face with dark thinking eyes' (p. 101); 'Ithaca' gives us Bloom's Wordsworthian method of salvation:

> It was one of his axioms that similar meditations or the automatic relation to himself of a narrative concerning himself or tranquil recollection of the past when practised habitually before retiring for the night alleviated fatigue and produced as a result sound repose and renovated vitality. (p. 720)

In less skeletally impersonal words: Bloom has a mental resilience that enables him to turn defeat, pain, or sadness, into triumph, pleasure, or solace. He can resolutely quell a vision of the world as female wasteland, sunken, grey, shrivelled, sterile, and poisonous, and quickly transform it into a scene of sunlight, of 'a girl with gold hair on the wind' come running to meet him (p. 61). Thoughts of his father's suicide are deftly overcome; and he is the only mourner at Dignam's funeral who can leave for the rest of the day's business sympathetic but also at peace. (He may seem pettily self-justifying when he excuses his failure to ogle the servant girl outside Dulgacz's with a scornful thought of her 'thick hams', when he answers Molly's rejection with the thought 'she's getting soft', or when he makes of Gerty's lameness the excuse for their missed encounter. But these also are examples of Bloomian assertion.)

The Dubliner's triumphs over Boylan and Molly's infidelity are inalienable, more so for being psychological victories that encompass all such situations of past and future. His is the age old problem of cuckoldry that confronted King Mark of Cornwall, Arthur of Brittany, Rabelais's Panurge, Shakespeare's Leontes, and possibly the first Odysseus. 'Caesar and Pompey, Mahomet, Belisarius. . . . worthies Time will never see again', Byron adds for us, 'They all were heroes, conquerers, and cuckolds' (II, 206). But only Bloom, among a host of horned literary and historical figures, can confront the fact of his cuckoldry with equilibrium by the end of his story. He puts aside Boylan's ego, and the man's sense of triumphant singularity at having robbed another of his wife's favors, with the derisive reflection: 'that each one who enters imagines himself to be the first to enter whereas he is always the last term of a preceding series . . . each imagining himself to be first, last, only and alone, whereas he is neither first nor last nor only nor alone . . . ' (p. 731). Boylan's physical act was neither large nor significant; given the human mind's ability to project to infinity (and so deny the pettiness of insult) it was hardly triumphant.

Bloom learns by reflection, as Panurge did from Rondibiles, that 'cuckoldry is one of the natural attributes of marriage' given 'the nature of women' (Bk III, ch. 32, p. 377). By accepting that adultery may be one corollary to the female physique and, as such, something beyond his power to control, he overcomes fears he feels at Molly's disloyalty. His defeat is impersonal, merely a defeat of nature and circumstance: because a nature in its free state is 'alternately the agent and reagent of attraction' Molly's act is inevitable, irreparable, but also 'As natural as any and every natural act of nature expressed or understood executed in natured nature by natural creatures. . . .' Not as calamitous as 'a cataclysmic annihilation of the planet in consequence of collision with a dark sun', it is also far less reprehensible 'than theft, highway robbery, cruelty to children and animals . . .' (pp. 732−3). Thus, Bloom accepts the most direct affront to the male psyche with 'abnegation and equanimity'.

As none of the cuckolds of literature who preceded him did, Bloom can convince himself (and all future humans in his position) of the insignificance of the act of physical faithlessness, of the negligibility and naturalness of this so-called crime against society. Where others in his situation could not, he can resolve that there will be no revenge, no retribution, no assassination, no duel, no suit for divorce or damages and, most of all, no real humiliation for him because chance, fate, and infinity are not within his concern. There has been no affront because of 'the presupposed intangibility of the thing in itself: . . . the futility of triumph or protestation or vindication: the inanity of extolled virtue: the lethargy of nescient matter: the apathy of the stars' (p. 734). Hence, there has been no defeat. Bloom's triumph is a victory of words and will. It may earn him the dubious position of the most self-vindicated of cuckolds in literature, but we still cannot deny him the fully heroic substance of his accomplishment won, completely, through the powers of his mind.

One could not claim the same mental achievements for young Juan who is always a creature of passion and instinct. His triumphs are nevertheless achieved without physical force and because of his passivity; and his mental exertions to prevail are of the same order as Bloom's. Juan has 'a sort of winning way' and, when he conquers, it is through this *unexerted* charm and naiveté of his. He even wins the Lady Adeline, we may presume, for not having tried to seduce her. His latent geniality or natural goodness is potent. His greatest acts are, like Bloom's, those of compassion and perception: as when he shows compassion for infidels or recognizes the singular courage of a beleaguered Pascha.

Through the poem Juan survives, prevails, and often triumphs because of his passivity and its corollary power — resilience or nimbleness of mind. On the raft after shipwreck he is the only passenger who maintains his equilibrium; hence, he is the only one to survive. Quick intuition saves him from the fury of Gulbayez and (subsequently) leads him to sense potential in Aurora Raby. His mental buoyancy helps him survive the ordeal of Haidée's end and his own slavery; he renders up the Greek idyll with abnegation, and he faces future 'adventures' with an equanimity not unlike Bloom's. 'Through Juan's natural passivity, the positive satirist exposes Wellington's claim to distinction'. The victor by force — Wellington's avatar Suwarrow — becomes the anti-hero, the classic hero at last seen through. The poet looks into the legend and his narrative, into Cervantes, into the daily news, 'to ask what true heroism consists of'.[32] He finds his answer in Juan's ability to survive by not acting, in his ability to prevail by an act of mind. Spaniard and Dubliner know that the value of life depends on its dignity not its success. Their passivity, championed against the wanton militancy of the old epics, reveals a far more potent, because resourceful and tranquil, power of mind. This is the source of true heroism.

What Kroeber claims of Wordsworth's achievement — through the reversal of epic values — in *The Prelude*, applies, directly, to *Don Juan* and *Ulysses* and their true epicality:

> *The Prelude*, then, is epic in its rejection of the traditional principles of epic narrative. Quietism is celebrated over heroic activity; imagination is rated above physical prowess; autobiography supersedes political history; individual adherence to basic, perhaps even primitive, loyalties is praised beyond individual sacrifice to social causes. Yet it is precisely these reversals of conventional epic standards, not Wordsworth's half-century of labor on his poem or references to and echoes of previous epic poems, that command for *The Prelude* the title of epic.[33]

Passivity, imaginative resilience, allegiance to one's own story, adherence to basic, primitive loyalties: these are the true heroics; the modern means to honor and dignity (or self-respect); the tools of triumph and salvation. With their mental feats, flung in the face of worlds that deprive them of all else, and in the face of literary tradition, Juan and Bloom supersede Odysseus and his martial fellows. Their epic achievement is greater than those of their heroic forebears for the simple reason that the adversary conditions despite which it occurs far exceed any the old heroes faced.

We need, therefore, to distinguish those differences in the modern hero's situation which necessitated the reversal of epic values by writers like Wordsworth, Byron, and Joyce. We also need to query whether the early Greek term for personal distinction has become (as a result of these differences) meaningless — or whether, as an abstract concept for timeless human goodness, it might yet be applied to a contemporary distinctiveness so distinct from ancient forms.

IV

The heroic hero manifests his personal ideal and exemplary worth within a welter of supporting conditions. Graced with a noble lineage, immediate parents of significant attributes, and a godly genealogy that could trace his blood all the way back to Zeus, he approached, full armed, his heroic goal. Chosen, blessed by the gods and communal goodwill, an Achilles or an Aeneas (though not, we must note, Odysseus) had friends and relatives to defend his name, and legends to extol his honor.

For moderns like Juan and Bloom there are no supports or contexts. Random humans, orphaned in effect, without roots and without name, unblessed and often inclined to arouse communal hostility, friendless and alone, the dispossessed Jew and Spaniard must nevertheless define themselves and assert their spirit if they are to be exemplars to their age.

The first Odysseus was a solitary figure. The *Iliad* says nothing of Odysseus's private life, and in the *Odyssey* (even among his shipmates) his situation is akin to that of Ahab in *Moby Dick*.[34] Given the standard hero's popularity, this trait in the archetype is an aberration, a response aroused by the peculiar environment of the *Odyssey* which subsequent epic chroniclers ignored. Juan and Bloom must prevail in isolation because Odysseus's singular fate has now become the condition of every modern protagonist. His experiences are fragmented, his encounters with others are brief, his 'loves' are fleeting, one-sided, farces of pen-pal writing, or spurned. Families in his world are not what they seem or should be; and bonds and ties, where they exist, are largely the creations of his own mind. Juan has charm, noble birth and a pretty face – all things which seem to make him welcome to European society. Yet he remains alone and without friends. He is alone at sea when still an adolescent. He is quickly deprived, by parental and societal cyclopeanism, of the two humans with whom he feels bonds of love (Julia and Haidée). Even Johnson, the good mercenary, turns out to be the friend who would abandon Juan in need (in the seraglio and in battle).

Names, as the Bible, Milton, and even Mr Shandy tell us, are important: for place, for purpose, for self-definition. We recall the great significance the early Greeks placed on naming. ('The name was an anticipation of the future *areté* of its bearer; it set, as it were, the ideal pattern for his whole life'.)[35] But, following Odysseus who devolved from Everyman to Noman and went home a ragged beggar,[36] Juan, despite his parents, christening, and legend, remains nameless. He is the nameless young stranger not only at the Turkish court, where one might expect such, but also during his happiest moments on the Greek isle. Bloom, of course, is the man whose name people forget or do not know. The one instance where his name is recorded, a newspaper obituary, lists him as 'L. Boom'.

Throughout *Ulysses* Bloom is the solitary voyager: a Jew in Christian Dublin; an isolated figure in a coach full of mourners, in a noisy and crowded presshouse, in a throng of gormandizers ('Lestrygonians'), in a bar of unconvivial Irishmen ('Cyclops'), in a place of entertainment ('Circe'). He is without legend and without friend. Not only is he not chosen, he is never (as Juan seems to be) welcome. When Stephen leaves him in 'Ithaca', Bloom feels 'a lonechill' like 'the cold of interstellar space, thousands of degrees below freezing point, or the absolute zero of Fahrenheit, Centigrade, or Réaumur' (p. 704). Asleep, he diminishes, curled up in a fetal-ball, to a nowhere point the size of a full-stop.

The modern hero's distance from the conventional model, the enormity of his task in defining a personal distinction as significant as the classical concept of *areté*, finds encompassing symbol in the subject of fatherhood. The issue, or non-issue, of paternity subsumes *Ulysses* and (though more obliquely) *Don Juan*, to come to an uneasy rest in the situations of the protagonists. *Ulysses*'s primary theme, Ellmann claims, is paternity: Stephen refuses to acknowledge Simon Dedalus and agonizes without relief over transubstantial and consubstantial fathers. There is a remarkable absence of fathers and father-figures in *Don Juan*, although old queens and unfulfilled mothers abound; an old Pascha dies with his seven sons and the only survivor of the Turkish town is a female child.

We might recall here the situation of the picaro. He begins without knowledge of his origins, and coincidental meetings with his male parent at a later time in his life are without significance or issue. There is no recognition or, if there is, it provides no sense of meaning or solace. There is only a sense that 'the revelation has come too late'.[37] In a recurring exercise without solution, Juan and Bloom exemplify exacerbated and more psychological variations of the same problem.

Juan is left without a legal father from a very early age. 'An only son left with an only mother', his one meeting with his physical father (if we allow for the veracity of gossip that Inez was indiscreet with Alphonso before Juan's birth) is a farce (he knocks him down) and without other issue. The boy's upbringing by Inez and a pack of emasculated monks provides no set of values, no foundation, even less familial sense, and only the urge in Juan to be a true father to someone while he himself is still a child.

Bloom mourns his sonless state; images of the dead Rudi wrapped in lamb's-wool haunt even his best moments. His rootlessness is reiterated in Virag-Bloom's suicide and exclusion from the community of Catholic burial, and in his triple baptism. 'Fatherhood in the sense of conscious begetting, is unknown to man', Stephen Dedalus says, giving word to the condition Bloom lives and to which he has grown resigned.

The question of paternity is never settled. In *Don Juan* Juan's adoptée is abruptly left in the worst possible hands of Lady Pinchbeck. The young Don himself is presumed an adult and left to the mercies of three English furies. Even the symbolic union of father and son at the end of *Ulysses*, supposedly the culmination of the book, resounds with unfulfillment. Stephen leaves abruptly, refusing shelter and a bed; we doubt he will return to Eccles Street, as he has promised, or that he will even recognize Bloom on the street the next day.

No relationships of lineage will countenance Juan and Bloom when they attempt to epiphanize their being. Nor will their environment provide the traditional supportive context for heroic self-affirmation. If anything, the alien aspect of the two elicits the hostility of their societies. No longer merely indifferent to the efforts

of the modern hero (as in the case of the picaro[38]), the environment is
hostile. European Society's welcome for Juan (in England and Russia
as well as in Turkey) is only skin-deep. There, and in Dublin City,
Iliadic wrath and revenge[39] are found; and the heroes become
odyssómenoi, victims of society's enmity – prey.

It is no coincidence that Juan's spaniel and tutor are eaten on the
raft. Clearly, it is Juan that the environment would like to swallow
up. Only poetic justice, not immutable Hardyesque law or social
kindness, makes Juan the sole survivor of the shipwreck. Again, it is
not for Juan's benefit that the Amundevilles bring him to their Great
House; nor is it Juan, but her own repressed desires, that Adeline
considers when she schemes for him. With Juan as the prey of three
women at the Abbey, we may guess that Byron planned a symbolic
denouément of societal rapacity.

Bloom's horror at the gormandizers of 'Lestrygonians' (where an
entire chapter becomes a communal sound of 'slurp, gulp, glurg'),
and the peristaltic movement of the episode's prose, suggest more
than just a Joycean disgust for pigs. Given the impending hostility
toward Bloom that shrouds the novel, we sense that it is Bloom's
innards those gluttons masticate. Their action recalls Dedalus's dire
prediction: 'Ireland is an old sow who eats her farrow'. And,
Promethean-style, it will be Bloom's liver, or heart, those callous
Dubliners will eat.

                                   V

Before such environmental hostility Spaniard and Dubliner show
forth their peculiarly modern version of the Greeks' 'complex notion
of human goodness'. 'The basic motive of Greek *areté*', Jaeger says, 'is
contained in Aristotle's words "to take possession of the
beautiful".'[40] To the Greeks, beauty was nobility; to have nobility
was to have the potential for winning the prize of the highest *areté*.
No ordinary man could have *areté*: it was the attribute of the
nobleman. In its oldest meaning, the term meant heroic valor: a
combination of warlike prowess and courtly morality. Gradually, the
term was used to describe excellence of non-human things (the power
of gods, the spirit of noble horses), but its primary application to
human excellence remained and evolved to suit the developing ideal
of man of the later Greek poets. When tracing the term's development from its first meanings in Homer, Hesiod, and Tyrtaeus,

through to its later applications in Simonides, Pindar, Solon, and Theognis, Fränkel deduces that the complex soon came to have 'a moral sense', and to refer to 'the eschewing of all that is ignoble'. The old sense of physical prowess remained, but the term also denoted moral and spiritual distinction: a nobility of mind coupled with a nobility of action.[41] Juan and Bloom may shun heroics and expressions of physical valor. But for all their passivity, acquiescence and equanimity, the two men possess cores that are not vulnerable. When manifest, these moral centers can be potent and nobly excellent. To this core in the character of each the classical concept of *areté* can be applied (as we shall see) without any violation of the term's essential meaning. 'The hero is he who is immovably centered', Emerson once said. Juan and Bloom are so centered, morally, spiritually and, where necessary, physically. When environmental hostility punctures through to this core in either of the two men, despite their earlier complaisance and non-resistance, they can assert themselves against the violation without vacillation – and with surprising force.

To a tyrannical, Cyclopean Sultana holding him prisoner and demanding performance, 'canst thou love?' Juan answers with defiance and suicidal self-affirmation:

'The prisoned eagle will not pair, nor I
Serve a sultana's sensual phantasy.

. . . Love is for the free!
I am not dazzled by this splendid roof.
Whate'er thy power, and great it seems to be,
Heads bow, knees bend, eyes watch around a throne,
And hands obey – our hearts are still our own.' (v, 126 – 7)

Most critics since Boyd have noted this core in Juan and how it surfaces in moments of extreme physical danger or moral threat. Suddenly potent, he is spurred to act of his own volition: as when he fights his way out of Julia's bedroom, or defies Lambro, or goes gaily to meet an unknown fate in the seraglio,[42] or guards the spirits during the wreck of the *Trinidada*, saying with insight and courage unusual for a young boy: ''Tis true that death awaits both you and me,/But let us die like men, not sink below/Like brutes' (ii, 36).

For Bloom, also, in moments of extremity, the center holds with a moral excellence worthy of the ideal Greek. In 'Circe' he displays unexpected pluckiness in protecting Stephen against the law (the two drunk Tommies and Irish watch): 'You hit him without provocation. I'm a witness. Constable, take his regimental number' (p. 603). At the climax of his story, amid anti-Semitic and xenophobic rant from a howling crew of Cyclopeans, Bloom can say righteously: 'And I belong to a race . . . that is hated and persecuted'. Efforts to undermine the courage of his statement by one of the 'citizens', lead to a larger affirmation: 'I am talking about injustice', says Bloom, claiming in the teeth of cynicism that life and history are not force and hatred but 'the very opposite of that. . . . Love . . . the opposite of hatred'. When the Cyclops' fury expands to physical threat, the alien Dubliner can still nervily claim a parallel that has all the sting such a moral truth can have on an immoral crew. 'Your God was jew. Christ was a jew like me', he says, calling forth the biscuit tins, the rocks, and the stones.

This may be Odyssean foolhardiness in Bloom, but it is also a manifestation of soaring moral courage in a limited, vulnerable mortal. It is a quality Byron and his generation would have recognized in kinship; one with which they endowed the characters of their best artistic efforts. It is certainly no mere coincidence of history or insight that Turner's *Ulysses deriding Polyphemos* (1829), picturing a thoroughly Romantic moment of Promethean defiance and daring, should have celebrated the same moment of assertion of the unquenchable human spirit in the archetype that Joyce was to single out for the highpoint of his *Ulysses*.

When Odysseus defied the Cyclops, as the Romantics would interpret the myth, he affirmed the will of man and manifested his particular *areté*. When Juan and Bloom confront essentially identical Cyclopeanism they, too, serve the ideal of man and manifest their *aretai*.

Summoning forth a core of commitment and strength and showing forth this essential being whenever societal one-eyedness penetrates to it, Joyce's advertising man and Byron's unlikely Don come to lay claim to a version of the Greek attributes of heroism that is both peculiarly modern and yet typically old. Jaeger's final clarification of the term justifies the coincidence of its application in classic and contemporary situation:

> The Greeks felt that *areté* was above everything else a power, an ability to do something. Strength and health [were] the *areté* of the body, cleverness and insight the *areté* of the mind. . . . It is true that

arete often contains an element of social recognition — its meaning then alters to 'esteem', 'respect'. But that is a secondary sense, created by the highly social character of all human value in early times. The word must originally have been an objective description of the worth of its possessor, of a power peculiar to him, which makes him a complete man.[43]

The last sentence is to our point; with it, old and new meaning, and old and new manifestation of the attribute, coalesce to serve an ever-evolving concept of human goodness. *Areté*, as Jaeger implies, is the act or attribute that defines the moment when a man's potential is fulfilled. At this moment selfhood is manifest, whether through an occasion of physical courage, moral heroism, imaginative affirmation, or spiritual will. Simply, it is a quality that has much to do with essential human goodness, distinction, in any age.

The parallel or relation that occurs between the *areté* of the early Greek man and the spirit of modern Juan and Bloom is one of type, gleaned by secular exegesis: it is the fruit of what prevails in common beyond the differences. In instance, and in interpretation by the respective times, the heroic qualities of then and now are distinct and dissimilar. But in essential function and type, as affirmations of personal excellence, they are the same.

The *areté* of the early hero was manifest in overt goodness and visible accomplishment of mind and body. The *areté* of the modern is a latent goodness; usually masked as a passive geniality and given to triumphs of instinct and insight, but, whenever vital, manifest as potent action, true and equally self-affirming. In early times honor came by social acclaim, for having fulfilled society's best intentions. In recent times, honor is personal satisfaction, at having fulfilled the self's best urges.

In their invincible moments Juan and Bloom show themselves to be complete, good men, much as the heroes of old did in their occasions of fulfillment. Beyond the distinctions of time and perspective, Byronic and Joycean retrospection on a timeless ideal, man, shows the line connecting diverging manifestations of noble *aretai*. Bloom and Juan continue the evolution of an ancient term for human goodness, they renew the human ideal, and they surpass its first manifestations. They are noble because they are good, and, however mortal and ordinary, they are extraordinarily Greek.[44]

VI

We are left to isolate those qualities that make Juan and Bloom good humans in only their era: qualities which, by virtue of being neither ideally Greek nor precedented (being human and barely significant in the old epic sense) become heroic by default because of the era — and, retrospectively, ultimately epic in any age. What attributes distinguish the modern *aristoi*? E. M. Forster said that a true aristocracy is made up of 'the sensitive, the considerate, and the plucky'.[45] And with precisely these characteristics Juan and Bloom place themselves among an elite — to perform 'little nameless acts of kindness and of love' that are uniquely democratic and ultimately heroic. Forster defined pluckiness as 'not swankiness but the power to endure'. Bloom and Juan endure, as Odysseus and Quixote did before them, but their endurance is not so much a Grecian *tlemosyne* or resistance to adversity[46] as it is the more Forsterian ability to endure through persistent adjustment, decency, and self-extension. One aspect of this endurance would be the ability to compromise, to lower one's expectations for the sake of survival (of self or another): to forget Haidée and pander to an old Queen, to forgive Molly, to befriend Stephen after being spurned.

This leads to a second attribute of human heroism: consideration. The quality implies both tolerance toward others and responsibility for others (a far more social, selfless form of the Greek *aidôs*). 'I resent violence or intolerance in any shape or form. It never reaches anything or stops anything. . . . It's a patent absurdity . . . to hate people because they live round the corner and speak another vernacular', Bloom says in too-many-worded 'Eumeus' (p. 643), echoing a less vocal feeling Juan has for pagans and aging women. Because of their tolerance each can create for themselves opportunities to be responsible for others, to perform those small acts of decency and sensitivity. Theirs is a selflessness which supersedes any fundamental egocentricity.

Saving Leila or protecting Stephen are but obvious examples of their selflessness. In countless ways the two men declare their willingness to extend themselves for others, to expose themselves and risk being hurt by those with whom they sympathize. Juan sees bonds between himself and numerous others, from a shipwrecked spaniel and a lonely sultana to a reticent Aurora against whom he has been warned. Even greater emotional resilience belongs to Bloom, who sees a Shakespeare's face behind the pathetically sad visage of Martin

Cunningham, and who is shown in 'Sirens' as having 'stretched [out] his string . . . more, and more' (p. 277).

Joyce said the footprint Robinson Crusoe saw in the sand was worth more than St John's vision of the eternal city. It is the promise of another human being with whom one can sense kindred feeling, for him as for the poet, that is of priceless value. Juan's and Bloom's expressions of kinship with strangers may seem petty and insignificant when compared with traditional epic achievement. But they are of the same sublimity as those acts of sympathy Wordsworth isolated as singularly vital and true in a democratic world. Charity (toward a Stephen or a Leila) is the real trophy of heroism, as Byron says,

> . . . reflect,
> That *one* life saved, especially if young
> Or pretty, is a thing to recollect
> Far sweeter than the greenest laurels. . . .   (IX, 34)

In comparison with these and other little, nameless acts of kindness and of love, 'Fame is but a din' – and the exiled young Don is sent from the Spanish ark 'like a dove of promise forth' (II, 8). French defines *Caritas* in Joyce as love freely given, without *quid pro quo*: 'an ability to live with incertitude . . . to relinquish the demand for certitude from the people and things around one'.[47] The words apply, no less, to the poem. Precisely their ability to love distinguishes Juan and Bloom in a world that cannot love, and among traditional heroes who would not have loved in such circumstances.

As their creators had maintained all along, and as such acts show, Juan and Bloom are good men. They are not god-like men or god-men as the Greek heroes were. But their geniality, an essential, youthful potency and ability to sympathize as Trilling once defined the term,[48] works to make them epic examples of humanity and to keep them unique. 'He is all-round in the sense of your sculptor's figure', Joyce said of Bloom, adding 'But he is a complete man as well – a good man'.[49] The same Bloomian amiability, 'a winning way', and innately genial impulses preserve Juan as a good man in a bad world.

Through involuted ways and via an intricate tradition Byron and Joyce force us back, replete with platitudes and contradictions, to the simplest terms for defining distinction in the Spaniard and the Dubliner. Their emphasis on natural goodness may recall in many

ways the old concept of the Good Man or Christian Hero evolved by
the eighteenth-century homilists, and by the Pelagian doctrine of the
goodness of the human spirit (which influenced Fielding so much).
The Christian hero was a man of moral courage and generous heart.
From the acts of selflessness they single out for special praise, Byron
and Joyce seem to be defining Christian behavior. We are aware of
the inherent contradictions and paradoxes even as we note the point:
for the pagans, the natural men, the thrice-baptized, and the atheistic
hedonists prove to be most Christian in the worlds of *Don Juan* and
Ulysses.

Kindness, empathy, christianity, tolerance, love, and communion
are all terms that have lost their meaning to habit and hypocrisy. Yet
it is a measure of Joyce's and Byron's paradoxic achievement that they
will employ such terms, more hackneyed than the epic tradition
against which they write, and make them the foundation of true
heroism.

In the poem and the novel, the authors have superimposed their
world and its concerns on the ever-mutating literary and historical
past. They have each placed a hypothetical modern man atop the heap
formed by hosts of heroes, and non-heroes, and anti-heroes, ever
declining under bourgeois ministration, from Achilles to Aeneas to
Pantagruel to Quixote to Tom Jones to Rameau's nephew. Whatever prevails, or strains through beyond the exegesis, is not much. It is
small, particular, mundane and shrouded in platitude. But, given the
Joycean and Byronic perspective, it is more heroic than epic measure
and infinitely more valid than its environment.

The epic thing about Juan and Bloom is, simply, their humanity. It
is something the Stephens, the Johnsons, the Suwarrows (like their
epic ancestors) do not have. To 'take possession of the beautiful' in the
modern world means to take possession of one's humanity, as Juan
and Bloom do, to prove it good and true. This is Byron's and Joyce's
'humanism'. The ordinary is extraordinary, eternity exists in a grain
of sand, and 'the commonplaces are blasted into truth by the language
of experience'. If the whole of *Ulysses* is an epiphany or continuous
showing forth of Leopold Bloom out of the commonplaceness of his
existence, then one needs make the same claim for Juan and his poem,
for:

> in the existence of both men the ordinary and actual are prepotent;
> both are in bondage to daily necessity and to the manifest absurdity
> of their bodies, and they stand at polar distance from the

Aristotelian hero in the superbness of his aristocratic autonomy and dignity. Yet both . . . transcend the imposed actuality to become what we, by some new definition of the work, are willing to call heroes. The way down, as Heraclitus said, is the same thing as the way up.[50]

The way up is through the way down. For Joyce as for Byron, the paradoxical truth of Heraclitus's statement applies with an adapted vengeance to their concept of the modern hero. They scan the past through the astigmatic lens of the present, and so reject it – only to search among the litter of one city and one continent of their times and find Ulysses.

Juan and Bloom, as insignificant humans, are most representative of humanity and the only heroes of *all* human time. Too human to be heroic, they are ultimately heroic and worthy of epic treatment because of their mundaneness; selfish slaves of their passions, they are the only ones with a real sense of community (Joyce's 'atonement') and love; without dignity of body, they are singular possessors of self-dignity in their worlds; judged suspect and alien by their environments, they are the good men of their times.

The paradox of their existence, and place, is part of the Romantic idea of organicism (organic wholeness) where contradictions are seen as part of one complex, but it belongs with an older and more complete concept of man which Byron places in the myth of Prometheus:

Like thee, Man is in part divine,
A troubled stream from a pure source;
And Man in portions can foresee
His own funereal destiny;
His wretchedness, and his resistance,
And his sad unallied existence:
To which his spirit may oppose
Itself – an equal to all woes,
And a firm will, and a deep sense,
Which even in torture can descry
Its own concentr'd recompense,
Triumphant where it dares defy,
And making Death a Victory.

Bloom and Juan may end their stories as grammatical stops,

Hardyesque specks in an epic immensity, too shrunken by epic example, too reduced and particularized by their creators, and too eaten away by their environments. But it is also true that Bloom and Stephen become 'heavenly bodies, wanderers like the stars at which they gaze',[51] at the end of *Ulysses*; and that Juan is left, at the terminal point of *Don Juan*, consorting with one frozen Aurora (Adeline) and another rose-fingered Aurora (Raby).

Too-human and small he may be, but the modern hero, because of the same diminished humanity, can also be immeasurably larger than his traditional predecessors and, without supernatural aid, larger than life and more cosmic than symbol. Dots and specks are the sources of ever-widening Promethean circles. The fullstop where Bloom ends describes his limited circumference. But it is also the size of a hummingbird's heart, Joyce tells us, and this much heart in a heartless world, Dublin or Europe, is of infinite value.

4 Society and its *Paideia*

The Homeric poems reflect Greek *paideia* in record and in example. They are our first sources for the nature of early Greek civilization, but they also were their era's primary manuals for true social living. As the *Iliad* was the guidebook for heroic behavior in times of war, the *Odyssey* was the exemplar of aristocratic manners in times of peace. The latter, in particular, portrayed courtly society in its best existing forms, and in the ideal form toward which the upper class of Homer's era could aspire. An educational force for one generation of Greeks after another, a model of human social behavior that has come to serve all subsequent times, the *Odyssey* is, among other things, an image of the best manifestation of the human spirit in community.

The history of Greek culture 'coincides in all essentials with the history of Greek literature: for Greek literature, in the sense intended by its original creators, was the expression of the process by which the Greek ideal [of culture] shaped itself'.[1] Beginning as a term for the communal schooling of future generations, *paideia* came to mean a conscious ideal of culture, a concept of social and civic perfection, an image man in community attempted to fulfill. *Paideia* was the attribute *areté* as it applied to a group, a community, a nation. It was the standard of behavior manifest at times of true society, and the ideal pattern civilized society pursued; it was the reason for social order, the ideal behind civilized behavior, and the source of human dignity.

It came from *humanitas* and meant the process of educating a man into his true form. It started from the ideal, not from the individual. 'Above man as a member of the horde, and man as a supposedly independent personality, stands man as an ideal; and that ideal was the pattern toward which Greek educators as well as Greek poets, artists, and philosophers always looked.'[2] By reflecting Greek *paideia* in the communal courts of Ithaca, Sparta, and Phaeacia, Homer represented and nurtured his community and helped the evolving ideal toward realization.

Following Homer, Joyce and Byron reflect the *paideia* of their times in *Don Juan* and *Ulysses*. They depict the old ideal as it has evolved and taken final form in their era. They represent the quintessentials of their societies, manifest in such city-courts as Ismail, Petersburg, London, and Dublin. They portray the end which, after years of striving, these societies have reached. But what we call culture today is an etiolate thing, a final metamorphosis of the original Greek ideal. Immensely more complex, infinitely more distant and ultimately far less than the Greek entity, culture is no longer the certain means of education, the indubitable 'process of man's progressive self-liberation', the promise of a perfect world's imminent realization.[3] For writers like Byron and Joyce the cultural process Homeric epic inaugurated has reached a certain point, an end-point. Hence the term culture, where it occurs in our discussion, will refer not to a positive process so much as to a complex of less-than-ideal notions and traditions (political, artistic, intellectual) which underly the particular way of life the writers witness in their age.

If early Aegean civilization stands as a *Blütezeit*[4] or highpoint in Western cultural history, then Byron and Joyce acknowledge as much in *Don Juan* and *Ulysses* when they use the Greek cultural ideal as the touchstone on which to test the communal virtues of their age. Ancient example proves modern devolution. Presided over not by Penelope, Helen or Arété, but by Gulbayez, Catherine, Molly, and Bella Cohen, the *paideia* of the fair cities of Europe is shown as having suffered internal collapse.

Poet and novelist survey their courts with a jaded eye, one grown all the more disillusioned because it has seen Homer's exemplary goal. They see no passage toward an ideal of Man, no image of human perfection, no desirable form to which the social behavior conforms. They see, instead, a reversing direction.[5] The ancient ideal has turned back on itself, into itself, shoring up its ruins from within. *Paideia* as the sense of cultural destiny has passed on to become *paideia* as the untrustworthy urges of communal ego.

Devolution preordains Byron's and Joyce's task. Where Homer's task was to admire, to exemplify, to educate, to proffer an ideal and show it as real for posterity, their role must be to criticize, to re-educate, to show up all that is false and hardly exemplary in their culture, and, by declaring the state of the communal ego to be not good and only likely to breed further wrong, to condemn contemporary society and deny it any right over the future.

Hippolyte Taine, in the preface to *Les origines de la France contemporaine,* said he would study the transformation of France (as a result of the Revolution) as one would the metamorphosis of an insect. The image holds true for what these authors attempt to do. They scrutinize their social milieu as the final product of the ideal Greek process. They reflect, through their study, the metamorphoses of the cultural ideal in the ages following Homer down to their own. Retroactively, through these transformations, they also summarily reflect on that original Greek concept of communal distinction.

I

The courts of Nestor, Menelaus, and Alcinous are greater and nobler than bickering Olympus. The lands of the Lestrygonians and Lotuseaters (and the inhospitality of Aeolus and Polyphemus) are perversions of the former's true community. If the *Odyssey* is our first novelistic survey of the environment, its supportive position toward the class it portrays is antipodal to the critical one which novels since the Enlightenment have assumed toward their milieus. A clear and inevitable reversal in writers' perceptions of the social entity has followed a more diffuse and gradual reversal in function of communal organization.

Alfred North Whitehead says that the social history of mankind exhibits great organizations in their alternating functions of conditions for progress, and of contrivances for stunting humanity. The history of Western Europe is one of the blessing — and the curse — of political organization, of religious organization, of social agencies for larger purposes. 'The moment of dominance, prayed for, worked for, sacrificed for, by generations of the noblest spirits, marks the turning point where the blessing passes into the curse.'[6] For the men of Byron's and Joyce's era, European social history has reached that turning place where order has become limitation, where progress has turned back on itself to become regression. Raymond Williams has documented how actual change in historical conditions prompted the changes in meaning of the term society: from a notion of active fellowship or association for a common purpose (in the sixteenth century), to a notion of specific laws governing a specific system of common life (in the eighteenth century), to the contemporary conception of society as a set of abstract and impersonal edicts intended not so much for social interaction as for determining individual behavior and governing civic institutions:[7]

Society itself, which should create
Kindness, destroys what little we had got:
To feel for none is the true social art
Of the world's stoics – men without a heart.   (v, 25)

The Romantics were the first to perceive the change in purpose
that had evolved in the social organization. They distinguished
society as an object, one established institution despite its various
manifestations in time and place, and spoke of the relationship
between the individual and his milieu as a problem. Society was
pronounced a completed, independent, distant and often overwhelming, organism; it was a process only when it entered lives to
shape or to deform them. They resolved that society should not be an
abstract framework in which men were defined but, rather, an entity
(even an actor, a character) that is seen, revealed, valued and judged
through persons.

Hence Stendhal came to define the novel as '*un mirror qu'on promene
le long d'un chemin*',[8] a critical mirror which reflects, from some
external vantage point, its environment's worst foolishness and
gravest faults. Like other writers since the early nineteenth century,
Byron and Joyce perceive their task to be the revelation and judgment
of society, whether manifest in Europe or Ireland. Anne Isabella
Milbanke reverently recorded the poet's first words to her: 'Do you
think there is one person here who dares look into himself?' The
moral Miss Milbanke was greatly impressed by Byron's astute
pronouncement on the inability of his society to take an honest look
at itself and on its need to do so. In 1906, when Grant Richards
expressed near-Milbankian nicety on behalf of Irish society over
Dubliners, Joyce offered a like sentiment: 'I seriously believe that you
will retard the course of civilization in Ireland by preventing the Irish
people from having one good look at themselves in my nicely
polished looking-glass'.[9]

Like the mirrors that preceded them, *Don Juan* and *Ulysses* reflect
truthfully. They tell truly of societal hypocrisy in their age, speaking
with paracletic vigor of the Dubliners' and the Europeans' rote-
behavior, their empty rules, their vapid politics. They penetrate
beneath the aspirations of social organization. Homer could passively
record and promise the imminent fulfillment of a social ideal, but
Joyce and Byron must reveal what lies beneath successive layers of
unfulfilled communal aspirations. The question of whether they will
find anything beneath the many layers persists and, as a result, their

methods become drastic. They purge, strip, flay and, finally, lay waste. Byron said ridicule was the only weapon the English climate could not rust. *Don Juan* would be known 'by and by for what it is intended – a *Satire* on *abuses*' of present, hardly rust-proof, society. On discovering in 1816 that (as he wrote to Moore) 'all the world and *my* wife are at war with me', the poet presumed the fault lay with the world. Through his last poem he resolved to conduct subversive war on the conspiratorial society whose formulae he knew so well.[10] Joyce, from the start, identified his 'holy office' as the purgation of a deceiving environment ('Myself unto myself will give/This name, Katharsis-Purgative'). *Dubliners* portrayed with grim exactitude the moral history (and this was no Hegelian history but a paralytic lapsing back) of his country. In a larger panorama of *Ulysses*, he would reveal the cant of an age and of a world of men.

If the novel is indeed a perpetual quest for reality, with the field of its research being always the social world and the materials of its analysis being always manners as the indication of the direction of a man's soul,[11] then both writers, surveying critically the manners of their age, conclude that the direction being taken by the communal soul or ego is not only unreal but wrong. Their purging is as much method for penetrating to the truth beneath appearance as it is solution for what they find. Greek epic poets could exemplify the *paideia* of their civilization, and Virgil could justify Roman order. Byron and Joyce can only destroy. They feel not just the general dissatisfaction with the 'public' that countless thinkers since Socrates have felt, nor merely the overall '*malade de sa différence avec son temps*', of the typical Romantic artist, but a bitter hostility to the civilization of their time and those past traditions that have supported it. Theirs is a literature 'overwhelmingly of discontent . . . pessimism and protest'.[12] Given the state of *paideia* in their age, its revocation is vital; destruction is the only positive act left for the modern artist.

There are no solutions, no promises, and no escape in *Ulysses*, only Joyce's creative intensity beating down 'like an aroused volcano upon an ancient city, overtaking the doomed inhabitants in forum and temple, at home or at brothel, and petrifying them in the insensate agonies of paralysis'.[13] Byron, who once said poetry was 'the lava of the imagination whose eruption prevents an earthquake',[14] implies that such a situation can apply to both writer and society, and reveals, in *Don Juan*, that the earthquake has taken place.

What were once inside, the base urges of the horde which Greek *paideia* controlled, elevated and transcended, are now outside. Gilded over by cant, these have become the maxims of behavior. Social aspiration to culture and civility has turned inside out to reveal itself as selfish inhumanity. The molten rock this event summons forth licks over the splendidly erected ruins illuminating and destroying, impartially, thoroughly, inexorably.

Their vision is harshly true but the authors feel no responsibility for the truth of what they see in *Don Juan* and *Ulysses*. No longer do they, as Homer did, participate in the life and manners of their environment. Nor is theirs simply an 'indignant-naif' stance; they are exiles literally and symbolically. Mankind provides the substance for their pictures, not they: as Byron says,

> Some people have accused me of Misanthropy;
> And yet I know no more than the mahogany
>   That forms this desk, of what they mean; *Lykanthropy*
> I comprehend, for without transformation
> Men become wolves on any slight occasion.   (IX, 20)

In Kiernan's tavern of Cyclopes, Joyce shows us just how.

Their perspective of society may seem initially to be that of the standard picaro outsider: Byron did map his hero's future travels to accord with the intent of picaresque journeys ('I meant to have made him a Cavalier Servente in Italy and a cause for divorce in England — and a Sentimental "Werther-faced man" in Germany — so as to show the different ridicules of the society in each of those countries'[15]); Joyce, also, did send Bloom journeying if not through the various levels of Irish society then through all the byways and sub-strata that make up Dublin's lower middle class milieu. But it is soon clear that the two writers' position is distinct and dissimilar from any picaresque perspective in the extent of its disaffection, and in its deliberate attempt to disassociate itself from what is witnessed.

When Homer sang he showed his approval and his organic relation to the essentials of his society. When the average picaro protests what he sees he is, still, the outsider dependent on the system he criticizes, the one who would reform but not change the status quo because, then, he would lose his purpose and place and one (even if critical) link with social organization. Byron and Joyce see no connection with the prevailing ethos, either for their heroes[16] or themselves, or their art. Social classes may be surreptitiously interdependent (as countless picaresque tales and stories by the likes of Dostoyevsky and Conrad have shown). Societies over the ages may even be connected by a common ideal. But these two writers refuse responsibility for current mores and deny all dependence on the civic organism. Theirs is the distant 'bird's eye view of that wild Society' (XIV, 14). Even when focusing on a particular depravity, it yet remains removed. Like that pre-epic poet who never got much past the front door during his singing, theirs is the perspective from the threshold. They refuse all invitations to join in the pseudo-civility or 'pseudo-syphilis' of their civilization (I, 131). Poet and novelist see no coincidence of history and literature; they will have nothing to do with the final metamorphosis of the Greek social ideal. Their disaffection with *paideia*, even the past ideal because of its present form, is complete.

II

Byron and Joyce single out for special mention certain practices, personages and institutions of society (and we will review these in turn). Their impulse in this must be reformative. However disassociated from their social milieu, they are still not aesthetes writing rarified expressions of disavowal. Alick West says reading *Ulysses* is a profound social experience, and Ellmann claims the book's writing constitutes a political act. [17] One need say no less for *Don Juan*. For by their declarations against civil pretense — by saying (to quote Byron) 'you are not a moral people and you know it' to European society, by questioning the cultural aspiration, by illustrating how 'improvement was not improvement' but regression — the poem and the novel execute the only truly social, political, moral acts in the too-political societies they portray. [18]

If the literature of the modern period is characteristically political, with the majority of its writers turning their adverse passions upon the condition of the polity, [19] then *Don Juan* and *Ulysses* follow suit. They consider political word and deed in their time only to hear the sounds of imperial bellicosity. Militaristic triumph and pride (and the theory that supports these) are emblematic of all other canted pieties of human organization: for if *paideia* has become communal ego, then the polity expresses the essentials of this ego in its aggressive chauvinism. And war, as the ultimate form of social aggression in any age, is nothing more than this imperial ego on a rampage.

'God made the country, and man made the town,'
So Cowper says — and I begin to be
Of his opinion, when I see cast down

Rome, Babylon, Tyre, Carthage, Nineveh,
All walls men know. . . . (VIII, 60)

Byron says. Men in every age may have established such city-structures as monuments to their civilization. But history has proved, at least to the disillusioned retrospection of these writers, that the end-purpose of construction is destruction. Human society builds in order to destroy, it organizes that it might more gloriously disrupt, it asserts itself most forcefully when it devastates its own creations. Social affirmation and social aggression are two sides of the same coin.

'Don't forget that he was a war-dodger,' Joyce noted of Odysseus while he was, himself, a neutralist in Switzerland during the First World War. 'He might never have taken up arms and gone to Troy, but the Greek recruiting sergeant was too clever for him.' Like the poet's, Joyce's pacifism has a precedent in Odysseus's reluctance to fight against Troy and in what some critics see as a general Homeric antipathy to war.[20] We must not forget, however, that Homer also had a special word for 'the joy of battle',[21] and that his spirited singing on the subject in the *Iliad* endowed a whole tradition of epic aggression and social bestiality.

Byron cast his siege of Ismail in direct response to this aspect in Homer's story of Troy:

O, thou eternal Homer! I have now
   To paint a siege, wherein more men were slain,
With deadlier engines and a speedier blow,
   Than in thy Greek gazette of that campaign;
And yet, like all men else, I must allow,
   To vie with thee would be about as vain
As for a brook to cope with Ocean's flood;
But still we Moderns equal you in blood;

If not in poetry, at least in fact. . . . (VII, 80)

For glorifying bloody conquest, Homer and his society lose size and stature. His siege of Troy was nothing more than what occurred at Ismail, his list of martyred warriors no more significant than the gazette lists of the Waterloo dead or some Turkish mourning list — the blood shed in all instances no different in color, no less in amount.

War-makers and war-mongers in *Ulysses* as in *Don Juan*, tyrants, oppressors, and rabble-rousing belligerents like the Cyclopes of

Dublin city, place far from the image of epic prowess. They are nearer the order of Rabelais's Furrycats: 'ruled by the sixth essence, which causes them to seize everything, devour everything, and beshit everything. They hang, burn, quarter, behead, murder, imprison, waste, and ruin everything, without distinguishing between good and bad' (Bk v, ch. x, p. 626). The poet's opposition to wars of conquest 'Sometimes call[ed] "murder", and at others "glory"', unequivocal since his depiction of Waterloo in *Childe Harold*, becomes bitter denunciation in *Don Juan*:

'Let there be light!' said God, and there was light!
'Let there be blood!' says man, and there's a sea!
The fiat of this spoil'd child of the Night
(For Day ne'er saw his merits) could decree
More evil in an hour than thirty bright
Summers could renovate, . . . (VII, 41)

As Roland proved to posterity, war is a 'brain-spattering, wind-pipe-slitting art' without other purpose. At Ismail, the Christian Cross 'red with no *redeeming* gore' is raised wherever the Crescent has been; and from Stephen Dedalus's 'gorescarred book' of history we know what colors the highest points in the tale of human civilization. Ismail's carnage, bracketed by the courts of Catherine the Great and the Sultan of Turkey, was the ultimate these two civilizations could produce in monument to themselves. Warfare is the social epiphany: the scarlet moment when society manifests its true self.

Joyce is more diffuse than Byron in his criticism of warring and jingoistic pride, but he is also more extensive. He makes no allowances for wars of liberation – having witnessed more revolutions than the Romantic poet, he is cynical of all human motives for strife. History is Dedalus's nightmare of belligerency and blood, a nulling repetition, without beginning or end, from which man does not awake. War is the end-product of such paranoic and venal fears as those manifest by Deasy: 'England is in the hands of the jews. . . . They sinned against the light' (pp. 33–4). It is nourished by the bullying sentiments that lead a pack of drunks to assault Bloom for urging tolerance: 'By Jesus . . . I'll brain that bloody jewman for using the holy name' (p. 342). It is glorified by the pomp and trappings of such events as the viceregal procession through the streets of Dublin: an unalloyed farce, replete with tin drums, horses, a wounded sailor,, and two smoking turds, worthy only of the rear-ended 'salute of Almidano Artifoni's sturdy trousers' (p. 255).

War-makers (the British Empire, made up of 'drudges and whipped serfs. – On which the sun never rises', p. 329), are emblemed by the two drunk soldiers in 'Circe', assaulting without provocation ('I'll wring the neck of any bugger says a word against my fucking king') and dealing the coward's blow to a faint Stephen (p. 595). Edward VII, a true king, carries a bucket labelled 'Défense d'uriner.' The Irish watch in the same episode, dealers in treachery, are the Suwarrows of *Ulysses*, the representatives of Dublin's civic pride, its force, its law. If the seeker of fame, especially the fame of physical victory, is a pig chasing the wind for Byron (VII 84), then bellicose patriot Robert Emmet, in Joyce's opinion, is such a pig. Bloom makes the final comment on war, social aggression, and nationalistic pride (all symbolized by the portrait and belligerent words of the patriot): he breaks wind.

For Joyce there is no redeeming motive for any form of aggression, only the reason of ego be it communal or individual. Passionate Byronic indignation seems too worthy for such absurdity. Cold laughter and ridicule are the only response. In *Finnegans Wake*, the Crimean War is reduced to a scatological joke, the Battle of Waterloo to an extravaganza in a waxworks museum, the World War to a prize fight.[22] And England's most revered hero, Wiley old Willingdone ('the best of cut-throats' according to Byron), sits for all posterity on a 'big white harse'.

III

The true perpetrators of bloody destruction, the nourishers of the communal ego, ultimately, are not the individual Achilleses, Suwarrows or Emmets, but the artists who give the words and the grand concepts or ideals to the sorry deeds and urges of their societies. Byron says:

> Yet I love Glory; – glory's a great thing: –
>   Think what it is to be in your old age
> Maintain'd at the expense of your good king;
>   A moderate pension shakes full many a sage,
> And heroes are but made for bards to sing,
>   Which is still better; thus in verse to wage
> Your wars eternally, besides enjoying
> Half-pay for life, makes mankind worth destroying.   (VIII, 14)

The condemnation here is for such as Homer, Virgil, and Horace –

artists who sang to patronize their king, their society, their nation. But it extends, also, to the likes of Southey the false poet ('Europe has slaves – allies – kings – armies still,/ And Southey lives to sing them very ill'); and to AE (Russell), Oliver St John Gogarty, and other members of the Irish literati who, according to Joyce, committed the crime of writing emotionally and falsely. All have written popularly, having placed themselves 'in service to' the depraved and foolish instincts and 'that outrageous appetite for lies' (VIII, 86) of their respective communities. Varying in stature and reputation, all are unpardonable criminals who provided their societies with the means and the lie by which the systems could justify their bestiality, exonerate their destruction, shore up their egos, and perpetuate the cycle of violence and pride.

With such false prophets providing society with its lie of distinction, deceit, not an ideal of culture, lies at the source of civic man as represented in *Don Juan* and *Ulysses*. Western society is a *pium desiderium*, [23] a system built upon (and feeding upon) wilful delusion, sanctimony, pride, games and tricks. Instead of cultural ideals and educational goals, the system has suspect motives and shady aims. 'I hate a motive like a lingering bottle,/With which the landlord makes too long a stand' (XIV, 58), Byron says, and his hapless Juan learns to his dismay that:

A young unmarried man, with a good name
    And fortune, has an awkward part to play;
For good society is but a game,
    'The royal game of Goose,' as I may say,
Where everybody has some separate aim,
    An end to answer, or a plan to lay –
The single ladies wishing to be double,
The unmarried ones to save the virgins trouble.   (XII, 58)

Fortuneless and without name, Dedalus also learns (as Joyce and the poet did before him) of the plans his society and church have for him, and of the hostility they reserve for him when he fails to do their bidding. [24]

Ulyssean duplicity is to be found in the civil body's manners. The other side of its illusory benevolence, its true aspect, is lycanthropy. Instead of the courtesy of Nausicaa, the respect shown Mentes, and the gracious hospitality of Nestor, Joyce and Byron show us cruelty – masked, of course, as fellowship and good order. Like

Henry James they, too, have imaginations of disaster, but it is social life they see as ferocious and sinister. They set forth, as he does, imaginary gardens of civility with real toads like Donna Inez, Sir Henry Amundeville, General Fireface – 'Who ate, last war, more Yankees than he kill'd' (XIII, 88), the callous priest at Glasnevin cemetery, and the Thersitean *alter ego* of the Citizen.

Pregnancy because it is indiscreet, but not infidelity, is condemned by toady-filled society in Byron's poem, and a country girl is sent to jail with two real poachers for having been 'a poacher upon Nature's manor'. In *Ulysses*, when the toads are not diseased and pathetic like Deasy, Breen, and Farrell, they act with typical communal spite: as when they see Boylan on the road to the cemetery and ask how Molly (referred to, insinuatingly, as 'Madame') is getting on and whether Bloom will be accompanying her and her lover on a concert tour; or when they pretend sympathy for Cunningham yet take gossipy delight in the source of his melancholy (his wife's alcoholism).

Children, above all, fall victim to social cruelty in these epics. As with Dickens and Blake, the perfect image of injustice is the unhappy child; like the historian Jacob Burckhardt also, Joyce and Byron connect the fate of nations with their treatment of children.[25] 'The world is full of orphans . . . orphans of the heart', Byron tells us (XVII, 1). The Dedalus children, Stephen's pupil Cyril Sargent, the younger Dignam, Leila, and the adolescent Juan, tell us much of the Dubliners' and the Europeans' essential urge to prey – upon their weakest members and future hopes.

The Great World is 'one polish'd horde,/Form'd of the two mighty tribes, the *Bores* and *Bored*' (XIII, 95). Boorish men (tutors, poets, politicians, Sultans, soldiers, Lenahans, Mulligans, Gallaghers, Boylans) and bored women (empresses, sultanas, and bored wives from Adeline to Molly) are its primary actors. As in Rabelais's world, warfarers, representatives of the law (Henry Brougham, 'A legal broom's a moral chimney-sweeper/And that's the reason he himself's so dirty' X, 15), usurers (Reuben J. the humpback usurer of 'Hades'), doctors who cannot heal society's sickness (Mulligan, the doctor at Catherine's court), clergymen (the learned reverend Peter Pith with his 'fat fen vicarage' whose 'jokes were sermons, and his sermons jokes', Father Dolan with his pandy bat), and women receive special mention.

Especially for the poet (but also for Joyce) the culprits who aid and abet the social illusion most, after the false writers, are its women. Women have traditionally been considered the reason for the formation of society. Homer, in the *Odyssey*, made Penelope and Helen the models of social elegance, communal morality, and domestic prudence.[26] The Teutonic and northern myths tend to place women at the center of civil organization. They also tend to see them as the source of communal problems: Kriemhilde recalls the singular role Helen ('the Greek Eve', xiv, 72) plays in the *Iliad*'s strife. (Butler, incidentally, perceiving that the *Odyssey* exalted 'high morality' through its women, guessed that it had been written by a clergyman before he decided on an authoress.) Joyce and Byron clearly follow tradition.

The poet finds in 'ladies' the image of society's ills: sanctimony, sentimentality, and fondness for 'appearances'. Teresa Guiccioli's request that he cease writing *Don Juan* arose 'from the wish of all women to exalt the *sentiment* of the passions – and to keep up the illusion which is their empire'.[27] Arch-model Donna Inez, 'Morality's prim personification', has 'A great opinion of her own good qualities' and, like her habitat, displays falsities, fancies, and the urge to serve others ill:

> . . . she had a devil of a spirit,
> And sometimes mix'd up fancies with realities,
> And let few opportunities escape
> Of getting her liege lord into a scrape.   (1, 20)

Her unctuous letter to Juan in Russia, warning him against Greek orthodoxy, recommending him to God, telling him he has a little brother, and praising 'the Empress's *maternal* love', is a consummate expression of civic sanctimony. Adeline, Byron's other model, playing her grand role, 'Which she went through as though it were a dance', until poor Juan begins to wonder 'how much of Adeline was *real*' (xvi, 96), provides us with the timeless image of the social feint. Joyce does not place pretense in the environment directly upon the Dublin women. Gerty MacDowell's embarrassing sentimentality, Mrs. Breen's feigned outrage in 'Circe', Mrs. Virag-Bloom's fondness for what is 'proper', and Molly's mockery of the marital bond are, nevertheless, all examples of dissimulation in *Ulysses*.

IV

'Are not Religion and Politics the same thing?' Blake asked in *Jerusalem*. Byron, resolved that 'Politics' was no more than 'the barking of war-dogs for their carrion', perceived the fatal link between it and religion: 'This is a patent age of new inventions/For killing bodies, and for saving souls' (I, 132). Joyce, of course, saw Dublin society as a treacherous alliance of clergymen, English masters, and craven Irish threatening (respectively) hell, jail, and social ostracism. In the war against Church and State, Stephen and Bloom emphasize the bloodthirstiness of each. They echo, in this, not only Bakunin's 'All religions are cruel, all founded in blood',[28] but the horror of Byron's Cain – at a God who craves carrion, 'scorching flesh and smoking blood' (I, i, 299), like so many human war-dogs. Poet and novelist follow Blake's advice: they tie king and priest, both symbols of the communal ego's urge to enslave, in a tether.

Far from representing a theory of goodness, organized religion in the two works is merely an agent of social division, exclusion, and dominance. Stephen was not supposed to kiss Protestant girls; in death, religion preserves the social distinctions: Protestants may not be buried in Catholic cemeteries, and suicides like Virag-Bloom's may not receive a Christian burial. Religious values mimic the secular yen for mastery. (' 'Tis pleasant, purchasing our fellow creatures,' as Byron says of the 'black old neutral personage of the third sex' who steps up to survey Juan, V, 27.) Dedalus remembers how the supervisor offered him not spiritual benefits but 'power' over other men as the lure for joining the priesthood, and he knows he must choose between two exacting masters, one English, the other Italian. Bloom's uncertain religious status recalls that of Boccaccio's Jew, who finally decided for Christianity because of its survival through social vice; it is a fair testament to religion turned secular device.

Don John Conmee, thinking fleshy thoughts while he reads his breviary, and Molly's confessors, joying in the details of her sins, represent the same breakdown of spiritual ideal as do Juan's priestly tutors, 'Those vegetables of the Catholic creed/[who] Are apt exceedingly to run to seed' (XIV, 81). In no mere coincidence, just after Inez's letter, Byron intones, 'Oh for a *forty-parson-power* to chant/Thy praise, Hypocrisy!' (X, 34) exhibiting a Joycean awareness of the extent to which spiritual and secular sanctimony support one another. Clergymen in *Don Juan* and *Ulysses* belong, thoroughly, to the fabrication that is society: at their best, they are the 'takers of tithes, and makers of good matches'; at their worse, they raven not for bodies but souls.

To know the fate of hallowed institutions of social order in these two works, we need consider just one: marriage or the family bond.

To Homer's advocacy in the *Odyssey* of the family as the first civic unit, the font of law and order, of loyalty, responsibility, and true succession, Byron and Joyce hold out what the social bond has become: farce. Families in contemporary Dublin are symbolized by the Dedalus family: motherless, homeless, its possessions in pawn, with an estranged eldest son, a drunk and irresponsible father, and a·brood of starving children. Marriage is an ever-pregnant Mrs Purefoy, or an apologetic Mrs Breen loyally following her insane husband about the city as he carries two tomes of the law and vows vengeance on the unknown mailer of a postcard that said 'U.P.' to him. Fidelity is Molly Bloom's tendency to be more promiscuous in thought than in deed.

The poet, after 1815, became even more uncompromising in his opinion of 'that moral centaur, man and wife'. The Amundevilles' union, he says in *Don Juan*, 'was a model to behold,/Serene and noble, – conjugal but cold' (XIV, 86). José and Inez, being exceedingly well-bred, live respectably as man and wife, 'Wishing each other, not divorced, but dead' (I, 26).

One could argue that Byron and Joyce are at odds on this issue since the latter seems to conclude on the side of the family: Molly will stay with Bloom, *Ulysses* implies, their marriage will continue in form and survive her passing infidelities. But the Blooms' marriage is intended as an expression of compromise, habit, and one-sided love. It is not a social unit, and there is no Bloom family. *Don Juan* depicts love as an institution of nature, and marriage as an institution of society.[29] The two are incompatible by virtue of the latter's precepts:

'Tis melancholy, and a fearful sign
    Of human frailty, folly, also crime,
That love and marriage rarely can combine.   (III, 5)

Bloom, in 'Ithaca', ponders sadly on the same dilemma; that Joyce did not marry Nora until copyright law required it, attests to the same perception.

V

The poet's invocation of Nature as foil to civic institution is pertinent. Society may claim communal dignity and a spirit of man, and ordered patterns of civilized behavior. But human nature is rarely as civilized as it claims: Homer portrayed Greek civilization at its height, but he also had to show Ulysses's soldiers forsaking physical dignity (and spiritual survival) to satisfy their passing pangs of hunger. Natural scenes in *Don Juan* and *Ulysses* highlight the massive discrepancy between vaunts of cultural stature – and human meanness: for it is not by the great catastrophes that the life of the spirit is brought into question but by the small ones. Juan's seasickness and Bloom's bodily functions, hence, raise radically subversive questions about the dignity of human nature. Or, as Byron succinctly says, 'I think with Alexander, that the act/Of eating, with another act or two,/Makes us feel our mortality in fact/Redoubled . . .' (v, 32). However civil human society may be, its claims to order, too, are checked at every turn by the natural disorder of the world. Where it exists in *Don Juan* and *Ulysses*, civic order is largely brute force: Lambro's 'police force', or two Tommies who would honor their king by defending a tart.

In their invocation of the natural, poet and novelist intend to do more than expose social pretensions to dignity and system. As we have said, they assert a natural configuration to balance a discredited social and spiritual ethic – and to surpass it. Byron's stanzas on Daniel Boone and the idyllic moments at Howth to which *Ulysses* returns are only part of what the two writers wish to proffer against the limited civilized arrangement. By refusing to deny the chaotic natural and the individual human as social systems have, their epics affirm a comprehensiveness to human life which society could never allow.

Promiscuity in Juan and Bloom is not threatening or dangerous as the prevailing moral code would suggest. It may be an intimation of uncontrol in the natural world, but it is not a threat until considered as such. Like the obscene letters Bloom sends to Martha (and those Joyce once sent to Nora), it is morally neutral, part of the amoral condition of the world. Vomit on a love-letter and blood in an orange-keyed chamber pot can be as significant, and more true, than those earlier social and religious relics of tears and blood-filled chalices.

Classical readers have often noted the numerous relationships Odysseus has with women. Juan and Bloom certainly fulfill Homeric pattern with their numerous female contacts: Inez, Julia, Haideé, Gulbayez, Catherine, Leila, Adeline, Fitz-Fulke, Aurora; and Milly, Martha, Mrs Breen, Mrs Purefoy, Gerty, Bella Cohen and Molly. What distinguishes the two men is that all their affirmative relationships are with natural women.

Don Juan repeatedly homes to an innocent, Edenic female: to 'Nature's bride' Haidée, 'Made but to love', speaking no scruples and asking no vows (II, 190); to Dudu, 'soft as a Landscape of mild Earth',

'Unconscious' enough to never think about herself (VI, 53–4); to
Leila, 'beautiful as her own native land. . . . the last bud of her race',
(XV, 29); to Aurora who, though in society, is yet 'scarcely form'd or
moulded, /A Rose with all its sweetest leaves yet folded' (XV, 43).
Bloom's story, meanwhile, begins with nymph-child Milly Bloom,
waxes half-lyrical in an encounter with the pure side of Gerty
MacDowell, sympathizes with pregnant Mrs Purefoy, and concludes
with thoroughly natural Molly in the pose of Gaea-Tellus.

In their natural aspect the women of *Don Juan* and *Ulysses* are not
mocked. Like the Nausicaa interlude in Homer, the aspect serves
positively: through it the women function in tandem with the heroes
to affirm a different configuration of value. Against the restrictive
prevailing ideal pillared by the likes of Inez, Adeline, Milbanke,
Mrs Dedalus and Mrs Virag-Bloom, Byron and Joyce propose the
natural woman. Woman, they say, need not be perceived as a
limiting, binding, unnatural force; the representative and reason for
society; the occasion for Man's ceasing to wander the limitless
universe to return 'home' to the closed hearthside and his neighbor's
laws. Society's pillars were once its greatest saboteurs.

Poet and novelist share an awareness, quite unusual in their
contexts, of the female principle as a power, an energy that does not
admit human law. As individuals, women in *Don Juan* and *Ulysses*
may be suspect or sweet. But as a sex or a symbol they are essentially
abstract, amorally outside, inscrutable and near cosmic in their
isolation from the mundane world.

'She walks in beauty like the night/Of cloudless climes and starry
skies;/And all that's best of dark and bright,/Meet in her aspect. . . .'
In *Don Juan* the poet advises young beginners to commence with a
'quiet cruizing o'er the ocean woman' (XIII, 40). He sees women as
finding true congeniality in abstracts ('In her first passion woman
loves her lover,/In all others all she loves is love'). His favorite, Aurora
Raby, to Juan's eternal regret, is as distant in aspect as in name.

Bloom's musings on Molly in 'Sirens', cuckolding him at that
instant, suggest the same sense of removed loss, of an alien,
self-sufficient principle that does not follow commonly understood
laws:

All is lost now. Mournful he whistled. Fall, surrender, lost. . . . In
sleep she went to him. Innocence in the moon. Still hold her back.
Brave, don't know their danger. Call name. Touch water. Jingle
jaunty. Too late. She longed to go. That's why. Woman. As easy
stop the sea. Yes: All is lost. (pp. 272–3)

Joyce reiterated this sense when he said that Molly, and the technique of 'Penelope', were to represent 'perfectly sane, fully amoral fertilizable untrustworthy engaging shrewd limited prudent *indifferent* Weib. Ich bin das Fleisch das stets bejaht'.[30]

The symbols (sea, heavenly bodies, dawn, universal matter) are clear. Byron and Joyce perceive true women as indifferent and fully outside the world of things, thoughts, and systems. It is as if, by invoking the female as natural principle and cosmic given, poet and novelist would return to a pre-society state, to a time when notions of order and concepts of *paideia* could not exist. It is as if they would expose what the female principle has become, in practice, in multiplicity, through the machinations of society and a limited communal rationality that cannot encompass nature or conceive of universal wholeness.

Bloom, when he thinks sadly of his daughter's inevitable maturity, and of her fate at the hands of society because she is part of a larger amoral order ('Destiny. Ripening now. . . . Will happen, yes. Prevent. Useless: can't move. Girl's sweet light lips. Will happen too' pp. 66–7), recalls the poet's like sentiment, as sympathetic as it is mystified:

> Poor Thing of Usages! Coerc'd, compell'd,
>   Victim when wrong, and martyr oft when right,
> Condemned to childbed. . . .
>
>   . . . who can penetrate
> The real sufferings of their she condition?
> Man's very sympathy with their estate
>   Has much of selfishness and more of suspicion.
> Their love, their virtue, beauty, education,
> But form good housekeepers, to breed a nation.   (XIV, 23–4)

'Ask any woman', Byron concludes, if she would choose to be 'Female or male? a school-boy or a Queen?'

As the pregnant country-girl at the Great House and the black-straw-hatted prostitute who haunts Bloom prove, society and nature are to blame for the breakdown, in the civilized world, of a universal principle into many, pathetic parts. The censure is not equal. The social ethic came later. It established the contradiction between the two sets of values. Byron and Joyce therefore, ever-conscious of precedent and place, decide on the side of nature because it, at least, does not deal in unctuous treachery and restriction.

As natural men and inviolate catalysis in a changeful society, Juan and Bloom are joined by women of the likes of Dudu, Leila, and Molly. 'The struggle against conventions in which I am at present involved was not entered into by me so much as a protest against these conventions as with the intention of living in conformity with my moral nature',[31] Joyce said in 1905. The naturals of *Don Juan* and *Ulysses* live in conformity with their individual moral nature, passively, without overtly challenging the alien system in which they find themselves.

They are constant but, by virtue of their place in an artificial complex (be this Spanish petty nobility, a Russian or Turkish court, nineteenth-century English society, or twentieth-century Dublin), they elicit violent responses to their naturalness and a spectrum of infelicitous acts on the part of society. As Juan and Bloom ruffle their respective milieus into unseemly responses at every turn so, too, do the natural women of their epics: Dudu's dreams disrupt a Sultana's ease and prompt murdering instincts, Molly sets the Dubliners a-gossiping and shocks them back into the century before, and Leila, we anticipate, will take London society by its ears.

They are all elements that induce the civil body to unmask: people mistreat them only to expose themselves, the communities judge them that they might be judged by us, the artful ones act to assert their values against an alien ethic only to undermine their own system. Each becomes (as Kroeber says of Juan) something akin to a Jamesian 'central intelligence', a lens for focusing and illuminating the action of others. As with what the Russians called the 'superfluous man', they introduce, by their mere presence, moral crisis.[32]

Like that piece of platinum T. S. Eliot spoke of in another context, Juan, Bloom, and the women who conform to their nature, do not act, nor do they change or compromise themselves. Rather, they trigger a chain reaction in the environment, and a host of unsocial overtures from the social institution. They are the pins placed in the Great Body, and the uproar that follows is inevitable: biscuit-tins are thrown, dogs bark, harem sleep is interrupted, eunuchs shudder for their lives, long-frozen champagne thaws, young girls presume, and sons home to an available mother.

The effects recall those of *Don Quixote*, where an insane knight leads others to act very strange: a peasant girl pretends to be a princess, a curate dresses up as a woman, and a barber goes in search of an absconded basin. To their societies, the naturals are the peculiar ones. Yet, by acting in conformity with their natures, they induce their milieus to exhibit characteristics which the social ideals would normally abhor, and to act against the concepts of culture to which the systems owe their being. It would seem we have variants of the 'Peter Bell' question. Which of the two sides in *Don Juan* and *Ulysses* (nature or society) is truly mad, or grotesque, or alien, or unreal? ' 'Tis strange – but true', Byron says, that 'Truth is always strange,/Stranger than Fiction' (XIV, 101). Seeming and being, appearance and reality, dishonesty and truthfulness, natural and artificial, normal and abnormal, these are the fluid questions, or keys, to *Don Juan* and *Ulysses*.

If the moments on the Greek isle in the poem and at Howth in the novel are idyllic occasions of appearance placed awkwardly within reality, then Lambro and the gormandizing Dubliners (both in the guise of Civilization) are the cruel semblances, shadows descending upon the truths of natural love. Natural catalysts thus cut both ways to highlight what is real and what is grotesquely delusive.

VI

Neither the semblance called Civilization nor the substance of Nature, we should note, escape the two writers' nihilistic purview. 'Alas! I see Nothing,' says Byron's Cain, one of Joyce's favorite characters in literature.[33] Like the novelist, the poet suggests 'that heroism has never been more than a sham and glory never more than a mockery even in the past'. Like Joyce also, he expresses this repeatedly until 'the strategy generalizes into an attack on nobility and meaningfulness of all human life, anywhere and in any age'.[34]

In 1820, Keats remarked that *Don Juan* gave him 'the most horrid idea of human nature' because it gloated and jeered at 'the most solemn and heart-rending' aspects of human misery. He found the shipwreck scene 'one of the most diabolic attempts ever made upon our sympathies'. A century later (1927), E. M. Forster expressed similar outrage and indignation at *Ulysses*'s pervasive realism, calling the book 'a dogged attempt to cover the universe with mud'.[35] Keats and Forster were shocked by approximately the same characteristics in both works: a vision that is often hideous in its honesty; a tendency to portray human behavior even at its lowest ebb, when it is grotesque, pathetic or horrible, and to surround such scenes with macabre laughter.

In *Ulysses*, we are given the scene of a palsied man extending his tongue to receive the Eucharist while a priest jabs fruitlessly at the air around the man's mouth. Tisdale Farrell, the most pathetically insane of the Dubliners, walks a mad and weaving line on the Dublin sidewalk which echoes the movement of human sludge through the alimentary canal. The poem, in a like vein of humor and horror, tells us of the shipwrecked people's grief: 'They grieved for those who perish'd with the cutter,/And also for the biscuit casks and butter' – and of how one died: 'Battista, though, (a name call'd shortly Tita)/Was lost by getting at some aqua-vita' (II, 61, 56).

Joyce and Byron are not jeering or throwing mud in these examples: they laugh that they may not weep. They refuse to ignore the true, ghastly side of humanity – in society or in nature. Human behavior, for all the claims of culturalists and naturalists, can be demeaningly brutish: people grub for life, or food, or liquor; they die not just unheroically but grotesquely, and they witness others' misery with some joy at having been spared themselves.

In *Ulysses*, an old crone twitches closed her window-blinds as Dignam's hearse goes by, glad to have escaped the banshee's visit this time. In Burton's eating-house, Bloom sees his fellows chewing, slurping, regurgitating, no different from a puppy outside returning to its vomit. In Canto II Byron notes how 'The longings of the cannibal arise' even among the most civilized, because 'man is a carnivorous production, And must have meals . . . like the shark and tiger, must have prey' (72, 67). Joyce, too, forces us to see the hideous relation between worms feasting in the graveyards and the human need for nourishment; between Plumtree's potted meat and Paddy Dignam's potted flesh. And Bloom is forced to see the obscene connection between two flies copulating on a restaurant's dirty windowpane ('flies stuck') and his memory of union with Molly on the seashore.

As nulling as they are pathetic, these episodes are part of the truth that lies beneath human nature and behind human civilization. Occasional macabre laughter, for poet as for novelist, is one way of containing the brutal truth. Human life, whether in the artfully urban or the naturally primitive, is 'solitary, poor, nasty, brutish and short'. When a shrivelled old woman crosses Bloom's path in 'Calypso', clutching a bottle, we wonder if the potion is to continue a minimal life, ease it, or provide an antidote to it. So, also, do we wonder at Battista's motive for getting at some *aqua vita*. 'Must I restrain me', the poet asks, 'From holding up the Nothingness of life?' (VII, 6). With Joyce, he depicts what is real, truthfully, to this point of nothingness.

Extreme realism in *Don Juan* and *Ulysses* undermines the natural
principle which the books affirm (and it is a paradoxic feat that the
writers can affirm humanity in spite of the clarity with which they see
life's meanness). But, more importantly, it is the ultimate annuller of
all civil idealism and cultural memory governed by the term *paideia*,
be this Homer's concept of civilized humanity as hero or contemporary society's artifice of community rule. 'I've stood upon
Achilles' tomb,/And heard Troy doubted; time will doubt Rome',
Byron says (IV, 101). And Bloom sees rats burrowed at the graveyard
waiting for Paddy – the avatar of Elpenor who had so longed for the
sacred ritual of burial.

By invoking the natural at its most mean (or, alternatively, at its
most distant and overwhelming), poet and novelist override the
artful. For them there can be no comfort, faith or honor in their
civilization, and they reject it. But they recognize that that rejection
destroys them, leaving them at home only with those manifestations
of nature most hostile to the survival of humanity, either in the
indifference of their grandeur or in the shocking kinship of their
meanness.[36] Nature prevails by default in *Don Juan* and *Ulysses*
because, given the truth about humanity, civilization cannot.

VII

'The leading passion of my life,' William Morris said, 'has been and is
hatred of modern civilization'. He spoke for most of the writers of the
nineteenth and twentieth centuries. Raymond Williams, citing
Coleridge's description of his civilization as 'a corrupting influence,
the hectic of disease, not the bloom of health', has noted that this was
part of the overall Romantic reaction against cultural claims of
progressive development and order. Trilling has discussed at length
the modern self's adverse imagination of the culture in which it has its
being, of its bitter discontent with civilization. Richard Poirier, also,
has spoken of how men of Joyce's era tended to perceive the cultural
inheritance as largely waste.[37]

Byron and Joyce are not singular when they address their culture in
hostile terms. Yet they do distinguish themselves in this regard from
other men of their centuries. Jacob Burckhardt, whose theory of
culture is presented in *Cicerone* (1855), contemplated the culture of
Europe as a ruin without renovative hope. It was to him, as Hayden
White says, 'like one of those crumbling Roman monuments which
stand in the midst of a Poussin landscape, all covered over with vines,

and grasses, resisting its reconfiscation by the "nature" against which it had been erected'.[38] Byron and Joyce join sentiments with Burckhardt – but with even less hope for the recurrence of the cultural moment, and even fewer explanations for its past occasions. Nor do they perceive civilization as an originally positive process whose particular manifestation in their era is reprehensible. For poet and novelist, the concept (and, where my discussion of them uses it, the term) applies to an achieved state of organized social life (material and spiritual) which holds within it, at once, the whole process of which it is the completed end, and the seeds and traditions which gave rise to the process.[39] Among other men who also contend with their culture, Byron and Joyce are unusual in the degree of their alienation, and in their extreme hostility to all its forms. In their respective centuries they are not only among the most articulate of the writers who quarrel with civilization, they are also the most comprehensive.

Where other men of the modern era show themselves hostile to a specific form of civilization as manifest in a finite period, Byron and Joyce carry their nihilistic perspective to its source, to the first social and cultural aspirations (or egotistical communal yearnings) of Western man, to Greece. They say, with Alfred Jarry in Ubi Roi, 'We won't have demolished everything if we don't also demolish the ruins',[40] and they do not cease in their destruction until they stand, literally and figuratively, among ruins and crumbled monuments.

Banished by their priggish societies for having seen truthfully, Joyce and Byron retort, with Coriolanus, 'I banish you!' – banishing herein not just the contemporary environment but the entire tradition of civil conduct and aspiration that has supported it since Homer. They perceive their rejection as the only positive, liberating option left. 'My mind rejects the whole present social order and Christianity – home, the recognised virtues, classes of life, and religious doctrine', Joyce said to Nora in 1904. 'Now I make open war upon it by what I write and say and do', he added, in a manifesto to what he felt to be Ireland's de facto dictate of exile.[41] Approximately a century before, the popular Byron found he was also popularly perceived as clubfooted, more distinctly marked than Cain, and he left England in response to an exile no less symbolic, and no less virulent. The poet vowed to Hobhouse that he would never return to 'your swindling Sodom of a Country', and declared, 'false England is unfit for me'.[42] Like Joyce, he made his exile final and 'denied any stake in the rejected world'.[43] The dust these two men shook from their feet as they passed by was, of course, from the ruins (which they had helped bring about) of civilization.

'Most men in a brazen prison live' Arnold said, and Wordsworth
told of how 'shades of the prison-house begin to close upon the
growing boy'. Michel Foucault, in his study of madness and
civilization in the century immediately preceding the modern era,
notes how institutions like the Hôpital Général were instances of
order, of 'monarchial and bourgeois order' which confined non-
conformists, the new lepers, until they conformed. These institutions
were conceived upon the notion that order was the equivalent of
virtue, and limitation the necessary corollary of ideal civility:

> There is, in these institutions, an attempt of a kind to demonstrate
> that order may be adequate to virtue. In this sense, 'confinement'
> conceals both a metaphysics of government and a politics of
> religion; it is situated, as an effort of tyrannical synthesis, in the vast
> space separating the garden of God and the cities which men,
> driven from paradise, have built with their own hands. The house
> of confinement in the classical age [the Age of Reason] constitutes
> the densest symbol of that 'police' which conceived of itself as the
> civil equivalent of religion for the edification of a perfect city.[44]

The frequency of prison-images in nineteenth-century works points
to the novel perspective of the age that followed the enlightened
order of Foucault's 'Age of Un-Reason':

> Men began to recognize the existence of prisons that were not built
> of stone, nor even of social restrictions and economic disabilities.
> They learned . . . [of] a coercion in some ways more frightful
> because it involved their own acquiescence. The newly conceived
> coercive force required of each prisoner that he sign his own *lettre
> de cachet*, for it had established its prisons in the family life, in the
> professions, in the image of respectability, in the ideas of faith and
> duty, in (so the poets said) the very language itself. The modern
> self, like Little Dorrit, was born in a prison. It assumed its nature
> and fate the moment it perceived, named, and denounced its
> oppressor.[45]

Self-exile, for Byron as for Joyce, followed self's vision. They
escaped to freedom from the contraption some call society and others
civilization. It was a mechanism for restriction, an active destroyer of
persons and relationships[46] — all, of course, in the interests of

building that perfect, walled city. Its power extended everywhere, ever falsely:

> . . . as swords have hilts
> By which the power of their mischief is encreased,
> When Man in battle or in quarrel tilts,
> Thus the low world, north, south, or west, or east,
> Must still obey the high — which is their handle,
> Their moon, their sun, their gas, their farthing candle.   (XII, 56)

To reduce the 'Great World' of civility, as the poet does here, was to undermine its reach; to reject it was to be positive; to escape it through exile was to affirm the self.

Juan's and Bloom's 'wrongs' are largely sexual. The evil of their societies is a fundamental and rooted inability to be honest, a refusal to care for the individual human life. Having seen the sham of unnature and inhumanity that is society, having reached behind culture to nature, and beneath nature to a brutishness that undermines all, Byron and Joyce can see no further and nothing further. Their *coup d'oeil* comprehends, nullingly, all human organization. Nothing survives beyond their exegesis. Society has always been of one type, and the cast is wrong.

The lie must therefore cease. The falsehood is no one place, no one time; it is not just the society of twentieth-century Ireland, nor just that of nineteenth-century Europe, nor even that of the post-Newton centuries, but the entity: civilization — Homer's, and since Homer. Its glory (of physical prowess or civic achievement) may have once been 'something' as Byron says, but it soon became 'nothing, words, illusion, wind' (III, 90).

Cultural ideals became communal rules, which became social etiquette:

> There's nothing in the world like *etiquette*
> In kingly chambers or imperial halls,
> As also at the race and country balls.   (V, 103)

Or, for that matter, in Irish stalls. Time levels, as it highlights the fatal connection between individual civilizations. 'The Tigris hath its jealousies like Thames' (VI, 11) and like the Lady Liffey. Husbands do not lose the compromised role assigned them by society over the ages or between class divisions: 'Emperors are only husbands in wives' eyes' (v, 115). Infidelity is an identical problem for the cuckold, be his household in Ithaca, Spain, or Dublin's Eccles Street. And 'that street in Hell . . . bears the greatest likeness to Pall Mall' (VIII, 26), Dublin City, and all Cities of Man including that *urbs aeterna* whose gold would never tarnish, and whose light would never fade.

Joyce said he was against every state and all organized civil rule because they were against the interests of the individual: the former concentric, where man is eccentric.[47] Byron listed among the 'great joys' of human order:

> War, Pestilence, the despot's desolation,
> The kingly scourge, the Lust of Notoriety,
> The millions slain by soldiers for their ration,
> The scene like Catherine's boudoir at three-score,
> With Ismail's storm to soften it the more.   (VIII, 68)

Hence civilization in its entirety must be laid waste in *Don Juan* and *Ulysses*; romped through from start to finish, and put to ruin by the individual word.

Poem and novel are encyclo-*paideias* of European civilization. Joyce shows modern society to be grim and self-destroying, but 'by merging Dublin with Rome and the glory that was Greece, by describing Paris in no better terms, and by portraying two unpleasant Londoners', he suggests that civilization itself has been repressive and life-denying.[48] Merging the civilities of Spain, Turkey and Russia, depicting these as immoral and destructive of their best hopes, showing English society as grimly unreal and an apotheosis of European lycanthropy, conjuring up Aeneas's dream of his city-site marked by white sow and farrow in nightmarish form at Ismail, and connecting all this with the glorious Aegean era, Byron's exegesis accomplishes no less an indictment.

By showing us, specifically, the final metamorphosis of the Greek cultural ideal in Seville, Ismail, Petersburg, London, and Dublin, the two writers point to what has been wrong with the ideal of culture since its inception. *Paideia*, even its best moments in Homer's Greece, held the seeds of an Ismail or a Dublin in it; as such, the concept is to be condemned along with its tangible tradition. Not only will there be no more epics glorifying war or a society modelled on an egotistical ideal, according to *Don Juan* and *Ulysses* there will be no more pretense (*paideia*). There will be, only, the isolated and truthful 'I'; and the domain of the bastard word.

5 Styles: Parodies and *Parallax*

Timon Let all my land be sold.
Flavius 'Tis all engaged, some forfeited and gone;
And what remains will hardly stop the mouth
Of present dues: the future comes apace:
What shall defend the interim? And at length
How goes our reck'ning?
Timon To Lacedaemon did my land extend.
Flavius O my good lord, the world is but a word:
Were it all yours to give it in a breath,
How quickly were it gone!   (II, 2)

The world is but a word. Or, as Montaigne, Byron and Joyce might
have it, *'nous sommes partout vent'*.[1] In *Don Juan* and *Ulysses* the
authors show us the essential windiness that subsumes, as with
Rabelais's island of Ruach,[2] the epic values and ideal manners of the
European tradition since Homer. At once critical and comic, their
method of exposure extends itself to the things that sustain the tale
called Western civilization: its literature, its learned disciplines and
discourse, its language. Reflecting and reducing these, their method
also comes to define its own manner of expression.

Poet and novelist are fully aware of the word as the first and final
product of the bankrupt culture they attack. They are also acutely
aware of their roles as dealers in the word. This dual knowledge
informs their presentations in *Don Juan* and *Ulysses*. Before one
distinguishes links in these two works' individual modes one must
therefore consider those perspectives (which have origins in the
eighteenth century) that lead Byron and Joyce to see style and
language as the objects of their art. One must also survey those
nineteenth-century philosophic concepts that underlie the singular,
parallactic perspective poet and novelist have of their art: its subjects,
its learned traditions, its literary antecedents.

I

Ezra Pound said true literary criticism comes from authors, but Byron and Joyce display scorn not only for their predecessors' exercises but for the art itself:

> Had they deceived us
> Or deceived themselves, the quiet-voiced elders,
> Bequeathing us merely a receipt for deceit?   ('East Coker', II)

they ask, of their literary inheritance. Not just Homer, Virgil, and Milton but Ovid, Dante, Petrarch, and even Shakespeare (Gulbayez's wish 'was but to "kill, kill, kill," like Lear's,/ And then her thirst of blood was quench'd in tears' V, 136; 'Hamlet, I am thy father's gimlet!' says a ghostly voice in 'Circe', stuttering a few lines later 'Iagogogo!' pp. 561, 567) are derisively summoned forth for the express purpose of exposing the vacuity of the literary enterprise. Literature is, for poet as for novelist (to quote *Finnegans Wake*) 'the hoax that joke bilked'.

Others, certainly, have parodied the conventions of literature. The novel has, from its beginnings, made books the object of its regard: *Don Quixote* was written about a man who had read too many books on knightly convention; *Shamela, Joseph Andrews*, and *Tom Jones* are all critical responses to literary style; Sterne wrote *Tristram Shandy* to deny the order and patterns of eighteenth-century narrative art. *Don Juan* and *Ulysses* distinguish themselves by their encyclopedic allusiveness. Where other writers may ridicule a particular convention Byron and Joyce burlesque literature. It is in its effete exclusivity a kind of enemy.[3] Major figures and primary genres (romance, epic, blank verse, lyric, drama, realism, naturalism, and prophecy) alike are parodied. The poet begins the practice which Joyce concludes, and each literary mode is pursued from its beginnings through its various manifestations to the point where it can be exposed as empty pattern.

Consider the fate of sentimental writing in both works:

> When amatory poets sing their loves
>   In liquid lines mellifluously bland,
> And pair their rhymes as Venus yokes her doves,
>   They little think what mischief is in hand;
> The greater their success the worse it proves,

As Ovid's verse may give to understand;
Even Petrarch's self, if judged with due severity,
Is the Platonic pimp of all posterity.   (v, 1)

In Donna Julia's platonism, in the harem, in Catherine's boudoir
practices, in Adeline's champagned state, in *Ulysses*'s poster-nymph,
in Bloom's love-letters, in Stephen's yearning for the ideal woman
(which hides his fear of sexual love), in the ha'penny manual on the
arts of love he buys, in the foolish tawdriness of Gerty MacDowell's
tawdry dreams, and, most of all, in the 'namby-pamby jammy
marmalady drawersy (alto la!)' noveletta style of 'Nausicca,' we see
the two writers' response to the tradition of amatory writing.

Not Petrarch alone, not a given convention like the lover's lament,
nor even contemporary love-stories, but the centuries-long literary
posture of sentiment in all its mutations—from Ovid, medieval and
Arthurian romance, Dante, Petrarch and Sidney through to their
own day—is the butt of their satire. 'I therefore do denounce all
amorous writing', Byron says in sweeping judgement, with Joyce,
and literature's quest for a symbolic Rose or mystical Grail finds its
apotheosis in Juan's and Bloom's search (on one level) for somewhat
more substantial female flesh.

Rabelais's great comedy and Flaubert's *Bouvard and Pécuchet*
presented similar encyclopedic critiques of literature. But Byron and
Joyce exceed the good-humored monk immeasurably in their distrust
of the enterprise, and they surpass Flaubert (whose subject was the
descent of literature and culture through the sentimentality of one
century) in the breadth of their critical response. Their comprehensive sweep questions the original impulse of literature. 'The
overvaluation of love is the beginning of the end of love; the
overvaluation of art is the beginning of the end of art.'[4] The literary
heritage has not merely grown weighty and cloying: it has always
been too artful, valued for its fabrications. If Western civilization is a
consummate sham, then the mimesis of this 'reality', an institution
licensed to traduce reality, has explicitly continued the falsehood.

Joyce's 'Scylla and Charybdis' provides the best illustration of an
attitude which the poet also shares. The episode, whose art is
literature, portrays an elaborate edifice of varying manner and mode
and is meant to be a microcosm of literary history, literary exercise,
and literary criticism. Yet it is founded on a supposition that is absurd,
it expresses an argument that Stephen does not believe, within a
framework of words that depends entirely on an artist's Dedalian

whims. By virtue of its unique place and technical versatility literature excels in the power to support the lie of civility. Poem and novel are therefore cast as polemics against the centuries-long fictive tradition in all its manifestations and mutations. 'Literature is now in the process of telling us how little it means.' Poirier's description of what he calls the twentieth-century literary phenomena inaugurated by Joyce and Eliot ('a literature of self-parody') applies accurately to aspects of nineteenth-century *Don Juan*: 'It proposes not the rewards so much as the limits of its own procedures; it shapes itself around its own dissolvents; it calls into question not any particular literary structure so much as the enterprise, the activity itself of creating any literary form, of empowering an idea with a style'.[5] Doubt is comprehensive in *Don Juan* and *Ulysses* and inclined to feed on itself. Doubting literature and its enterprise, the writers doubt human discourse, the disciplines of learning and art, and language itself.

Poem and novel can be read as picaresques of the writing modes of human society. As the works romp through the cultural heritage and contemporary mores in critical review, so, also, do their authors mockingly pass through the various stylistic maneuvers they have inherited. Their intention in this is not so much to satirize as it is to portray how inadequate, individually and cumulatively, the things they parody are to their proposed function: true communication.

When Byron parodied elements from epic, lyric, drama, or romance, he wished to sound the hollow note of each as much for his time as within its first context. He wished to show how impossible it was for a writer of his age to employ any of the traditional genres for the accurate representation of current reality, but he also wished to question whether any of these modes was ever fully adequate to its task.

By assaying each style in turn and, in effect, by placing them together in a single work in the hope that they would support one another and make up for individual limitations, the poet implicitly provides for a startling, denying historical perspective. Far from aiding one another in the representation of reality, the various modes of the literary art throughout history, like their examples in the poem, merely serve to cancel out one another.

Joyce attained this perspective of literary style in history early; Byron's implication became Joyce's conclusion and, surpassing the poet's range, he applied the perspective to all human discourse. Each of *Ulysses*'s chapters is devoted to the exploration of a particular rhetorical technique (narrative, catechism, monologue, dialectic progression, argument and so on). Each of the eighteen episodes assays in turn a given technique, denounces its Cyclopean monocularity and carries its peculiarities to meaningless extreme. Each chapter makes a new beginning in style, and accomplishes a new end for style.

'Oxen in the Sun', with its parodic tracing of the English styles from medieval Latin translations and Anglo-Saxon to Newman's prose, ending in 'a frightful jumble of Pidgin English, nigger-English, Cockney, Irish, Bowery slang and broken doggerel',⁶ is a microcosm of what happens to all the traditional modes in *Ulysses*. The English styles, for all their elegant developments and mutations over nine hundred years, individually denied one another over the years and, together, were able to produce only a monument of anti-style and gibbering incommunication.

The styles, like the genres of literature and traditional modes of human discourse, are inadequate by themselves and suicidal in their limitation—able, only, to undermine each other and deny their common purpose of communication. They are failed attempts at portraying truth. From the Joycean (but also the Byronic) perspective the styles are each, in their own way, rhetorical wind; together, they suggest the impossibility of true representation.

II

'Heat is in proportion to the want of true knowledge', the narrator of *Tristram Shandy* says, in explanation of how the size of a stranger's nose leads to a discussion of a Strasburg steeple, the attributes of God, Aquinas, and the devil. 'The stranger's nose was no more heard of in the dispute — it just served as a frigate to launch them into the gulph of school divinity, — and then they all sailed before the wind' (Bk IV, ch. 4). In Mr Shandy's obsession with abstract learning (metaphysical, legal, physiological or philological), in Uncle Toby's hobby horse of military science, Sterne expresses what he sees to be the clear connection between the exercise of the learned disciplines and the stirring of true wind. Before Sterne, Swift (in *Gulliver's Travels*) had depicted the vapidity of the scientific theories of his day. Rabelais, also, exploited swollen abstruse learning and false theory on foolish subjects.

When Byron and Joyce satirize erudition in *Don Juan* and *Ulysses* they are, certainly, within a tradition for abusing the windier aspects of learning. Far more disillusioned than any of their predecessors and functioning at a time when the learned disciplines had had several more decades to further abstract and specialize, they are also quite distinct from the tradition. Their diminution, not limited to scholastic knowledge, extends to the arts and to all the major occupations (and preoccupations) of human culture. In their comprehensive rejection, poem and novel are without precedent. Retroactive cancellation, in *Don Juan* as in *Ulysses*, applies inexorably to cultural disciplines (or distractions). As Joyce devoted each of eighteen chapters to the exploration of a particular rhetorical technique so, also, did he devote each chapter to a specific art and its system, from theology, history, philology, economics, botany-chemistry, religion, rhetoric, and architecture to music, politics, painting, medicine, magic, navigation, and science. 'One system eats another up' in *Ulysses*, 'Much as old Saturn ate his progeny' – just as Byron had predicted.

The poet, hardly as methodical as Joyce, nevertheless proceeds from criticism of past literature and contemporary poetry to adverse commentary on metaphysics, philosophy ('System doth reverse the Titan's breakfast,/And eats her parents, albeit the digestion/Is difficult . . .' XIV, 2), pharmacology and physical science. In Canto XII, he expresses plans for a Joycean romp through all the other learned arts from music and painting to 'physics', politics and astronomy: 'But my best Canto, save one on Astronomy,/Will turn upon Political Economy' (XII, 88).

> Throughout *Don Juan*, traditional forms and systems are reduced to nonsense by showing their inability to take the measure of man and his world. Plato's philosophy becomes no more than 'confounded fantasies'. . . . The grave philosopher himself becomes a 'bore, a charlatan, a coxcomb . . . a go-between'. . . . 'History can only take things in the gross.' . . . Science fares no better. Newton's 'calculations' of the principles of nature . . . have led only to mechanical contrivances which balance one another out: rockets and vaccination, guillotines and surgery, artillery and artificial respiration. Religion, metaphysics, psychology, social custom, law, all received systems of thought, are sieves through which existence pours in the fluid, shifting world of *Don Juan*.[7]

The overvaluation of art leads to the end of art, as the critic said. Every art Joyce and Byron include in their works bludgeons itself by its own technique and limited specialness; and, through its inability to take the measure of man and his world, calls into question the efficacy of every other art.

Joyce said the progress of his book was like the progress of some sandblast:

> As soon as I mention or include any person in it I hear of his or her death or departure or misfortune: and each successive episode, dealing with some province of artistic culture (rhetoric or music or dialectic), leaves behind it a burnt up field. Since I wrote 'Sirens' I find it impossible to listen to music of any kind. . . .[8]

His last sentence tells us much about the method he employs and even more about the method's intention. Having put music on the page in 'Sirens', turning musical sound into words, Joyce irrevocably destroyed an essential quality of music, the quality that made it distinct from the other human arts. Philosophy, theology, medicine, pharmacology, astronomy, and all the other cultural exercises summoned forth for treatment in *Don Juan* and *Ulysses* follow the same route. The method dissolves them all, puts them on the page, levelling them to one medium. Civilization's learned systems of thought, its most advanced arts, are all brought down to words. Poet and novelist pre-empt each of the given disciplines' particular domain and deny their specialness; they level all into a uniform series of ink-swirls, or so many gusts of sound.

Don Juan and *Ulysses* are quite literally about descent through language.[9] The most enduring elements of their culture are reduced to their lowest common denominators: words and sounds. Literature, literate discourse, erudite and artistic systems, all are contracted to their ultimate platitudes, to clichéd patterns of speech and imprecise words. As Eliot says in 'Burnt Norton' and as Joyce and Byron knew too well,

> Words strain,
> Crack and sometimes break, under the burden,
> Under the tension, slip, slide, perish,
> Decay with imprecision, will not stay in place,
> Will not stay still.

The world is but word, words are but sputters of sound, and 'sounds are impostures' (p. 622).

In the poem the word, turned 'quaint and mouthey', is the medium for Donna Inez's hypocrisy, the vehicle for Suwarrow's rant, the craven tool Southey uses to patronize a swollen despot. In the novel the word is emblemed by a newspaper house full of windbags clattering and banging upon an original integrity of language, gusting empty sound in support of clerical and secular authority, drugging its readers with too many facts, and blasting them into catatonic stupor with the melodramatic echoes of meaningless headlines. Even at its most precise in *Ulysses*, in the scientific catechism of 'Ithaca', the word is amorphous, dehumanized, barely able to communicate what it must.

Submerging all in a sea of words, *Don Juan* and *Ulysses* appear to drown their own medium. Intending, at first, to upset the complacency of human traditions by reducing all through language, Byron and Joyce are propelled to raise subversive questions about language itself and, by implication, their *métier*. The speech the Evangelical quack utters at the end of 'Oxen in the Sun' predicts headlong descent and doom on a number of counts:

> Come on, you winefizzling ginsizzling boozeguzzling existences! Come on you dog-gone bullnecked, beetlebrowed, hogjowled, peanutbrained, weaseleyed four flushers, false alarms and excess baggage! Come on you triple extract of infamy! Alexander J. Christ Dowie, that's yanked to glory most half this planet from 'Frisco Beach to Vladivostok. The Deity ain't no nickel dime bumshow. . . . He's the grandest thing yet and don't you forget it. Shout salvation in king Jesus. You'll need to rise precious early, you sinner there, if you want to diddle the Almighty God. Pflaaaap! Not half. He's got a coughmixture with a punch in it for you, my friend, in his backpocket. Just you try it on.   (p. 428)

This jabbering golliwog spewing forth a mess of utterance is the mongoloid fetus which the English styles have puffed forth after a nine-hundred year gestation. It is an apocalyptic phantom of pure wind. Powerless to live (communicate) the phantom is also powerless to die (be silent). It predicts the end of the English language. Inherent in its testament is the gathering doom of all linguistic exercise. More incoherent than its chaotic origins, more puny than had been anticipated, and much more grim in its promise, Joyce's *enfant terrible* of gibberish (of sound without meaning) threatens imminent self-destruction upon those writers like himself (and Byron) who have borne witness to the coming event.

The question of the two writers' nihilistic perspective and method leading, ultimately, to their own destruction has been addressed before. Eliot said Joyce had destroyed his own future by showing the futility of the English styles because 'now there was nothing left for him to write about' – or with. Auden's remark that *Don Juan* could only have ended with the author's death, implies a possible fear for the writer's writing himself to death: once established in his method, Byron could not write anything else nor put a stop to his habit – in the end, the method of *Don Juan* would have turned on the poem and on the poet, destroying both. But, as we know, Joyce went on to write *Finnegans Wake*, and to plan another work on the sea; and Byron, undisturbed by the prospect that his poem's manner might catch up with him, saw himself cantering on over a hundred, or a thousand, cantos into eternity.

In two of the most remarkable turnabouts in literature, poet and novelist evade self-destruction, refuse to render up the word to the abyss they prepared for it, and affirm the validity of their calling. Their nihilism spurs creation. Having demonstrated that the creation of shapes is an exercise in factitiousness, they are spurred on by their discovery; they respond not only with ironies about man's futile inventiveness but with wonder 'at the human power to create and then to create again under the acknowledged aegis of death'.[10] Exercising the same creative compulsion, they work the debased word up from the apocalyptic hell into which they had once chased it, to an unrivalled place in the artist's rarefied domain. How they accomplish this, and on what grounds, must be discussed further.

III

In a vacuum and ever on the verge of becoming meaningless sound, the word (to the Byronic and Joycean perspective) is also most free. A bastard, without tradition or discipline, it is also responsible to no tradition of styles and tied to no disciplines whose facts and techniques it must represent. Invulnerable to further reduction, it admits no external demands and can turn on itself, feeding on its own sounds and assaying anything.

Some eighteenth-century writers suspected literature of being an elaborate game. In the modern era language itself is the endless game, with orphaned words as its tokens – a game whose only requirement is to keep permutating and defying its original rules. The focus has shifted from universal and overarching structure to the particulars themselves, structureless and without foundation. Words are intoxicants for Byron and Joyce, things of rare and strange device, as they once were for Rabelais who, Anatole France said, played 'with words as children do with pebbles'. *Don Juan* and *Ulysses* indulge their creators' verbal urge; their events often merely further the indulgence. Bent, like Rabelais, on the destruction of all complacency and structure that once limited the play of words, poet and novelist pun, travesty, etymologize and alliterate. Internal rhymes, double-entendres and Freudian slips pave the way for making obscene jokes, wisecracks and, guilelessly, settling private scores. In a story of how some fruit made people swell up, Rabelais punned *patrem omnipotentem* into *ventrem omnipotentem* (Almighty Belly), and he told of how there was very little difference between a woman '*folle à la messe*' and '*molle à la fesse*'.[11] In *Don Juan* Byron ends a long monologue on the uses of the word 'fifty' with:

> At *fifty* love for love is rare, 'tis true,
> But then, no doubt, it equally as true is,
> A good deal may be bought for *fifty* Louis.   (I, 108)

He sends Don José from Inez 'like a lineal son of Eve . . . plucking various fruits without her leave'. He tells of how Julia '.whispering "I will ne'er consent" Consented', and of how Juan's position as *cavalier servente* to Catherine is 'the highest in the nation/In fact, if not in rank' (IX, 52). Joyce, in *Ulysses*, has Stephen play with 'ugling Eglinton', two beds, and 'Mr Secondbest Best'. He has Bloom, during the hour of his cuckolding, say something is a point for the wife's admirers to consider, when he means the wife's advisors (p. 313), and has him react with alarming sensitivity to M'Coy's innocent question on a concert tour: 'Who's getting it up?' (p. 75). 'I rerepugnosed in rererepugnant', Bloom gurgles (p. 538), when the events in 'Circe' wax too Freudian.

The examples are endless. We should note here that the teller of the *Odyssey*, also, was addicted to puns, jingles and quibbles. Joyce defended the use of word-plays by remarking that the Holy Roman Catholic Apostolic Church was built on a pun. His comment exonerates a long, reverberating impulse that passed from Homer and the Bible through most of literature to find particular expression in Rabelais, Enlightenment comic writing, *Don Juan*, and *Ulysses*, until it became, as one large Freudian pun, the echoing motion of *Finnegans Wake.*

Between Rabelais's wielding of the word as device and that of Byron and Joyce stretches an eighteenth-century tradition of learned wit. Wordplays and puns were the staple of this wit's exercise, and in some ways *Don Juan* and *Ulysses* can be read as orphaned progeny of this art which reached its apogee in Burton's *Anatomy of Melancholy,* Swift's *Tale of a Tub,* Pope's *Art of Sinking in Poetry* and Sterne's *Tristram Shandy.* Learned wit is the witty development of intellectual issues (from logic to canon law) and can be traced to a mentality formed under scholastic or quasi-scholastic influences. The forms of this wit owe their character to intellectual habits of a pre-Enlightenment world of thought (like the ratiocinative techniques of abstruse medieval learning)[12] against which the Enlightenment set its face. The publication of the English Rabelais was responsible for the sudden increase in the wit's exercise during the eighteenth century.

We have noted in other contexts how distinctly Byron's and Joyce's efforts recall eighteenth-century writers from Swift and Fielding through to Sterne and Smollett. Although Smollett is usually excluded from the catalogue of those who practice the art of learned wit, it may well be through his perverse expression of the wit in *Humphry Clinker,* his misspellings, malapropisms and name plays, that *Don Juan* and *Ulysses* come closest to the tradition. (Joyce acknowleged Smollett as his direct forerunner in the use of misspellings to suggest another, usually bawdy, meaning;[13] it is no accident that one of his protagonists bears the first name of Humphrey.)

Even as one acknowledges the Enlightenment's precedent here, one must mark the gulf that separates Byron and Joyce from that age and its traditions. The eighteenth century pilloried scholasticism and certain forms of abstruse theorizing. *Ulysses* and *Don Juan* exhibit reverence for no form of learning. During the Augustan age it was deemed responsible to be a learned, literate man. But Byron tried hard to hide the extent of his reading and knowledge; while Joyce read volumes of obscure and antiquarian texts[14] not to make himself more literate, nor even out of curiosity (as did Rabelais and Sterne), but in order to make himself seem strange, to set himself apart from his Dublin peers.

Poet and novelist see themselves as the only learned men (by default) in an era where erudition, not merely on the downturn, has hit rock bottom. For them learning is completely discredited; it is something with which they arm themselves through compulsion; it is weapon, instrument, means of distinction from the herd. They may recall the eighteenth century's like practice when they abuse learning, they may borrow certain devices from the Augustan tradition of wit, but they are without that age's values. Having seen through all mental exercise, Byron and Joyce are free of all theory, they have no need for predetermined ideas. Words play by themselves in *Don Juan* and *Ulysses*, without preconceived notions from the learned arts to start them on their way; they suffice.

IV

'First we feel', Anna Livia Plurabelle says as she wanders out to sea, 'then we fall'. Considered from a number of angles, *Ulysses* and *Don Juan* would appear to be about falling,[15] and specifically about sinking in poetry or prose. As Swift had warned in *A Tale of a Tub*, and as Pope had illustrated in *Peri Bathous*, the actual language of *Don Juan* and *Ulysses* (dragging a variety of things with it as we have seen) sinks.

With Martin Scriblerus Joyce and Byron plunge, taking their readers with them: leading them 'as it were by the hand, and step by step, the gentle downhill way to *Bathos*; the Bottom, the End, the Central Point, the *non plus ultra* of true Modern Poesie!' They agree wholeheartedly with the scribbler's contention that, as there is an architecture of vaults and domes, so also should there be one of making dikes and digging ditches; as Longinus documented a poetic art of rising to sublimity so, also, should there be developed an art of sinking in expression.[16] *Don Juan* and *Ulysses* are such developments: they rise in language to epic, lyric and rhetorical heights, only to descend. There is a Joycean and Byronic twist here, however, for if the language of their books plummets to the depths it does so wilfully, to plumb and measure the deeps of trivia and then, audaciously, to rise.

Before Eliot, and even before Heine, 'Byron had expanded the comic syllepsis of the Augustans'.[17] A Byronic equivalent of Pope's famous couplet of reduction, 'Here, thou, great Anna! Whom three realms obey,/Dost sometimes counsel take – and sometimes tea' would be the description of the paragonic Donna Inez:

> Her favourite science was the mathematical,
> Her noblest virtue was her magnanimity,

Her wit (she sometimes tried at wit) was Attic all,
Her serious sayings darken'd to sublimity;
In short, in all things she was fairly what I call
A prodigy – her morning dress was dimity.   (I, 12)

Or take the rainbow over the *Trinidada*:

Brought forth in purple, cradled in vermillion,
Baptized in molten gold, and swathed in dun,
Glittering like crescents o'er a Turk's pavilion,
And blending every colour into one,
Just like a black eye in a recent scuffle   (II, 92),

the 'heavenly chameleon' looks like that other 'celestial kaleidoscope',
Hope. This frequent collapse (through shifts in perspective and
language) of the lofty into the commonplace for critical, as against
merely comic, effects marks a clear kinship between Byron and
twentieth-century writers.

Joyce uses variations of the eighteenth-century anti-climax and the
Byronic collapse into matter-of-fact for the description of Dedalus.
The prose of the climax of *A Portrait* passes through a series of
Fieldingesque rises and falls. Stephen approaches the wading girl,
hears inner music and 'one long-drawn calling note, piercing like a
star the dusk of silence. . . . A voice from beyond the world was
calling'. The voice belongs to one of his churlish friends. The young
man's soul soars, his body is purified, an ecstacy of flight makes his
eyes radiant, his breath tremulous, then he and his prose descend to
'O, Cripes, Im Drownded'. Again, having seen the bird-girl and
passed heavenward, with his soul swooning amid heavenly flowers,
Stephen sinks down to a naturalist description of tea-table swill:
watery tea-dregs in jam jars, crusts sopped in dripping, stale
breadcrumbs, overturned dishes.[18] The same occurs in *Ulysses* when
Dedalus's triumph in the Library and vision of the birds ascending is
juxtaposed, moments later, with the reduced circumstances and prose
of a conversation with starving Dilly Dedalus over the pawn-cart.

In *Peri Bathous* Pope tells how his favorite poet of Bathos compares
the ocean to a lady in a ruffled bed; of how the triumph and
acclamations of the angels at the creation of the Universe suggests, to
the bathetic imagination, the rejoicings on Lord Mayor's Day; his
parting shot in Chapter XI provides the remarkably profound verse:
'Ye Gods! annihilate but Space and Time,/And make two lovers

happy'. Examples as good, but reaching far beyond the critical intents of *Peri Bathous*, litter Byron's satiric poetry and Joyce's prose. Bad poets like Martin Scriblerus sink unconsciously into their bathetic deeps. Byron and Joyce write in reduction wilfully, cathartically, seeking to reach successively lower levels in the realm of linguistic experience. The poet recalls for us 'Lord Mount Coffee House the Irish peer/Who killed himself for love (with wine) last year'. He tells of how, in Regency England, 'A lady with her daughters or her nieces/Shines like a guinea and seven-shilling pieces'. And he puts the ladies to bed at Norman Abbey with

> Peace to the slumber of each folded flower –
> May the rose call back its true colours soon!
> Good hours of fair cheeks are the fairest tinters,
>   And lowers the price of rouge – at least some winters.   (XIII, 111)

The exercise reaches its ultimate heights (or depths) in the language that describes Bloom in triumph, just after he has vanquished the Cyclops, clambering onto the jumpseat of a car in the four o'clock sun:

> When, lo, there came about them all a great brightness and they beheld the chariot wherein He stood ascend to heaven. And they beheld Him in the chariot, clothed upon in the glory of the brightness, having raiment as of the sun, fair as the moon and terrible that for awe they durst not look upon him. And there came a voice out of heaven, calling: *Elijah! Elijah!* And he answered with a main cry: *Abba! Adonai!* And they beheld Him even Him, ben Bloom Elijah, amid clouds of angels ascend to the glory of the brightness at an angle of fortyfive degrees over Donohoe's in Little Green Street like a shot off a shovel.   (p. 345)

It does not ultimately matter whether we term these examples bathic profundity, mock-heroic juxtaposition of elevated and commonplace tones, Augustan comic syllepsis, diminuendo, or buffoonery. What is significant is the singular perspective they reveal. Where Pope did not, Byron and Joyce plumb the depths; they sound the deeps for size and potential. They gauge the elasticity of language: the levels to which it can sink; the extent to which words, divorced from all tradition and rule, can be played between solemn and frivolous contexts, their potential for expressing at once serious and comic intent. They wish their reductive writing to be comic, critical — and affirmative.

Ulysses's 'Nausicaa' episode criticizes the sentimental, 'namby pamby . . . alto la' style of 'true story' novels — but it also waxes lyrical on occasion to affirm the kind of rapturous lyricism that a youthful and artistic imagination can bring forth. *Don Juan*'s 'Isles of Greece' outburst does the same thing: it is affirmative of a certain youthful exuberance and its lyrics function as a positive expression of the heroic lay — yet it is also something Southey might have written. 'And must thy lyre, so long divine', asks the Southeyesque poet bathetically (and Byron, seriously), 'Degenerate into hands like mine?' (III, 'Isles', 5).

Clearly, the poet and Joyce would have their cake and eat it. Falling implies the potential not just for mindless and irresponsible play but for ascent. Not only may the most absurd subject be deemed fit within its context, any manner of expression, however low, may be deemed valid and uplifting in certain circumstances. The way up, to re-invoke Heraclitus, is through the way down. Language, sunk in bathetic oblivion, rises. Words, at play in a vacuum, turn serious.

Joyce must have been aware of the reverse symbolism inherent in his figure of doom at the end of 'Oxen', for he made the medicine-seller babble with Pentecostal fervor and inspiration. Good Christian in training that he was, he was also certainly aware that the other side of Babel's curse was the gift of tongues. We are not too surprised therefore when we hear him exclaim to Eugene Jolas: 'I have discovered that I can do anything with language I want.'[19] A century before this, Lady Byron had expressed a similar sentiment, though critical, of the poet: 'He is the absolute monarch of words and uses them, as Bonaparte did lives, for conquest, without more regard to their intrinsic value'.[20]

In direct opposition to Lady Byron's observation, what distinguishes Byron and Joyce here is precisely that, having annihilated the tradition of styles and so pre-empted the word's extrinsic functions, they are fully aware of the intrinsic value of words — in the hands of a morally earnest writer. Seen at the bottom of a heap of human maneuvers, they are impotent wind; seen as the first component of human aspiration they are prepotent. Where other writers approach things and concepts first, and then invoke words to describe these, words come first for Byron and Joyce: through them they approach the world and its contents.

In 'Eumeus' Stephen, Joyce's emblem of the morally earnest if somewhat crabbed artist, expresses this sense of words as a primary reality: 'He could hear, of course, all kinds of words changing colour like those crabs around Ringsend in the morning, burrowing quickly into all colours of different sorts of the same sand where they had a home somewhere beneath . . .' (p. 644). In *Finnegans Wake*, Joyce reiterates this sense when he assembles a room full of prefixes, suffixes, phonemes, and syllables to see what sort of suggestive, euphonic combinations of worlds they will make. Byron puts the same perception of words as isolated and prepotent entities into poetry when he says in *Don Juan* – as 'That which make thousands, perhaps millions, think' – 'words are things' (III, 88).

Whatever their plays, their postures, their comic effects, whatever their attitudes to past literatures, stylistics, disciplines, whatever their doubt, poet and novelist write in earnest in *Don Juan* and *Ulysses*.[21] They pass well beyond the Enlightenment's concern over the inadequacies of language, its ambivalent fear of and delight in the word, its moral fervor that the word ascertain truth, its suspicion that the word could and would lie. Doubting, playing, they go through the bottom of their skepticism for everything including the writer's medium until they see that in the hands of a morally earnest artist words are indeed things.

Byron and Joyce feel ultimately responsible as writers precisely because of the vacuum in which they write; because they feel no responsibility to be epically substantial, no dependence on tradition, no obligation to any discipline. Subsequent sections will consider this point in its self-conscious context, but it should be noted here that the word has its inalienable place as primary reality for the morally earnest artist; that it exists as truth rather than as the medium to truth; that it is his substance, his weapon, the vehicle of his earnestness; and that, as all this, it also comes, at least for him, to represent reality truthfully.

V

Byron and Joyce are critical, ironic and objective in *Don Juan* and *Ulysses*. Their subject is 'out there', and they seek to isolate their style and its medium from the subject. But ultimately, like Montaigne, they appear to discover only themselves, their own self-consciousness and its postures. Detached, they yet incline toward self-dramatization.

We ought now to consider the essential stylistic perspective *Don Juan* and *Ulysses* share. The next sections will survey their individual modes of presentation, and some distinctly similar aspects of these as they relate to earlier writers and yet distinguish Byron and Joyce from them. Later sections of the chapter will note the philosophic concepts that support these related modes, and show how the word and its world and the writer's 'I' function together to delineate a singular linguistic universe.

Don Juan is not experimental in the same way, and to the same extent, as *Ulysses* is. There are no extensive challenges to space and time in the poem, none of the fracturing of scene or attempt to render simultaneity of perception (as in the 'Wandering Rocks' episode). Nor, for that matter, is there any modernist symbolism. Nevertheless, along the order of *Tristram Shandy*, there are toyings with chronological time and, to a lesser extent, spatial order.

Juan sets out from home as Odysseus, only to be confronted two cantos later by Lambro, as Odysseus, returning home. There may be a regular, largely continuous narrative, and no real disintegration in the continuity of exterior events, but the commentaries do intrude on the story's sequence and interrupt its spatial pattern. Again, although there may be no multiple reflections of consciousness and time-strata like those in *Ulysses*, Byron's Orlando-esque plans for continuing Juan's history past a century do suggest a like regard for a human consciousness uncircumscribed by spatial presence and mortal existence in time.

It is virtually impossible to separate the narrative proper of *Don Juan*, which is usually within time, from the authorial commentaries which are usually without time and place. The poem exists on several levels: we have Juan's story, and Juan's picaresque reactions to what he experiences; we have the poem's narrator-persona, who comments on Juan, Juan's encounters, and a host of other random subjects; we have Byron himself, controlling Juan's history and representation from a distance, manipulating his narrator's mental wanderings, and speaking out, when least we expect it, in his own voice.

The poem shifts among these levels, often scorning heroic journeys, literary personae, and literary enterprise itself, to achieve yet greater variety of effect. M. K. Joseph provides the best estimate of the poem's layers and range in his analysis of Canto III.[22] The canto has, as its first layer, the epic action of Lambro's Odyssean homecoming. Once removed, is the theme of Greek freedom and decadence shared by two embittered patriots (Lambro and Byron) but beyond this there is also satire on law, trade, and the great man of action or contemplation as embodied by Lambro the sea-attorney and the poet as a kind of Levantine Southey. At another level, the events on the island after Lambro's return give rise to reflections on love, marriage, female inconstancy, and family life. At a yet farther remove comes a satire on the Lakers and a declaration of allegiance to Pope and Dryden. At a fifth remove comes the 'evening voluntary' and a personal declaration of religion. 'On another level again, there is Byron the man, actually riding at twilight through the Ravenna pinewoods, recalling "Boccaccio's lore and Dryden's lay".' And as a seventh, and all-embracing level, there is Byron the poet arranging, controlling, digressing and conscious of digression, and finally cutting the canto in two with a reference to Aristotle'.[23]

Selected pages of *Ulysses* – its first page, the chapter entitled 'Proteus' – may be read similarly, as existing in layers and communicating on multiple levels that are distinct but not always separable. The book expands the method epitomized by *The Ambassadors* which Lubbock defines as 'the type of novel in which a mind is dramatized – reflecting the life to which it is exposed, but itself performing its own particular and private life . . .'.[24] Stephen's and Bloom's minds, each in perpetual tension with the other, prevail; as a kind of commentary on these two, we received fractured representations of the minds of Molly and some subsidiary Dubliners. But, written in a kind of impressionistic shorthand, there are yet other planes of narrative in *Ulysses* for which interior monologue must mix with third-person objective statement. Joyce is not interested in presenting life through the eyes of merely one or two or three of his characters; he rejects the single point-of-view in narrative (Jamesian or Victorian) for texture, dimension, and a multiple-layered effect: 'Wandering Rocks' shows us individual action within the totality of relations existing at the moment: 'the traditional unity (of the nineteenth-century novel) is broken; in its place is the unity of Dublin'.[25]

Action, narration, recollection and cerebration combine for its presentation. Homeric pattern of significance and Dantesque levels of suggestion mix with symbolic echoes, nuances, repetitions and epiphanic highlights; all these, in turn, are knit together with quotidian existence, its occasional defiances of time and space, and the selected Dubliners' mental exercises as they experience this existence – until Joyce is able to make of his presentation the tiered workings of his age's consciousness.

Don Juan and *Ulysses* are post-Lockean, like that important example before them, *Tristram Shandy*. Sterne called the *Essay Concerning Human Understanding* a history book 'of what passes in a man's own mind', and tried to demonstrate some of the literary possibilities which the essay suggested.[26] Locke's theory of the natural association of ideas is central to the experimental modes of most modern literature. One need only examine specific expressions of it in Sterne, Byron and Joyce to perceive how much this theory underlies their related modes – and yet how distinct its presence is in each.

> – '*Bonjour!* – good-morrow! – so you have got your cloak on betimes! – but 'tis a cold morning, and you judge the matter rightly – 'tis better to be well mounted than go o'foot – and obstructions in the glands are dangerous – And how goes it with thy concubine – thy wife – and thy little ones o' both sides? and when did you hear from the old gentleman and lady – your sister, aunt, uncle and cousins – I hope they have got better of their colds, coughs, claps, toothaches, fevers, stranguaries, sciaticas, swellings, and sore eyes. – What a devil of an apothecary! to take so much blood – give such a vile purge – puke – poultice – plaister – night-draught – glister – blister? – And why so many grams of calomel? santa Maria! and such a dose of opium! pericilitating, *pardi*! the whole family of ye, from head to tail – By my great aunt *Dinah's* old black velvet mask! I think there was no occasion for it. (Bk VIII, ch. 3)

We travel, in this example of near automatic writing in *Tristram Shandy*, along a train of private thought sparked by public expression: from a character's spoken words of greeting, to comments and thoughts and questions on the weather, health, the dangers of 'obstructing glands', wives, concubines, children legitimate and illegitimate, old relatives, illnesses, the excesses of an apothecary, and the velvet mask of great-aunt Dinah, who was got with child by the coachman. We cannot tell where the public utterances break down to become private thought, or where thought-associations become word-associations and then sound-associations. Yet Sterne only began exploring the literary possibilities suggested by Locke's theory; he did not exhaust them because they were inexhaustible. He was the rebel who set up the license under which others like Byron and Joyce were to operate, each in his own way.

A passage from *Ulysses* will illustrate this point: the occasion in 'Lotus-Eaters' where Bloom, having collected his letter from Martha and opened it, meets M'Coy (pp. 73–4). Because of his guilt concerning the clandestine affair with the typist, his curiosity about the letter's contents, and his knowledge that M'Coy will importune him to do something or lend a suitcase, Bloom's first thought is 'Get rid of him quickly'. M'Coy stays, to direct a series of questions at Bloom: where he is going, what he is doing, how he is, why he is in mourning, of Dignam's death, the time of the funeral, and whether Bloom knows Hoppy, and Bob Doran and Bantam Lyons who conveyed the news of Dignam's passage while on a binge in Conway's. Bloom registers M'Coy's questions in haphazard fragments (being preoccupied simultaneously with getting rid of the man, guessing what Martha has enclosed in her letter as he turns it over in his pocket, and anticipating the moment when a young woman across the street will climb into a hansom with her escort and reveal hidden curves); his responses issue from his own pre-occupations but serve nevertheless as adequate retorts to M'Coy's probes:

> Doran, Lyons in Conway's. She [the woman] raised a gloved hand to her hair. In come Hoppy. Having a wet. Drawing back his head and gazing far beneath his veiled eyelids he saw the bright fawn sky shine in the glare, the braided drums. Clearly I can see today. Moisture about gives long sight perhaps. Talking of one thing or another [M'Coy]. Lady's hand. Which side will she [the woman] get up?
> — And he said: *Sad things about our poor friend Paddy! What Paddy?* I said. *Poor little Paddy Dignam*, he said. [M'Coy, reporting his speech with Doran.]
> Off to the country: Broadstone probably. High brown boots with laces dangling. Well turned foot. What is he [her escort] fostering over that change for? Sees me looking. Eye out for the other fellow always. Good fallback. Two strings to her bow.

M'Coy jabbers on and Bloom has a moment's respite to alert himself for the occasion of the woman's display, only to miss it because of a passing tram, curse, and recall other such occasions missed:

> Watch! Watch! Silk flash rich stockings white. Watch!
> A heavy tramcar honking its gong slewed between.

Lost it. Curse your noisy pugnose. Feels locked out of it. Paradise
and the peri. . . . Girl in Eustace Street hallway. Monday was it
settling her garter. Her friend covering the display of. *Esprit de
corps.* Well, what are your gaping at?
  — Yes, yes, Mr. Bloom said after a dull sigh. Another gone.
  — One of the best, M'Coy said.

When Bloom says 'Another gone' he is referring to another sight of
delectable flesh missed by him. But to M'Coy, mulling over
Dignam's fate, this is also fit response to the death.

The range and complexity of Joyce's effects in this passage, and
others like it, defy critical delineation. Three distinct actions (opening
the letter, meeting M'Coy, watching the woman), a conversation, a
report of an earlier conversation, an answering of questions, Bloom's
mental exercises of registration, speculation, recollection, and a
continuum of word and thought on subjects ranging from the
weather to Brutus and the English rich, are recorded; they are
recorded simultaneously, interlaced with one another, over a period
of a few minutes and one printed page.

It would seem difficult to find effects of this sort, or even of those of
the Sterne passage, in *Don Juan* — and certainly not in the narrative
proper. But the commentaries of Byron and his narrator suggest a
streaming of association in thought and word that is of the same order
as that employed in *Tristram Shandy* and *Ulysses.* The poem's
monologues shift back and forth, in like manner, from external event
to internal speculation, and, from there, to memory, passing subjects,
practical advice, and then back to the present event.

In Canto II the poet begins to describe the Greek coast. A 'small
ripple spilt upon the beach' presents to his mind the image of
creaming champagne, sending him off on an eulogy of old wine,
'wine and women, mirth and laughter, / Sermons and soda-water the
day after' and, from there, to the speculation in his own voice that
men must get drunk and, as such, can use some advice — that hock
and soda-water are the best hangover cure. The narrator conjures
himself back to his subject with Shandean aplomb: 'The coast — I
think it was the coast that I / Was just describing — Yes, it *was* the
coast' (II, 181). Other lines from the poem's digressions exhibit a like
conversational haphazardry and shifting between external and
internal planes:

> But to my subject — let me see — what was it?
> Oh! — the third canto — and the pretty pair —   (III, 81)

> Kind reader! pass
> This long parenthesis: I could not shut
> It sooner for the soul of me, and class
> My faults even with your own! which meaneth, Put
> A kind construction upon them and me:
> But *that* you won't — then don't — I am not less free.   (VI, 56)

The author is an issue in these works and, because of their forms, a part of their presentations. *Don Juan* is neither just third-person objective narrative nor just the digressive monologues of its narrator, nor even is it a mixture of these two. There is authorial presence in the poem, not just in relation to event, character, or persona's preoccupation, but in Byron's tendency to slip in (through and despite his narrator), to be present in the poem in his own right. *Ulysses* is not pure stream-of-consciousness representing the ultimate literary manifestation of artistic objectivity via Locke's theory and Dujardin's example (only Molly's soliloquy in the entire book is consistently stream-of-consciousness), but rather an admixture of this, third-person narrative, reminiscence, reported speech, Jamesian first-third person, blank copying from printed sources, rhyme, and dramatic colloquy. Through all this we are aware of Joyce: not just as he relates to his characters, nor yet as he relates to his novel's central concerns, but there, in the book, in his own shoes.

Beneath the layers and reflections of *Don Juan*, its various manner and more various deflections, is the poet himself:

> The Byron who rides through the Ravenna woods is also, in a different way, the Byron who broods over Marathon. The reflections on marriage and the family hearth which enlarge Lambro's story are also an expression of Byron's own nostalgia for his household gods. . . . And the Byron who burlesques Southey in the form of the poet is also the Byron who digresses directly to attack the Lakers, and who himself, as poet, is consciously manipulating all the complex levels of the poem.[27]

The author is no less present, and no less manipulative, in *Ulysses*.

Joyceans have already noted how much of Joyce's own experiences and opinions (on Irish nationalism, marriage, drunkenness) went into forming the book's two protagonists. The novelist's concerns are manifest everywhere: sometimes placed with coy distance in the mouth of subsidiary characters, as the subject of hoof-and-mouth disease is in Deasy's; sometimes directly conveyed, as in the novel's repeated illustrations of burgeoning Cyclopeanism. Authorial detachment that courts ironic commentary (in *Don Juan*) and stream-of-consciousness (in *Ulysses*) clearly also posits omniscient artistic presence.

VI

Chapter 2 noted how Byron and Joyce use digressions and random inclusions to annul the pithy selectiveness of epic organization. We need now examine their digressiveness as it relates to their overall presentations; how it distinguishes them from a large group of writers who also employed digressions, and helps define the unusual perspective they share of the author as he relates to his work and its order.

Don Juan and *Ulysses* function by accretion. They exceed any and all literary traditions of digressiveness in the wilful, unpredictable extent of their growth by inclusion. The expanding commentaries of the poem, like the gigantism of 'Cyclops' and the amorphous spreading of 'Eumeus', are obvious examples of what is a much larger method. Each writer combines the trick of rapid association of ideas with a flair for expropriating expressions from any source at hand, and with an excellent memory for recalling exactly and then developing anything read or heard. Because of this, plots and plans serve *Don Juan* and *Ulysses* best in their absence, or in and as their creators depart from them.

'You ask me for the plan of Donny Johnny? – I *have* no plan – I *had* no plan – but I had or have materials', Byron responded, to a query on his poem's plan.[28] The poet was half-joking, for the poem was formed as much of Juan's story and certain related subjects as it was of the contents of the poet's mind (its preoccupations, distractions and recollections) during any given moment of composition. The narrative in Canto III is that canto's only digression; Byron's freewheeling commentary forms the body of the canto, spreading spatially like the fingers of a hand, expanding amorphously with total disregard for fixed subject. A lyric on Greece, itself a tangent from the main story, suggests comments on fame and writing; these lead in yet another direction to criticism of the moralistic Lakers and the 'drowsy frowsy' *Excursion* which suggests, even more tangentially, a digression on digressions and on Wordsworth's ability to sometimes wake (while calling for a boat to sail the deeps of air and drivelling seas to set it well afloat). All this appears to focus for a moment in the story line (in Juan and Haidée's isolation at twilight), only to spawn forth a variety of allusions on the evening angelus, the Ave Maria, pantheism, Ravenna's wood, Boccaccio's specter huntsman, Hesperus, the day's decay, loss, and the flowers on Nero's grave.

Ulysses carries this refusal to be confined by any subject further, and the story of the novel's accretion (by a third more its original size) is probably unique in literature. For all his intricate plans, plots, and parallels, much of Joyce's material started out as trivia encountered by chance. 'My head is full of pebbles and rubbish and broken matches and lots of glass picked up "most anywhere" ', he admitted to Harriet Weaver, and from the example of how a nonsense question Sylvia Beach once put to Joyce became a line in the novel ('Your corporosity sagaciating O.K.?' p. 425) we know how much of this trivia became *Ulysses*. Not content with the material presented to his pen by mind and external event, Joyce sought out volumes of other semi-facts from newspapers, outdated compendia, and unreliable friends. *Ulysses* grew outward in a variety of directions like some yeasted mixture, as *Don Juan* had, limited only by the ability of the author's mind to contain and collate the tangential materials.

There is an aspect of simultaneity to their augmentative growth. Joyce implies as much when he speaks of his creation of portions of *Ulysses*: 'the printer, for some reason, sends me now proofs of *Circe*, *Eumeus* and *Penelope* at the same time without having finished the composition of the first two and I have to work on them simultaneously, different as they are, so that I remind myself of the man who used to play several instruments with different parts of his body'.[29] In Byron's poem also, composition takes on a flat, spatial quality that transcends the narrative line. The contents of the two works expand, spreading outward more than progressing sequentially, and narrative becomes a contracting device.

Jack's beanstalk growing each time the boy looked at it and the voracious threshing machine at Hardy's Flintcomb Ash, provide two accurate images of how the accretive method of *Don Juan* and *Ulysses* functions. Novel and poem burgeon out to touch upon scores of disparate things, although the ultimate motion is to pull the extraneous material back inward, crablike, to make it relevant to the first intent. More and more is allowed to enter the vortex of each work, ever-greater amounts are made priceless to the given situation with each imaginative swoop. The effects recall not so much the intrusiveness of *Tom Jones*'s inter-chapters as the rollicking inclusivity of *Gargantua* and *Tristram Shandy*. Rabelais's inclusiveness was meant to suggest merry disorder; Joyce and Byron, like Sterne, use theirs to assert order.

In all his digressions, said Sterne, 'there is a master stroke of digressive skill' possibly overlooked by his reader 'because 'tis an excellence seldom looked for, or expected indeed, in a digression. I fly off from what I am about', he says, 'as far and as often too as any writer in *Great-Britain*; yet I constantly take care to order affairs so, that my main business does not stand still in my absence'. Later, he claims his diversions are the structural aspect of his book:

Digressions, incontestibly, are the sunshine; – they are the life, the soul of reading, – take them out of this book for instance, – you might as well take the book along with them; – one cold eternal winter would reign in every page of it; restore them to the writer; – he steps forth like a bridegroom, – bids All hail; brings in variety, and forbids the appetite to fail.   (Bk 1, ch. 22)

Basic to its form, Sterne's digressions comprise the more significant part of his book: they are the sources of its variety, factors in its entertainment, integral aspects of its method, and representations of the artist's domination over his material.

One could say as much for the digressiveness of *Don Juan* and *Ulysses*. One could also claim much more – for poet and novelist carry their accretiveness to the point where the distinction between 'digression' and 'main business' is annulled. Sterne played off the devices of narration and digression against each other. But one cannot isolate particular passages in these works, not even the blank transcriptions from nineteenth-century history books and Dublin newspapers, and show them as clearly digressing into irrelevance. Nor can one say that the multiple inclusions flesh out the main structures of Homeric narrative. To the Byronic and Joycean perspective, their Odyssean parallels could not exist as structural devices without the teeming external additions. To their ideal reader, everything is germane in *Don Juan* and *Ulysses* – as Dedalus says, 'A man of genius makes no mistakes. His errors are volitional and are the portals of discovery' (p. 190).

'Why Man the Soul of such writing is its licence', the poet said, adding '– at least the *liberty* of that *licence* if one likes – *not* that one should abuse it — it is like trial by Jury and Peerage — and Habeas Corpus — a very fine thing — but chiefly in the *reversion* — because no one wishes to be tried for the mere pleasure of proving his possession of the privilege.'[30] When Byron speaks of trial he is asserting the writer's right to assay any subject. When he mentions the license of this writing he means, simply, the writer's liberty to include anything in the body of his work — a privilege that is coupled with an ability to make anything seem part of the whole. It is expression and proof of the writer's possession of ultimate control that he can portray a lack of control.

Critics of Joyce may claim that he seized the license Byron speaks of here only to abuse it, through too much randomness and too much assaying. But Joyce's manner was, precisely, to collate numerous disparate shreds (events, comments, techniques, even 'programmes, pawn-tickets, press-cuttings [and] handbills'[31]), 'to assemble discrete details on little scraps of paper — we obtain the idea of their numerousness from the fact that the notes he never used at all weighed some twenty-five pounds — and then fuse them in his head for many, many hours before starting to write'.[32] 'I am stitching away like a cobbler', he wrote to Harriet Weaver, in description of how the diverse minutiae of *Ulysses* were intricately sewn into larger order. Despite its puzzles, mysteries, intricacies, banalities, flotsam, and gobbledy gook, *Ulysses* conveys one impression. The reader who bogs down in the labyrinth of interlocking trifles, who worries about who the man in the macintosh was or how a wedding announcement becomes a list of trees, is in the position of Forster's character, Fielding: they have had the experience (of multifariousness) and missed its meaning — order.

Friedrich Schlegel said that the essential characteristic of the *Roman* is chaotic form;[33] he found such works to be syntheses of apparent chaos and underlying order, confusions artistically arrayed. Certainly, we read *Ulysses* or *Don Juan* for the created wholeness that exists beyond and through their diversions. And the wholeness exists because the artistic mind, exulting in confusions and minutiae, perceives it as such. Order is an artistic perspective; to appear disordered is an artistic right. By seeming to digress, be random, uncontrolled, trivial, impromptu, and inclusive to the point of chaos, Byron and Joyce show the domination of their immortal minds (those fiery particles, as the poet would say) 'over a congeries of material facts'.[34] They also exhibit the audacious will that lies behind the ability to see order where there is none.

VII

The poet's and the novelist's expressions of right to any subject, over all subjects, deserve closer scrutiny. Their compulsive assaying, the demands they make on their readers' attention while sounding off upon a host of diverse issues, and their overweening expression of authorial will, clearly mimic the attitude of Montaigne toward his writing. Indeed the overall tone and manner of their expansive compositions connect *Don Juan* and *Ulysses* directly with the Montaignesque essay and its presentation of the free play of mind. Of his ideas Montaigne says, '*Les fantasies de la music sont conduites par art, les miennes par sort*'. But if they are guided by chance, their treatment as subjects betrays an alarming degree of authorial will. 'I take the first subject that chance offers', he says on one occasion, but he eschews any duty to treat subjects fairly: 'I take one, sometimes only to lick it, sometimes to brush the surface, sometimes to pinch it to the bone. . . . And most often I like to take them from some unaccustomed point of view'.[35] The essayist's subjects depend on nothing but his mind: 'I undertake to speak indiscriminately of everything that comes to my fancy without using any but my own natural resources'. He admits his proclivity for tangential discussions ('My style and mind alike go roaming'), but he also defends these with 'I do not portray being: I portray passing. Not the passing from one age to another . . . but from day to day, from minute to minute'. He claims that his digressiveness is part of his evolving style, 'My book is always one'. Indeed, his self-confidence as a writer – even of his right to be accomplished in ignorance – is without limit; his impositions on the attention of his reader know no bounds. 'I apply myself to make use of vanity itself', he says with Byronic and Joycean audaciousness, 'and asininity, if it brings me any pleasure'.[36]

Byron and Joyce follow the cardinal rule 'Do What You Will' of Rabelais's Abbey of Thélème to become most like Montaigne. They please themselves in their assays; testing subject and reader to each one's limits; insisting always on an attentive audience whom they might manipulate, like their subjects, at will. 'It is the inattentive reader who loses my subject, not I', they also say, and Montaigne's 'I' appears, authoritative and wilful, in a Byronic and then Joycean voice, in two of literature's most detached, ironic, (apparently) objective works.

Byron, who enjoyed Montaigne, said he wanted a form for *Don Juan* that was large enough to swim in and talk on any subject that he chose, 'from a tyrant to a tree'. In it he would combine the attitude of Montaigne with the technique of the *improvvisatore*:

> . . . speculating as I cast mine eye
> On what may suit or may not suit my story,
> And never straining hard to versify,
> I rattle on exactly as I'd talk
> With anybody in a ride or walk. (xv, 19)

He would be the direct, accomplished speaker (even in ignorance, like the French humanist):

> I'm a philosopher; confound them all!
> Bills, beasts, and men, and – no! *not* Womankind!
> With one good hearty curse I vent my gall,
> And then my Stoicism leaves nought behind
> Which it can either pain or evil call,
> And I can give my whole soul up to mind;
> Though what *is* soul or mind, their birth or growth,
> Is more than I know – the deuce take them both. (vi, 22)

Given the poet's tongue-in-cheek wilfulness of tone and the unpredictability of his subject, *Don Juan* makes for dangerous reading. We cannot be certain that it will not turn suddenly and rend its own audience. Its reader exists, like Montaigne's, as captive pawn, witness to any and all loquaciousness, to be teased, shocked, ignored, and always threatened with being pinched to the bone.

Joyce makes like claims upon his reader's attention – and exhibits the same disdain for his reader's well being. Subjects exist in *Ulysses* to be exorcized, topics are conjured forth to be dissipated, and foolishly tenterhooked readers are importuned and possessed but for their own mockery. Its author breaks the book's texture which he has taken such pains to establish, for no other evident reason than that he has got the reader to trust it. Contemptuous of smooth surfaces 'he fractures them to display power over his world, himself, his reader'.[37] Joyce also never forgets to exercise his privilege as artist writing to please himself and disturb his reader. Writing from eighteen different angles, he shocks us into awareness of the act of authorial choice seventeen more times than necessary. The reader of *Ulysses* thus takes

on an aspect suspiciously close to that of martyr – or masochist.
'*Je suis moi-même la matière de mon livre*' Montaigne warns his reader,
in case a person should neglect to notice how large a percentage of the
essayist's words are first-person constructs expressing his own
predilections. 'It is not my deeds that I write down, it is
myself . . . my essence'. Where another writer may look in front of
him, he adds, 'I look inside of me; I have no business but with myself, I
continually observe myself, I take stock of myself, I taste myself'.[38]
Montaigne's commentators Auerbach and Highet[39] have emphasized the extent to which the essays fulfill his aim at autobiography.
The Frenchman may have claimed (in 'On Experience') that he found
within him no self or continuity of personality, he nevertheless
remains his own best subject. His self-confidence becomes a form of
self-revelation; and his writing turns inward to speak of the workings
of its creator's mind. Objective, ironic Byron and Joyce follow
Montaigne's example to reveal themselves and center on their own
experiences and acts of writing.

Byron intended that the chief interest of his poem should be not in
the hero's living his life and dying his death, 'but in the poet's writing
the poem'.[40] He and his persona are always at the forefront of the
poem, and Byron 'who painted nothing else than himself', as
Coleridge once said, reveals himself no less in *Don Juan* than does the
creator of that other monument of modern objectivity, *Ulysses*, in his
portrayal of the experiences and predilections of James-Stephen and
Joyce-Bloom. Joyce may seem more oblique, but it is also true that a
primary subject of *Ulysses* is the writing of *Ulysses*, and that he is more
the matter of his book than the poet is of his poem.[41]

Nor is it simply a question of our learning a number of
biographical facts about these two writers – that Byron swam the
Hellespont as Leander once did, that Joyce and Nora slept head-to-toe
in a bed that wriggled on its quoits – as we learn Montaigne's height,
health, education, and that the essayist seldom dreamt. If we leave out
the narrative element, Joseph notes, '*Don Juan* becomes an inde-
finitely extensible medium for personal apologia and topical
commentary, not unlike the *Cantos* of one of Byron's modern
counterparts, Ezra Pound'. Mary Colum marked *Ulysses* as belong-
ing to the Confessional class of literature. 'Like Rousseau, Joyce
derived everything from his own ego. . . . like Rousseau, he has a
passion not only for revealing himself, but for betraying himself; like
him also, he deforms everything he touches.'[42] Common precedent
for this is the Montaigne who promised his readers psychological self-

description long before Rousseau trumpeted his 'task' as daring and unprecedented.

As self-centered and self-revealing presentations, *Don Juan* and *Ulysses* belong with an older and various tradition of personal apologia-cum-confessional literature, one which is part of the yet larger movement toward self-consciousness which Schiller saw as the fate of post-Homeric man. Before we discuss this movement and its implications for the stylistic perspective shared by *Don Juan* and *Ulysses*, we ought first to distinguish between the situations of these two works and that of Montaigne's essays.

Montaigne was the first to describe thought describing itself thinking. He was also one of the first writers to make himself his own subject. Eliot found the Frenchman to be fluid, insidious and the least destructible of adversaries — 'You could as well dissipate a fog by flinging hand grenades into it' — and he claimed that the essayist does not reason so much as charm, insinuate and design. Montaigne feints. In fact, he reveals himself far less than he purports to do. Too often, he uses the pretense of talking about himself to conceal his person and the insubstantial nature of its portrayal. When he does reveal himself, it is by intention only.

Byron and Joyce often reveal themselves unintentionally, compelled by their situations. Self-centeredness is largely a device for Montaigne, for revealing what he wants to, for pretending to reveal, for not revealing. With the poet and the novelist it is as much method, chosen intentionally for dealing with a possible absence of objective reality, as it is philosophic necessity. Unlike the Frenchman's *Essays*, *Don Juan* and *Ulysses* are monuments of the post-Enlightenment world-picture, where the mind has invaded fiction.

Auerbach noted that Montaigne, for all his self-irony, cannot completely conceal his delight in his own person. His 'is a calm and self-rooted consciousness of his individual self, free from pettiness, arrogance, insecurity, and coquetry'.[43] We cannot say the same for Byron and Joyce. They may assume such a manner in their writing, but they do not have the self-contentment of the French humanist. The self-confidence Montaigne exhibits belongs, at least partly, to the confidence of his age. The self-confidence Byron and Joyce exhibit is an act of will, isolated, based on nothing around them, an artistic pose in an unconfident world. Where Montaigne is skeptical, they are cynical; where he may have seen human folly, they have seen cosmic nullity; where he is self-centered and, occasionally, self-revelatory, they are fully self-conscious.

VIII

The early Greeks manifest an anthropocentric attitude to life as witnessed not only by the subject of their sculpture, painting and poetry, but that of their philosophy and political theory. Man is still our primary concern, but the focus has since shifted to human personality and selfhood. The Greeks did not discover the subjective self, they realized the universal laws of human nature; their intellectual principle was not individualism but, to use the word in its classical sense, humanism.[44] The difference is crucial. Not the Grecian principle of Man, but its shrunken metamorphosis, man in the singular and the diminutive, an 'I' confused by its own solemnity, now holds center stage. The subjective self has somehow become eminently more verifiable than the external world, and subjectivism has become the intellectual principle of the modern world's consciousness.

Schiller, as Chapter 2 noted, distinguished the change in aesthetic perception that occurred between the early Greeks and ourselves. His naive poet perceived nature as an imitable unity to which he also belonged. His sentimental poet finds nature inimitable, separate from him, and so seeks unity — until he comes to doubt the external world and speculate that the unity he seeks is, in truth, a product of his own mind. The latter poet reflects upon the impression that objects make upon him: ideas refer to apparent external conditions which are, in turn, referred back to the ideas, and the poet finds his motives in himself and in pure reason, which draws everything out of itself, and to itself refers everything. The naive poet may have looked outward and perceived unity, but he was also limited because of this to a single relationship with his subject, and to a single treatment of it. The sentimental poet is not so limited: finding no imitable external world, he is free to construct his own image, or images, of it and then act accordingly toward it.[45]

Coming close upon the heels of Schiller, and quarrelling with him as to whether Shakespeare's works manifest naive objectivity or experienced subjectivity, Friedrich Schlegel renamed Schiller's antithetical terms Classical and Romantic (in effect, he redefined the terms, giving the contrast three stages) and pursued the theory to its logical extreme.[46] The Classical poet was one who subordinated himself to his material. The Romantic poet dominated it through his personality. We will return to Schlegel's theory of romantic irony elsewhere, but it should be noted here that it was Schlegel who saw romantic expression as characterized by constant reflections of the work of art in itself: its artist is free to intrude upon his work, and the mirror he holds up reflects his own image as much as it does the world (such as it is) as seen from the perspective of this image. (It is significant that Schlegel's examples were the reflections of Yorick, Shandy and the author upon one another in *Tristram Shandy*, and the entire tradition of the comic novel inaugurated by Cervantes.[47])

The change from unity to disunity (or from objectivity to subjectivity) was not a static event. A movement of increasing self-consciousness, it evolved. Once the self began to turn inward, whether with Schiller's post-Homeric genius or Schlegel's romantic poet, the introspection could not stop, and the self-dependency could only increase. *Ulysses*, Proust's *Remembrance*, and Woolf's *Waves* are late manifestations of a self-reflective movement that had begun well before them, to reach them by way of the Romantic poets (and Sterne) who were the first to perceive the creative potential of introspection.

Man has fallen not so much into sin as into the highly original sin of self-consciousness. 'The alienated man cut off from nature by his conscience is the Romantic equivalent of post-Edenic Adam.'[48] Northrop Frye's comment implies a corollary: the self's startling ascent to power. When nature not only ceased to suggest imitable unity but proceeded to fade as an external experience, self-consciousness grew to replace it and the self gained in creativity until it became prepotent.

'In looking at objects of Nature', Coleridge said in the *Notebooks*, 'I seem rather to be seeking, as it were *asking* for, a symbolic language for something within me that already and forever exists, than observing anything new'. Keats implied that whatever the imagination seized as beautiful had to be true because the imagination, like Adam, assigned names and values. 'In the intense instant of imagination, when the mind, Shelley says, is a fading coal, that which I was is that which I am and that which in possibility I may come to be' (Dedalus, p. 194). From such comments, it is clear that the self provides the artist with substance, patterns and values; that it has the power to realize, of itself, that which it conjures forth from its own recesses.

Forced into self-consciousness, the artistic genius of the nineteenth and twentieth centuries turns fully inward to find, there, freedom and self-sufficiency. Self-conscious perception, freed of the external world and its mimesis, finds in itself both the substance and the method for endless self-reflection: art. 'Gaze into your omphalos', Stephen advises all artists. Bloom, in 'Lotus-Eaters', does so literally and farcically; his creator, figuratively and solemnly, employs a narcissistic art. Young Juan's unconscious narcissism, meanwhile, serves as clear symbol of his creator's conscious narcissism. *Don Juan* and *Ulysses* are overwhelmingly self-conscious. Introspection pervades both their content and their technique of expression. They are, to borrow Hazlitt's phrase for *Don Juan*, written about themselves and about their own writing. The technique they each employ for this introspection also turns inward. The poem turns on its story in its commentaries, the commentaries turn inward on the hero's creator, and the poet's act of writing itself becomes lost in the expressions on writing and on its writing. *Ulysses* introspects as much in subject as in technique. When Dedalus quotes Maeterlinck, '*If Socrates leaves his house today he will find the sage seated on his doorstep. If Judas goes forth tonight it is to Judas his steps will tend . . .*' (p. 213), he refers to the prevailing inclination of human perception, once fallen, to look outward and find only itself. But his words here, like Best's subsequent recollection of Mallarmé's Hamlet reading the book of himself, point to the book's inwardly involuting technique. While Stephen talks about Hamlet he is really talking about himself, and while he does that Joyce speaks through him about *Ulysses*;[49] throughout all this the book itself introspects on its own creation. Joseph's comment on the series of reflections and counter-reflections in Byron's poem refers as well to Joyce's technique:

> It is, in fact, characteristic of much great art to be 'about itself' in this way. It bounds and impersonalizes itself by insisting on its own nature, not by trying to sustain an illusion; or perhaps we should say that the illusion is so persistent that it survives even when the sleight of hand is revealed. All art is about life: all art is about art. These statements are equally and simultaneously true.[50]

What distinguishes *Don Juan* and *Ulysses* from countless other self-reflective works of art, within and without their periods, is that self-consciousness invades their technique to a degree where it becomes, oddly enough, distant.

The poem and the novel reflect upon themselves, their creators, and their own writing; they do this to the point where involution in writing becomes an independent process. We sense, reading either work, that somebody or some thing has set an inwardly-turning process in motion and then left it, to spin on itself. Far beyond the self-consciousness of technique Hazlitt perceived of *Don Juan*, the poem and *Ulysses* are only about their own writing. Like haunted musical instruments playing by themselves, the two works write of themselves, themselves. Self-consciousness or introspection, at least in this regard, becomes distant, self-sustaining, linguistic, pure activity.

IX

Don Juan and *Ulysses* represent two peaks in this post-Lockean, post-Kantian world. In an era where the mind has invaded fiction, they are each representative of a kind of internal problem-solving: attempts to find a form where none can exist, attempts to find this form through the exercise of mind and self when mind and self each possess the power to destroy themselves.

Kant, even as he focused on the activities of the human mind, spurred on the movement toward self-consciousness. By pointing to the limits of a reason the eighteenth century has believed infinite, he cast doubt not only on the mind but on any and all subjective achievement:

> Himself the supreme product of Rationalism, Kant was destined historically to overcome it: in him reason attained the ultimate clarity necessary to the discernment of its own limitations, and he prepared the way, directly and indirectly, for Romanticism.

A philosophy which establishes an idea or ideal as primary, which lays emphasis not on external phenomena but on our subjective modes of perceiving them, is but a short step removed from a philosophy which views all objects as being the product of the subject. Thus Fichte completed the destruction of objective reality which Kant had begun, and carried German philosophy to the dizzy heights of absolute idealism. From Fichte's position, it is but a step to the formula 'das Leben ein Traum', which became so important in Romantic thought and poetry. From Fichte, again, it is only a step to the ironical attitude in which the ego looks with a superior smile upon the non-ego, the creator upon his creation.[51]

Byron and Joyce are among those artists who inherited the tension in attitude toward human perception inaugurated by Kant and Hume and documented by Schiller and Schlegel – that of seeing, at once, the ultimate potential of the mind's activity and the self's creativity, and the imminent destruction of the same by their own insubstantiality. For these artists the mind is its own place, fair substitute for the Grecian sense of *polis* and connection now lost to them. The ego to which this mind belongs, through its own exercises in consciousness, creates all it envisions. Yet they are also aware that the self can consume itself by the very energies that define its being; and that the mind is a fevered vacuum which ultimately expends and dissipates itself.[52] Byron and Joyce absorb Kant but, absorbing Schiller's and Schlegel's theories also (and practising them to exhaustion), they subsume and subvert the first motion toward giving human consciousness the highest palms. With the external world dissipated in its favor, human consciousness proves, ultimately, to be hardly more reliable.

The ultimate substance and only verity, the human mind is yet the most unpredictable, comic thing in creation. Expended in its own best activity, it destroys itself and the self to which it belongs. Hence notions of what is comic or grave, substance or vacuum, profound or trivial, springing as they do from this same mind, merge; they are merely interchangeable terms to the prescient artist. Loss of consistency in tone and in communication, a consequence of the artist's having seen through the achievements of human perception, becomes his virtue.

Byron's ambivalent tone in *Don Juan* makes for a disconcerted reader; it also suggests acute self-consciousness, uncertainty, in the poet. Canto XI's solemn eulogy on Freedom and 'Freedom's chosen station' shifts abruptly to the free-born sounds of 'Damn your eyes! Your money or your life!' from footpads who have seized their freedom too literally; a discourse on the female predicament is followed abruptly by 'This was Juan's earliest scrape'; and the lyrical heights of the 'Isles of Greece' shifts to the notation 'Thus sung, or would, or could, or should have sung,/The modern Greek in tolerable verse'. Examples of sinking in language to disconcert the reader, these are also expressions of the poet's inability to maintain consistency of tone.

In the midst of describing the seraglio, Dudu, Lola, Katinka, and pins in women's dresses, Byron stops to ponder 'What are we? and whence came we?' Canto XV speaks of stuffing with sage that 'very verdant goose' (society), of ghost-stories and other shudderings, when the poet takes a sudden leap to the sublime in a stanza that sounds like a compressed paraphrase of the ninetieth psalm:[53]

> Between two worlds life hovers like a star,
> 'Twixt night and morn, upon the horizon's verge:
> How little do we know that which we are!
> How less what we may be!   (xv, 99)

The poet intends his uncertainty, his abrupt changes in level, to be obvious to his reader. He knows he cannot maintain the same tone – and that he must not. When Francis Cohen objected to 'the quick succession of fun and gravity' in *Don Juan* and to the sensation it gave the reader 'of being scorched and drenched' at once, the poet was quick to claim, in a Joycean mixture of grossness and acuity, that that was his intention, an express purpose of heightening, not leveling, the contrasts in communication. He asked of Cohen:

> Did he never play at Cricket or walk a mile in hot weather? – did he never spill a dish of tea over his testicles in handing the cup to his charmer to the great shame of his nankeen breeches? – did he never swim in the sea at Noonday with the Sun in his eyes and on his head – which all the foam of the ocean could not cool? did he never draw his foot out of a tub of too hot water damning his eyes and his valet's? did he never inject for a Gonorrhea? – or make water through an ulcerated Urethra? – was he ever in a Turkish bath – that marble paradise of sherbet and sodomy? – was he ever in a cauldron of boiling oil like St. John? – or in the sulphureous waves of hell? (where he ought to be for his 'scorching and drenching at the same time') did he never tumble into a river or lake fishing – and sit in his wet clothes in the boat – or on the banks afterward 'scorched and drenched' like a true sportsman?[54]

In his medley of conflicting effects, impressions, perspectives, Byron found the means for meeting the new subjective requirement of sincerity in art.[55]

'Sometimes I'm trivial', Joyce once said, 'and sometimes I'm quadrivial'. His *Ulysses* exhibits the same self-conscious and intentional poise, between any two extremes of frivolity and earnestness, in its communication as does Byron's poem. Dedalus the artist takes a walk along the strand and urinates in an expression of his defiance. Yet, the lyrical intensity of this episode's tone and language, its intricate mixture of symbols for past, future, death, creation ('seaspawn and seawreck'), words, and artistry, convey a profundity of content unrivalled in literature.

We have already noted how 'Nausicaa' sinks in language only to communicate, at once, smarmy novellettism and lyrical height. Consider now a yet more effective example of Joycean extremity in communication: his assumption of conflicting tones to heighten, not cancel out, each other's effect. This is the passage in the chapter on the English styles where Joyce appears to parody the manner of Thomas Browne and the Authorized Version of the Bible:

> Remember, Erin, thy generations and the days of old, how thou settedst little by me and by my word and broughtest in a stranger to my gates to commit fornication in my sight and to wax fat and kick like Jeshurum. Therefore hast thou sinned against the light and hast made me, thy lord, to be the slave of servants. Return, return, Clan Milly: forget me not, O Milesian. Why hast thou done this abomination before me that thou didst spurn me for a merchant of jalaps and didst deny me. . . . But thou hast suckled me with a bitter milk: my moon and my sun thou hast quenched forever. And thou hast left me alone forever in the dark ways of my bitterness: and with a kiss of ashes hast thou kissed my mouth. (p. 393)

From one perspective this is parody, farce, triviality. From another, it serves as fully sincere remonstration and lament, a valid use of Biblical manner for an appropriate (albeit secular) emotion and mood. The passage puts a parodic cast on Biblical style, Irish rhetoric of loss, Stephen's mother-complex, and Bloom's cuckoldry by a merchant of jalaps; it is yet the expression of a sympathetic artist's sadness and regret for Ireland, Bloom, Stephen, Molly, motherhood, the fallen world, human folly, and for the artist himself. Mockery is sympathetic, profound, transcendent; trivia becomes quadrivia.

We might consider the two writers' tendency to communicate serious and comic effects at the same time and to slip back and forth between two extremes of tone, a continuation of the democratization of style which was inaugurated (as Auerbach sees it[56]) by Dante and the Christian era's mingling of styles inherited from antiquity. We might even consider the two writers' descent from sublimity to comedy — and from there to profundity — variations on the eighteenth century's exercises in linguistic sinking. This is hardly sufficient however. For unlike the eighteenth century writers poet and novelist mean also to be polemically affirmative, like Dante, of the lowest forms of expression. But where Dante achieved consistency of style no matter how low his content and his forms of usage, Byron and Joyce seek inconsistency of style with the compulsive self-consciousness of too many perspectives.

X

Byron and Joyce learn from the comic-epic novelists (Cervantes through Sterne) that if life is a serio-comic situation it warrants a like style. They learn from Montaigne not only of their right to declare with wilful abandon on any topic but also of their right to speak tongue-in-cheek of any subject.[57] They learn from Ariosto the advantages that can be achieved by mixing solemn with light until they are indistinguishable: by moving, often in the same sentence, from the elevated and romantic to the commonsensical and pragmatic; by treating their material in general (as Voltaire said of Ariosto) 'with gay badinage' — giving voice to 'the sublimest things only to finish them with a twist of pleasantry'.[58]

They learn from Rabelais, most of all, to tease their readers with flippancy at crucial moments, to suggest bone-marrows and hidden significances only to warn that they must only be read for entertainment (or, in Joyce's instance, for puzzles) because they compose, like Homer, during meals. Coleridge's comment on Rabelais is pertinent:

> It is in vain to look about for a hidden meaning in all that he has written; you will observe, that after any particularly deep thrust, as the Papinamia [Bk IV, ch. 48], for example, Rabelais, as if to break the blow, and to appear unconscious of what he has done, writes a chapter or two of pure buffoonery. He every now and then, flashes you a glimpse of a real face from his magic lantern, and then buries the whole scene in mist.[59]

Don Juan and *Ulysses* are also written in a manner of transcendental buffoonery. They stay poised on the verge between the comic and the serious, parody and profundity, triviality and quadriviality. It is useless to try and define where the line between earnestness and mockery falls. Joyce would be the last to deny the significance of anything in his book; he would also be the first to deny the ultimate significance of any one thing in *Ulysses*. The poet wrote to giggle in *Don Juan* — but to giggle with moral earnestness.

Poet and novelist have each learned with Wilde, too well, the importance of being earnest. Auden called the blithely savage poet of *Don Juan* 'the master of the airy manner'; but three lines from the poem convey its Wildean tone: 'However, 'tis no time to chat/On general topics: poems must confine/Themselves to Unity, like this of mine' (XI, 44). Joyce deadpanned to the same effect in *Ulysses*, and in regard to his writing of it. Questioned too closely on the significances of his book, he responded: 'I am afraid I am more interested, Mr. Connolly, in the Dublin street-names than in the riddle of the universe'.[60]

Friedrich Schlegel's theory of romantic irony remains the best description we have of the perspective that nurtures this manner. Schlegel said philosophy was the true home of irony, and that transcendental poetry alone could rise to the heights of philosophy. The latter (ancient or modern, verse or prose) is characterized by a pervasive irony 'throughout, as a whole, and everywhere'. Its mood (*im Innern*) 'surveys everything and rises infinitely above everything' that is limited, even above its own art, virtue, or genius; and, in its externals and execution, it mimics the manner 'of an ordinary good Italian buffo'.[61] Romantic irony implies buffoonery, assuredly, but a transcendental variety; the ironic expression transcends the external world that may not be there, the self's substitute creations, and the creator's own self-consciousness in the act of creation.

There is an inherent paradox to this manner arising partly from Fichte's concept of '*intellectuelle Anschauung*', the attitude of superior self-contemplation (where artistic self-consciousness is meant to control, not merely accompany, inspiration, and where the artist is not supposed to lose himself in his work no matter how subjective its material), upon which Schlegel built his theory.[62] Self-consciousness includes, ultimately, the ability to distance oneself from the self and its creations, to be aware of one's own self-consciousness; and romantic irony, as Schlegel first perceived it, is a form of super-objectivity born out of the very subjectivity Schiller documented in his essay.

Schlegel found Shakespeare to be 'the centre, and core of romantic poetry', and he balked at Schiller's categorization of the bard as a natural objective artist. To him the bard was '*interessant*' (fully subjective): he had the special intimacy and high visibility in his work characteristic of a 'modern' poet. Schlegel soon concluded that he and Schiller were both right: Shakespeare could be 'objective' and '*interessant*' at the same time, transcending his literary creations yet immanent within them. Like a Deity in relation to the universe, a transcendental artist can be utterly detached and behind his work yet fully self-revelatory and himself the matter of his work.[63] Thus Schlegel saw beyond Schiller's formulation to the point where artistic self-consciousness would nurture ironic objectivity toward the self — to the point where the ego, all powerful, would rise above itself. Romantic irony becomes 'that objectivity in a romantic work of literary art which nevertheless shows forth plainly the literary creator in all his artistic power, glory, wisdom, and love toward his creation'. Goethe's *Wilhelm Meister*, 'where the poet is said to be smiling down upon his own masterpiece from the heights of his genius', significantly enough, is the prime example of this irony.[64]

The cornerstone of Dedalus's aesthetic theory in the *Portrait* (on the Flaubertian artist who 'like the God of the creation, remains within or behind or beyond or above his handiwork, invisible, refined out of existence, indifferent, paring his fingernails') would seem to be a recitation of Schlegel's central thought. Joyceans will be quick to point out, with some justification, that Joyce uses this statement on the artist to mock young Stephen and illustrate his doctrinaire aestheticism. The fact remains that many of Dedalus's notions on art, even in *Ulysses*, can be traced to Schlegel. What Stephen says about Hamlet as an occasion of authorial self-revelation connects closely with Schlegel's comments on Shakespeare's high visibility in that play. Indeed Joyce's own quizzical treatment of Dedalus everywhere subsumes the perspective of romantic irony.

Romantic irony is 'a clear consciousness of an eternal agility, of the infinitely abundant chaos'. It implies 'constant self-parody', 'permanent digression', exhaustive duplicity (like Dedalus's notion of art as a duplicity mirroring duplicity) and license. In it, everything is 'both playful and serious, both frank and obvious and yet deeply hidden. . . . [It] is the freest of all licenses, for through it one rises above one's own self; and it is also the most circumscribed, for it is absolutely necessary'.[65] Bound by his ironic perspective on creation, the artist is also most free. He sees the limitless potential of his material, and his own eternal agility, as spectator and master, in regard to it. Neither subject nor style can limit his prospect. He may seem distant, objective, when he is most subjective; and freedom means, above all, freedom of style — or freedom from style.

To the ironic perspective of such an artist, no one style is sufficient. Be it an old style from an abused tradition or a brand new invention, any mode is insufficient because it requires subjectivity: that the writer devote himself to its formula and lose himself in its manner. The ironic artist cannot be bound. He must write in a style that has no requirements, or limitations, or tradition, or anything else that might jeopardize his objectivity: his stance is above style. 'A change of subject requires a change of style', Berlioz said; and critics have noted how J. M. W. Turner's manners are almost as many as his pictures.[66] For complete objectivity in *Don Juan* and *Ulysses*, Byron and Joyce find that they must write without a style while assaying every mode that swims into ken during a given situation.[67] Poem and novel do not share a particular style because they cannot have a particular style. They share, only, a parallactic view, a propensity to be without specific style. Theirs is a neutral style, one that allows their creators to manifest chameleon-like agility of expression: an ability to keep changing style according to the material at hand, the mode best suited to this material, and the passing perspectives of both. They range over a fluid artistic domain, changing manner and perspective continuously, sharing only the radical device of the undependable narrator.

Don Juan's motto '*Difficile est propriè communia dicere*' would fit *Ulysses* as well. It is indeed difficult to speak of common things in an appropriate manner, especially when these are of as diverse a cast as those which form the content of the two works. Novel and poem are satirical, saturated medleys.[68] The Homeric poems combine style-components and manners from diverse ages and cultures, but *Don Juan* and *Ulysses* are more stylistically multiple than these. Numerous modes and elements from their literate heritage and linguistic environment are absorbed, in passing, from epic and lyric to bastard slang and coy obscenity, until each forms not so much a literary cosmos as a literary chaos.

Their absorption of numerous and diverse components of expression, combining as it does with their inconsistency of tone and medley of content, would seem to make *Don Juan* and *Ulysses* works that have fulfilled the final rules Pope laid down for the bathetic writer:

He is to consider himself a *Grotesque* painter, . . . He is to mingle
Bits of the most various, or discordant kinds, Landscape, History,
Portraits, Animals, and connect them with a great deal of
Flourishing, by *Heads* or *Tails*, as it shall please his Imagination, and
contribute to his principal End, which is to glare by strong
Opposition of Colours and surprise by Contrariety of Images.

His Design ought to be like a Labyrinth, out of which no body can get clear but himself. And since the great Art of all Poetry is to mix Truth with Fiction, in order to join the Credible with the Surprizing; our Author shall produce the *Credible*, by painting Nature in her *lowest simplicity*; and the *Surprizing*, by contradicting *Common Opinion*. In the very *Manners* he will affect the Marvellous; he will draw *Achilles* with the patience of *Job*; a Prince talking like a Jack-pudding; a Maid of honour selling *Bargains*; a footman speaking like a philosopher. . . . (*Peri Bathous*, ch. v)

The poet of bathos and the transcendental buffoon coincide; only intention distinguishes one from the other. The former creates his effects unconsciously; the latter gives the impression of such effects as proof of his control over the material. Byron and Joyce turn Pope's joke, with the audacity that informs their ironic manner, into a method for dealing with the problem of not writing in any one style.

XI

Henry James said that what one sees from the house of fiction depends on which window one is looking from. The distinguishing mark of *Don Juan* and *Ulysses* in this regard is that their windows keep changing, and that their style keeps adapting to the changes. Nothing, or almost nothing, remains constant — as much in poem as in novel:

> a love which at one moment seems the source of the greatest good becomes a painful trap; spirit and vitality which make their possessor in one incident attractive lead him in the next to brutal and destructive actions; pleasure turns pain and pain turns pleasure; what is now comic becomes in an instant tragic, and what was tragic with a sudden shift of perspective becomes meaningless.[69]

Perspectives shift continuously in *Don Juan* and *Ulysses*. Their creators apply the concept of parallax, of the shifting point of vision and the inconstant impression, to their subject, their tone, their mood, and most of all their style.

Poet and novelist do not merely combine a most various set of stylistic traditions. Nor do they merely parody them all. They assay and pass through them, showing how the modes and elements function well in ideal environments and poorly in not–so–appropriate environments; how within a limited situation any one can be proven valid, and how for any sustained, more multiple, more objective communication, none serves.

> Apologue, fable, poesy, and parable,
>   Are false, but may be render'd also true
> By those who sow them in a land that's arable,   (xv, 89)

Byron says. Within their limits, under particularly supportive circumstances, each of the styles can be shown true. But by themselves, in a vacuum or non-supportive context, or when used sustainedly for diverse situations, they prove sterile. In *Ulysses*, the struggle between characters who represent opposing ways of envisioning one and the same event turns into a struggle between these opposing modes themselves, as part of the way of telling the story.[70] It is, as Odysseus's vision of the wandering rocks proved, all a question of perspective. The same shifting vision that serves to cancel out the literary styles individually can be reversed to affirm them all. The parallactic view that can perceive them supportively in certain limited circumstances can also perceive their cumulative shortcomings.

If these modes did not function truly in particular situations, however short and limited their roles, they would not contribute the tension between styles that Joyce wants. They would stand, only, as parodic grotesqueries. Goethe's remark that Byron's literary manner in the poem was a form of action, of a wire cutting through a steel plate, suggests just this tendency which the poet shares with Joyce: that of passing through the various styles, proving and disproving, acknowledging, parodying, and ultimately rejecting them for their subjectivity. Throughout all this the modes remain tools for the ironic artist, not vehicles.

If, like Blake before them, Byron and Joyce beat upon the wall until Truth obeys their call, then what they seek, above all, is truth of style. They assay virtually every mode of writing known, finding each functional on occasion, parodying each for being deficient and subjective. They reject all the styles, cumulatively, as too 'stylistic' for their intentions. The action of assaying the modes, however, contributes greatly to the truthful manner of expression of the transcendentally ironic artist. An ironic subsumption of all the styles known to man makes for complete objectivity (truth) of style: for writing without style.

Pater said that all art aspires to the condition of music, where content and form coalesce. The authors of *Don Juan* and *Ulysses* seek the same coalescence of tenor and vehicle, mood and mode which, long before Pater gave it word, Wordsworth for one had tried to effect. Given the immensely diverse nature of their materials, this means they must keep adapting their expression to their content, however many and various these adaptations may be. They must assume, on a moment's notice, any style that best fits a current situation, casting it off for another, more apt mode when the situation changes.

Aptness of style, the ability to make one identity of matter and form implies, at least for Byron and Joyce, adeptness in style, the adeptness of a virtuoso. *Don Juan* changes its modes rapidly to become an expression of action that is as rapid and lively as life. We have the poet's own words on the appropriateness of his manner, as a kind of action itself, to his changing material:

> As to 'Don Juan' — confess — confess — you dog — and be candid — that it is the sublime of *that there* sort of writing — it may be bawdy — but is it not good English? — it may be profligate — but is it not *life*, is it not *the thing*? — Could any man have written it who had not lived in the world? — and tooled in a post-chaise? in a hackney coach? in a Gondola? against a wall? in a court carriage? in a vis-a-vis? — on a table — and under it?[71]

'Sirens', in *Ulysses*, presents a pinnacle in Paterian 'at-one-ment' of content and form, but almost any section in the book bears witness to this union of substance and style in an ongoing action of expression. The novel's style changes episode by episode, in harmony with the theme; the eighteen episodes give the impression of having been written by eighteen different people; technique tends more and more to become subject, and 'by the time we reach "Ithaca" the form of the episode is as much the substance as the actual interchanges between Bloom and Stephen'.[72] An energized adaptiveness effaces creator and subject alike: ductility becomes the vehicle for expression.

Don Juan and *Ulysses* have no style — as we commonly understand the term. Their authors write them without style and, as they pretend, without effort. They accomplish this by claiming for themselves an ever-extending, fluid domain where the patterns of composition can shift and change according to the terrain, where any mode can be assumed or allowed to fall into disuse. Style, as that manner shared by Byron and Joyce here, is the adept ability to adapt and fuse all styles; it is to have a singularly good internal ear which permits the artist to find a place of equilibrium behind and between them all.

In *Don Juan* and *Ulysses* the authors write their own particular versions of what occurs between the acts — of loving, of warring, of living, of dying, of acting, of writing. Adapting Ariosto's notion of his work as a lucid interval of mind in the rushing oppositions of universal madness,[73] they write of the lulls between tensions and, most of all, of how the lulls feed the tensions.[74] The metaphor is most appropriate with regard to style. Poet and novelist write for the tensions that are created between their rapid changes in style, and for the further versatility in mode these tensions will nurture. They achieve, thus, a form of drama.

Joyce is able to translate what he learned from Ibsen (and could not transfer to *Exiles*), into the tension of modes he achieves in *Ulysses*. Poirier says the drama of *Ulysses* is only incidentally that of Stephen, Bloom, and Molly; more poignantly it is the drama of Joyce himself making the book. The trial and dispensation of techniques 'in itself constitutes the drama of the novel'.[75] Barzun notes that Byron writes a dramatic verse that is unrivalled,[76] and, in truth, the poet's dramatic communication of the activity and tension of on-going life in *Don Juan* springs, largely, from his rapid changes in mode.

XII

Through all the varied subjects, attitudes, concerns, manners and intentions of *Don Juan* and *Ulysses* the focus remains on the writer, his pre-eminent personality, his omniscient power. The writer can reduce everything to words and sounds. The moral artist has the ability to make words, impotent playthings, prepotent. The author exerts wilful control over his content and his reader. Artistic self-consciousness is creation in an uncertain world. The artist's mind, its own place, makes quadrivia of trivia. Its self-conscious perception sees through its own ego's creations. Its parallactic vision, changing and circling, encompasses all. For it, styles exist as tools, used or destroyed through its motions of transcendental buffoonery.

The normal condition of things is paradoxic disorder. The earnest artist's abnormal power of personality, however, can preserve the conflicting parts in balance, to provide unity in the form of the ironic overview. As early nineteenth-century Romanticism had always said he must, the artist plays God. The question for *Don Juan* and *Ulysses*, specifically, is whether this play-acting ever becomes more true than anything else.

Joyce took quite seriously the romantic view of the artist as a word-combining surrogate for God. Stephen Dedalus would be the priest of the Imagination, an acolyte and disciple of his all-powerful creator. That Joyce perceived himself as a godlike figure behind his work seems clear not only from his manipulations in *Ulysses* but from his intention in *Finnegans Wake*: he was the writer of the Universal Book, the Paraclete summarizing scripture and uttering the new truth in tongues of flame.

Byron, very differently, expressed contempt for the professional writer, 'the pen peeping from behind the ear, and the thumbs a little inky', and for bards who 'burn what they call their "midnight taper"' all for a piece of wretched paper (I, 28). Nevertheless he saw himself, at least in regard to *Don Juan*, as its omniscient creator who wielded control as much over its contents and expression as over its reader. A short, sharp comment concerning Gulbayez ('Her first thought was to cut off Juan's head;/Her second, to cut only his – acquaintance' V, 139) plays maliciously with the reader's mind much as Stephen in *Ulysses* (embodying his creator's 'cruel playful mind like a great soft tiger cat's' as Yeats once described it) plays with his audience in the Library and sends the librarian off to tend to the Church's needs (the clergyman Dineen) without telling him, much as the man wants to know, *which* of Shakespeare's brothers was the bard's cuckolder.

In his poem, Byron comes to perceive the sustaining power of literature – and its creators:

> 'Tis strange, the shortest letter which man uses
> Instead of speech, may form a lasting link
> Of ages; to what straits old Time reduces
> Frail man, when paper – even a rag like this,
> Survives himself, his tomb, and all that's his.   (III, 88)

His perception is remarkably similar to Dedalus's conclusion that literature is 'the eternal affirmation of the spirit of man'. *Ulysses*'s greatness is its 'community of speech' – achieved despite its patterns of loss and frustration, and despite the conventions that have strained and screened human speech, style and language. For Byron and Joyce, both exiled writers, 'the most deeply known [and perhaps only] human community is language itself'.[77]

'*Don Juan* is among other things a triumph of memory, like Joyce's

Ulysses', Donald Low notes, while observing how Byron's poem expresses the poet's perception of Regency England and a historically identifiable experience of expatriate living. [78] The poem's later cantos frequently circle out from political and social facts the poet recalls, in much the same way as *Ulysses* starts out from Joyce's memory to become a vicarious experience of life in Dublin in the early nineteen-hundreds. Poem and novel alike depend on their authors' memories for their bare contents. They owe their beginnings not to immediate experience but to memory, memory of a very specific kind. Their cumulative effect is to substantiate this memory. Poet and novelist recreate the worlds of Regency England and turn-of-the-century Dublin from, to a large degree, the substance of their recollections. These worlds exist as vicarious, yet largely true, experiences; yet they are creations formed primarily of whatever the mind and its exercise of language could conjure forth from two expatriates' memories. Novel and poem, as such, become feats of human memory and the individual artist's word.

Lysander used to say that 'children play with knucklebones, men with words'. [79] For the modern artist, the play has become deadly earnest, the only valid occupation in his world. The Romantics said that since man had invented his civilization, the artist had a professional concern in shaping and directing its forms. The artist wrote to extend the consciousness of his audience, his commitment extended beyond writing to the world as a whole. The 'one talent which is death to hide', hidden, meant death to a way of life and true civilization also. For all his 'giggle' and devotion to a life of action, Byron felt he wrote with moral responsibility in *Don Juan*. Joyce as we know carried the Romantic concept of artistic dedication to its heights: his commitment was to forging the apperception of his race, to the truths of civilization. Without any Miltonic qualms of his vainglorious ambition, Joyce set out to rival the Almighty with the power of his word: *Ulysses* would form the consciousness of the age; *Finnegans Wake* would be a lisping conscience of the race.

The committed artist's 'true words are *things*', Byron said, from the start, in his 'Childhood Recollections'. The artist sustains whatever his moral sensibility tells him is valuable in the world. Sustaining his world, he may also create it. Martha's letter in *Ulysses* lamenting 'I do not know that other world' points to the letter-link between word and world, between language and life. Ellmann tells us how words become *Ulysses*'s (and Joyce's) world:

Words are expatriated and repatriated like Dubliners. Joyce exploited all these nuances, and the pun becomes the key to his work – a key both aesthetic and political, both linguistic and moral.

Each pun in effect wreaks havoc with space and time, and with every form of settled complacency. Words are fractioned by ineptitude, yet the force that fractions also draws the world together. Near-misses of sound, sense, and finally, of form constitute the fabric of creation. Out of malapropisms, spoonerisms, bloomisms, the world is born.[80]

Life is a linguistic experience. The creators of *Don Juan* and *Ulysses* are writing of life; even more, they are creating it. From mind, memory, words, comes existence, not vice versa. Byron and Joyce write primarily, as we have noted, about the writing process. Their writing exhausts life. But writing is also the moral endeavor of the modern world, the only epic process left: it consummates life. Dedalus tells how 'in the virgin womb of the imagination, the word was made flesh'. Joyce protests of how difficult everything is 'when your life and your book make one'. Words are made flesh, consubstantial with the author.[81] They make the artist as he makes them; they form, flesh, his existence.

'Since 1922', Joyce said, 'my book has been a greater reality for me than reality'. Byron, in 1821, expressed a like sentiment for external reality: 'As I grow older', he said to Shelley, 'the indifference – *not* to life, for we love it by instinct – but to the stimuli of life, increases'. [82] The focus of existence becomes trained upon the writer, his words and what they form. The book receives the most deference, to become greater reality than reality. The world is but word. Joyce wished to make of a book an entire self-supporting world, a reality which would be a paradigm of some inaccessible truth. 'Dublin, 1904, was his *Vision*', and one reads *Ulysses* on the cosmic scale or not at all.[83] The artist's truest things are his words: his book is his world, and the cosmos so formed plays to cosmic truth. Or, as Byron must conclude for us,

> What a sublime discovery 'twas to make the
> Universe universal Egotism!   (XI, 2)

6 Conclusions: Paradox and *Nostos*

T. S. Eliot wrote the nineteenth century's epitaph and credited Joyce with having killed the period. He displaced the Romantics specifically, but behind them Milton and Spenser also, to a place outside the mainstream of English poetry. They were unlicensed heretics who had deviated from the proper tradition and, thanks to his propaganda as aided and abetted by Pound's discovery of newness, the years *entre deux guerres* saw Donne as a Metaphysical Ariel cast out these recently unmasked Calibans.[1] In 1818 Byron, sounding like an unlikely Cassandra, predicted somberly of the poets who would follow him and his peers: 'The next generation,' he said, 'will tumble and break their necks off our Pegasus, who runs away with us; but we keep the *saddle*, because we broke the rascal and can ride'.[2] In retrospect, this statement by the poet of *Don Juan* rings startlingly true. It is an astute anticipation of the problems in keeping saddle that the heirs to the limitless Romantic vision would face; it is also a most fit response to the modernists' attempt to justify their poetry through a self-serving rewriting of literary history.

Eliot's summary dismissal of the ethos of an entire literary age, and Byron's shrewd pronouncement of the prospects of post-Romantic poetry (whether that of the *fin-de-siècle* romantic decadents who could not ride poesy's mount, or that of the anti-Romantic makers of newness who thought they could) bring to mind the polarized polemics of nineteenth and twentieth-century literary criticism. Since Arnold, Eliot, and Pound issued charges against their predecessors, there have been discussions on how these two centuries exhibit diametrically opposed positions on poetic influence, poetic diction, poetic distinction, and poetic tradition. These issues were never irreconcilable; they should never have been used to assert positions which prevailed at the expense of each other, nor yet to denote two eternally contraposed, antithetical periods in literature.

Thomas Hardy's puny thrush flung out its soul in song upon the corpse of the nineteenth century in evensong 'Of joy illimited'; its small and impossible hope projected toward the oncoming century, but it also harkened back to a century of great hope. It is appropriate that Hardy, the writer who continues to make things difficult for compartmental criticism by refusing to remain a nature-loving and somewhat romantic Victorian, should provide the statement that dissolves all contra-Romantic critical biases: 'Romanticism will exist in human nature as long as human nature itself exists. The point is (in imaginative literature) to adopt that form of romanticism which is the mood of the age'.[3]

There is a basic, essential continuity to the literature of the two periods. We cannot accept the notion that Joyce and his contemporaries annihilated the nineteenth century any more than we can deny that they were dependent upon the very things they set themselves up to oppose and bludgeon. Wilde, Woolf, and Auden exempted Byron from the general judgment on his century. An eminent body of critics has maintained the vital connection between the two centuries and distinguished the Romantic roots of much Modernism.[4] It is customary nonetheless to regard Byron and Joyce as typically antipathetical. Before we can bring these two writers home to their rightful place in one epoch, to observe those final distinguishing points about *Don Juan* and *Ulysses* that serve paradoxically to place them conclusively in one literary era and yet show them as distinct among other products of their respective centuries, we need review two related subjects: the extent to which Joyce's concerns reveal nineteenth-century, Romantic impulses; and the extent to which Byron's efforts anticipate modernist concerns.

I

Like Flaubert's self-admitted, paradoxical, and ultimately incestuous liaison with Madame Bovary, and following Wilde's rickety refrain on each man's urge to kill the thing he loves, Joyce was in love with the century he so devastatingly dissected. We are never more aware of his condemnation of it than when we trace this to the concepts on which his mind was nurtured. We are never more aware of his unbreakable link with the Romantic age than when we consider his antithetical starting-point and continuous innovations.

Joyce combined a fully Romantic view of the artist with what he called 'a grocer's assistant's mind'. 'His beliefs and attitudes,' Kermode says, 'froze in his early twenties'.[5] He never ceased believing that he was the priest of the imagination — a thoroughly Romantic percept which came to him by way of the dicta of Symbolism and Aestheticism. In his sense of nation, his love-hate for Ireland, his aspiration for personal distinction, his notion of *Heldenleben* and of the treachery of friends, his concept of love in the Tristan-Isolde sense, his sense of the potential connection between love and politics (in the kind of brotherhood manifest by Bloom), he further revealed his Romantic roots and manifest his work as a continuation of the titanism of the nineteenth-century artistic personality. Indeed, far from denying the connection, Joyce put himself directly, *naively*, in the line of the powerful personalities of the age before his own'.[6]

The Joycean epiphany has specific attributes that go beyond Aquinas to suggest a distinctly Wordsworthian conceptual basis. When the *Portrait* and *Ulysses* record moments of eucharistic significance in quotidian life, and invoke theological terms for a naturalistic aesthetic, they demonstrate what Abrams sees as *the* Romantic characteristic: that of reinterpreting and assimilating traditional religious concepts and schemes into a world-view founded on secular premises.[7] Moreover, when Joyce's late work displays a thoroughly modernistic evocation of Freud's science, it behooves us to recall not just the Viennese Tweedledee's (Joyce's epithet) debt to literature, but that psychoanalysis is one of the culminations of Romantic literature and its passionate devotion to research into the self.[8] The too-conscious, unconscious night-world of Joyce's Most Freudian *Finnegans Wake* becomes, as such, at once literal and symbolic representation of the Romantic belief '*la vida es sueño*'.

Like so many modernists, Joyce began writing under the sway of decadent romanticism, freed himself by an anti-romantic reaction, and later reconciled himself with his predecessors.[9] 'Chamber Music' was born of the turn-of-the-century romanticism and pale-grey colors of the Celtic twilighters. In Dedalus's postures and prose, Joyce expressed his adverse opinion of this form of romanticism. With his perception of artistic role and purpose, Joyce declared himself on the side of the century whose guiding percepts and aspirations he knew so well.[10]

If he is credited with having killed the Romantic age it is precisely because so considerable a part of his fabric is formed of the things he is supposed to have destroyed: not just that era's values but even the postures of its most legendary poet. Dedalus's '*Non serviam*' echoes Manfred's 'I will not serve';[11] Cain and Abel portrayed as light-bringing Shem and conforming Shaun is a debt owed to Byron (and acknowledged, in 1931, when Joyce proposed to George Antheil that he write an opera for John Sullivan based on *Cain*). The sense of persecution by the Dubliners recalls the poet's belief that he had been hounded from England by rancorous Pharisees: 'If the Christ they profess to worship reappeared, they would again crucify him,' the poet said to Trelawny, much as young James would draw parallels between himself, Parnell, and Christ. The novelist, in his alienation, echoed Byron's defiant indifference to 'public attunement'.[12] Denied the opportunity by birth and birthplace to be a 'lord among men', he resolved to be so through his art: he scorned the rabblement as much as Byron did the '*bestia trionfante*'; and despite his claims of socialist art, he wrote for no less of an élite, urbane coterie of readers than did the poet of *Don Juan*. Like Byron, Joyce vowed to be famous in his time. Like Byron also, he chose exile that he might better be, with Dante and Petrarch, a citizen of the world.[13]

Mont Blanc countered any abysses seen in the youthful, exuberant Romantic age, for 'in their ignorance and folly, the Romantics missed a great opportunity to be as miserable as we are'.[14] Certain poems of Byron nonetheless strike chords which we usually identify with *fin-de-siècle* despair and contemporary *Angst*. His brooding noble malefactors anticipate the haunted figures of modern literature: Lord Jim, Joseph K., Cathcart, even Dedalus and his *Agenbite of Inwit*. If guilt-ridden, overwhelming anxiety is the hallmark of the modern ego, then the Corsair's obsession foreshadows the secret encumbrances under which Kurtz, Ahab, and even (on the absurd level) Humphrey Chimpden Earwicker labor. The Byronic precedent behind the Dandyism-Aestheticism of Gautier, Baudelaire and Wilde is indisputable. More pertinent is the poet's explanation of the object of his, Brummel's, and others' dandyism: 'The great object of life is Sensation – to feel that we exist – even thought in pain – it is this "craving void" which drives us to Gaming – to Battle – to Travel – to intemperate but keenly felt pursuits . . .'.[15] Byron's words on the 'hunger of the imagination' could be a manifesto of Huysmans and Wilde; they also point to some characteristically 'modern' voids like Jim Bricknell's insatiable hunger in *Aaron's Rod*, or the old man's sense of consummate emptiness in 'Gerontion'.

Again, take the poem 'Darkness'. To the jaded modern eye dulled by the sight of too many wastelands, it might seem that the poet is largely concerned with atmospherics and lighting (or lack of lighting) effects. Yet in its (albeit temporary) mood of horror, in its notion of a world without a moral comment, reward, or punishment, where no human feels any concern for the race's imminent extinction, 'Darkness' is a small but remarkable anticipation of the malaise and sense of indifference that followed the Great War. Indeed, the poem's slowly extinguishing world, rolling in pitch, recalls specifically the universe of *Finnegans Wake*: dark, nightmarish, perpetually creating and extinguishing itself without regard to its individual components.

We adopt the form of romanticism that is the mood of the age, as Hardy said, and *Don Juan*'s pervasive skepticism, which itself arose partly from the disillusionment of the displaced generation that followed Waterloo, is found to mirror the bitter mood of the age that had just discovered (as Henry James said) what the treacherous years really had in store for them all along.[16] In the carefully orchestrated Norman Abbey dénouement of the last cantos, with the Bores and Bored squared off in their corners, and three women (a virgin, a seductress, a third married but treated 'less like young wife than an aged sister') designing upon unsuspecting Juan, we can detect a distinct foreshadowing of Wilde's best drama, where form dissolves content into pure farce. The poem's random method and private-public conversational tone presage the poignant-ironic, grandiose-slangy tone and technique we now locate in the Laforgue-Eliot type of poetry.[17] Auden felt the poem's satire looked forward to that of Lawrence, not backward to the Augustans.[18] Certainly, if *Don Juan* is 'a precursor of a new kind of novel writing',[19] then it is to be linked not so much by content to the novels of social context (of Austen, Dickens, and Thackeray) as by form and technique (its openended-ness and integrity) to more recent experimental novels.

'Before me now lies Byron and behind,' Lawrence Durrell says of the on-going debt of his century to the poet of *Don Juan*. The poet's message, 'Somewhere in *Juan*', has not reached us yet, he adds. Nor, we might add, has modernist criticism come to terms with the poem's epic precedence. Pre-empting its historical place and period, *Don Juan* is, at once, an inheritance of and a vanguard to the modern period, and to future literary generations.

One could say that it is to nineteenth-century Europe what *Tom Jones* is to eighteenth-century England: a mirror like a comedy, a voyage like an epic, and a storehouse of facts like a history.[20] One could even continue the formula and add that *Ulysses*, written to fossilize Dublin's social history for posterity, treating its content at once epically and with mimicry, serves the twentieth century the same way. This would not imply that the three counter-epics are identical, but that they function congruently with regard to the centuries which fostered them: as keys to the eras' primary concerns, and ironical commentaries on the ages' sentiments. Yet even here the suggestive paralleling breaks down to highlight the problems inherent in placing influences, distinguishing precedents, and marking periods.

Byron did not see his major poem as exemplary of nineteenth century writing – or as a brilliant anticipation of a new literature: he declared himself in the line of Dryden and Pope, and said he was employing an Augustan tradition of satire to cure contemporary sentiments (to which his own *Childe Harold* had contributed) and cant. Joyce may have seen himself as the innovative genius of the twentieth century, but he was also emphatic about his living relation to the Continental past and careful to denounce both his literary competitors and contemporary tastes. His work connects back not only with Romantic literature but with eighteenth-century experiments in novel-writing, and in his structural techniques he does not break so much as resume a tradition.[21]

Between Byron and Pope stood Voltaire, Rousseau, Kant, German transcendentalism, the French Revolution, and Napoleon; between Joyce and the two centuries to which we have linked him were all these and, in addition, Bergson, Freud, and first, ever, world war. As Leavis says, the eighteenth-century element in Byron is essential to his success, yet it also has the effect of bringing out how completely the Augustan order had disintegrated.[22] For Joyce also, the eighteenth and nineteenth-century elements were essential to his efforts; yet his harkening back to the past had the added effect of reiterating his age's distinctions from it: because of its time *Ulysses* developed Romantic themes to a point of mania, showed nineteenth-century concerns exacerbated past hope, and made of eighteenth-century experiments in novel-writing a pattern of excessive innovation that was incomprehensible to a generation of readers.

Precisely in their acknowledged reversion to past principles of literature do the two writers manifest most clearly their individual contemporaneity. By looking back to earlier centuries' concerns in writing, they distinguish themselves from contemporary habits. In the way in which they assume these past patterns, they disclose the passage of time and reveal their respective ages' particularities. Because of their links to earlier centuries *Don Juan* and *Ulysses* function best as, at once, the exemplars of and the ciphers to their own eras. Byron the Romantic declares sides with eighteenth-century satirists and, beyond Byronism, proves to own remarkably 'modern' characteristics. Joyce the arch-modernist exhibits in his thought and writing the most telling Romantic elements and eighteenth-century precedents; refusing to accept his age alone, as it is, he typifies it. Poet and novelist subsume three centuries between them. Mirroring contemporary issues and facing ever forward, Janus-like, they point back (all the way to Homer) to earlier literary examples and traditions. Attempts to classify Byron or Joyce within a specific literary period, and link them to a definite time, are self-defeating — undermined by the very writers who best illustrate these periods. The distance and paradoxical reflection that results from their unusual situations between centuries remind us of what we might forget: the continuum that is literature.

II

If *Don Juan* and *Ulysses* are precedented to some degree (as Chapters 1 to 5 imply) and if both their creators connect with the nineteenth-century vision, we should be able either to place them within a particular genre or else to distinguish those attributes that make each of the two works singular in their times. Poem and novel provide a paradoxical response to the problem: they exhibit Romantic concerns and modernist characteristics to remain individually unique and more like one another than most of the works with which each has been compared; they succeed in being, at once, related to earlier works and genres and yet, quintessentially, *sui generis*.

Cultural periods are united by their questions, not their answers. Dominant problems addressed, not the individual philosophies designed to solve these, unite men in a given age.[23] *Don Juan* and *Ulysses* certainly ask the same questions — of the cultural inheritance, of contemporary life, of the individual. In the texture of their responses to these questions, however, they distinguish themselves from other products of the post-Enlightenment world. In the function which Byron and Joyce perceive to be theirs, they show their exclusive affinity across a hundred odd years. Poem and novel respond with aggressive novelty to the problem of representing their era's consciousness while yet criticizing past traditions and current mores. Their creators perceive themselves as the consciences of their age: the estimators of the race's inheritance, the summarizers of its accomplishments, the judges of its taste. As a result, *Don Juan* and *Ulysses* become two related landmarks, each singular in its historical time, of the post-Kantian consciousness and its literature.

In their influential positions as the conclusive consciences for their times, Byron and Joyce employ paradox and produce effects of composite cumulativeness. The qualities of being paradoxical and cumulative are hardly novel in literature: indeed they are the primary characteristics of romantic art in any age. Nevertheless, the two qualities also serve to focus the singularity of *Don Juan* and of *Ulysses* within their centuries, and to highlight their ultimate relation to one another. Comprehensiveness is *Don Juan*'s most obvious quality. Literary motifs from every age of European literature throng together with half-remembered historical facts and half-admitted autobiography, with scraps of legends and shreds of myths. To its 'wilderness of the most rare conceits' (XVI, 3) and multiplicity of styles is added an orchestral range of tones, from piccolo to double bass. Like the 'rich confusion' of the Sultan's palace (V, 93), the poem defiantly renders the Romantic view of a complex world too large in all directions.[24] Byron called his poem a 'Capo d'Opera', '"full of pastime and prodigiality"'; when sending a stanza to Murray he referred to it as 'a brick of my Babel'.[25]

Ulysses, also, shows as its primary characteristic a need to be as prodigiously multiple as its world and the Western heritage. It accumulates all the great motifs of cultural history to provide a mirror not just of Dublin or Ireland, but of Europe and its millennia.[26] Its author plays at being prophet, bard, confessor, sociologist, and chronicler simultaneously. The book describes itself as a 'chaffering allincluding most farraginous chronicle'. Even the confused array of its early critical readings testify to its multifariousness: Edel thought it was an attempt to arrest time by immortalizing one day, while Wyndham Lewis found it to be an acceptance of flux; to Edmund Wilson it depicted the confrontation of mind, body, and spirit, while to Tindall it portrayed unifying familial and historical cycles; some found it an all-inclusive record of man's universal failure, yet others found it a celebration, like the Book of Kells, of life and art; Lawrence complained that reading Joyce's conglomerate was like being put into a large bag of cotton and shaken very slowly; and Bennett said he finished the book with the sensation of a general who has just put down an insurrection.[27]

Petronius's *Satyricon*, Rabelais's human comedy, Fénelon's *Télémaque*, and Flaubert's last testament (as earlier chapters note) exhibit analogous, if not as extreme, impulses to mix disparate styles and include cumulatively. Romantic art as a whole distinguishes itself by its tendency to mix and add, for as a comprehensive reflection of its milieu, it is by nature and by destiny a *Mischgedicht*.[28] *Don Juan* and *Ulysses* are nevertheless distinct from their antecedents and among their contemporaries. They assume the romantic license of infinite variety in art and carry it to its limits; their encyclic expression thus surpasses all literary precedents to fulfill their declared ironic roles as the encyclopedias of Western tradition:[29] they are true, circular, and terminal.

Poet and novelist write not merely cumulatively but culminatively. They distinguish their inclusiveness in *Don Juan* and *Ulysses* by making it form a complex exclusivity, an exclusivity which subsumes the perspective that they are the last chroniclers of Western tradition.

> The thought of what America would be like
> If the classics had a wide circulation
> Troubles my sleep. ('Cantico del Sole')

Byron and Joyce share Pound's nightmare. They see themselves as writing just before the popularizing of art, an imminent event that might well be synonymous with the annihilation of art.[30] As hybrid mixtures, as Babels, as works that indiscriminately yoke high and low styles, pay no regard to fitness of subject, gladly include the meanest contents, and are ignorant of the principles of purity and propriety, operating under the general principle that 'more is better', *Don Juan* and *Ulysses* are frightful harbingers of this abysmal event. But purpose, place, and high effectiveness keep poem and novel as threats, images of the nightmare of conspicuous consumption in art – preserving them therein from becoming the real thing – mass chaos.

Poet and novelist beat literature to death in one last rescue attempt. They are, as they perceive themselves, learned men in an unlearning age writing the final books that will at once summarize and dispel the literary inheritance. The poem is, as Boyd says, 'heir of all the ages'. *Ulysses*, written as his final fiat, at a time when Joyce did not know he would go on to write *Finnegans Wake*, is, first and last, an epic epitaph of all that has preceded it. No less than any of the men of their respective generations, Byron and Joyce see themselves as elected spokesmen for Western tradition at a time of profound cultural crisis. But more than any of their contemporaries, they see their acts as terminal points. Having perceived the imminent dispersion of art among the masses, worse, having anticipated the spurning of the literate tradition as irrelevant to contemporary life by the same, and having themselves contributed to the ruination of literature and its ideals, Byron and Joyce shore up the ruins one last time. *Don Juan* and *Ulysses* are summations of Western tradition, critical, withering, destructive summations – and threnodies.

'It is a peculiarity of the imagination,' Foçillon said, 'that it is always at the end of an era'. If these two writers' sense of termination seems to form part of the recurring, endemic inclination Kermode discusses in *The Sense of An Ending* (1967), in reality their situation is at once more specific and more complex. Their 'sense of an ending' stems not so much from an apocalyptic vision of the world's end as from a loss of faith in the world's word. Poet and novelist perceive 'end' most acutely in terms of literature. Not only do they not see (as Yeats did) a new age coming upon the heels of the decadent one in which they live, they see no new literary effort or movement following them.

Don Juan and *Ulysses* are monuments of culminative literary record like the Homeric poems. Like Homer their authors blend conflicting traditions, materials, and formulae from the diverse past. Like Homer, living at 'the end of a long succession of invasions, migrations and destructions, in which customs and language had suffered many changes',[31] they sacrifice purity for multiplicity so as to represent and preserve a various inheritance. Much as Homer was the Greek people, with his poetry representing the range of early Hellenic consciousness, *Don Juan* and *Ulysses* stand for the post-Enlightenment consciousness as it has evolved and mutated: they preserve the Dubliners and the Europeans, like exotic animals amid their habitat in a zoo, like an insect species in a showcase or snakes in a reptile museum pinned according to mutations, in an aspic of their own mores and follies.

There is one crucial difference. *Don Juan* and *Ulysses* do not merely represent their time's consciousness as the Homeric poems did – they function as the recorded consciences of their age. The poem and the novel evaluate their own contents, weighing as they summarize, and telescoping as they perceive.

Homer looked to the future and wrote, ultimately, in example: to preserve certain ideals of behavior for a new, more vital if less literary age, and (as it turned out) to spawn a literary tradition that would continue for centuries after him. Byron and Joyce write, ultimately, in conscience. They write retrospectively, remorsefully, for literature may have no future. They write compositely, exegetically, to test the cultural past and then save whatever might remain (and should survive) beyond the testing. They look back critically and, having first destroyed, they shore up the ruins retroactively. Among all the writers who composed cumulatively and sensed an ending, Byron and Joyce are unique in this their revisional interpretation of the European tradition.

Joyce once referred to *Finnegans Wake* as his 'Irish dung-heap'. *Don Juan* and *Ulysses* can likewise be seen as the litter-heaps of a divine human comedy. They are layered archeological sites composed of successive series of cultural effort like Schliemann's Troy. They are compost heaps, weighed down by the rubbish of the human past, and by the fragments of its achievements.

Earlier chapters of mine have noted this layering. Not one myth but portions from disparate myths are layered together until they produce, because most jumbled, the best pattern for the modern story. Not the first Odysseus but a composite of all his mutations in literature since Homer prompts the Odyssean figure of the contemporary world and contributes to the current definition of personal distinction. Not the epic hero but every literary hero since the epic prototype began its slow descent to democratic meanness and anonymity, every variant of mock-hero and anti-hero, is summoned forth. Together, these are addressed by current questions until they yield – Juan and Bloom. Not one writing style or genre but a thoroughly critical, parallactic view of them all provides the base and medium for the earnest contemporary writer.

This layering by Byron and Joyce, a kind of secularized exegesis, telescopes to focus on contemporary issues while yet demonstrating the cumulative ineffectuality of past formulae. Like the experiment (conducted during Joyce's lifetime) which attempted to discover what the typical woman looked like by photographing thousands of women and then combining all the negatives into a single print called 'Eve',[32] *Don Juan* and *Ulysses* superimpose their cultural-cum-literary inheritance by category. In the attempt to glean those things that might withstand contemporary or future chaos, they begin with the oldest archetype and layer this with successively more recent mutations and variations up to the present. But they do not want the types of the past to explain the present; nor yet do they merely want a multiple type composed of everything that has preceded them. They want to see what will remain of these types, already battered by the highly critical juxtapositions with later models, once they are confronted by current problems.

Because of their place within the post-Enlightenment world, poet and novelist must think in terms of echoes not images, failed types not ideal examples. Because of their function as the consciences of the dispossessed world that followed Kant, *Don Juan* and *Ulysses* must run composite tests and validate their own contents, destroying much of the past as they propose to summarize it, and remaining poised always to fasten on or seize as exemplary whatever strains through their layered debris.

This is indeed an unusual, and unusually violent, form of cumulative summary. Not only do Byron and Joyce fail with their peers to assimilate what they borrow from the past, they force the unassimilated substances from the past into close proximity, yoking type and anti-type by violence together, and berating them with complex modern questions and situations. Whatever withstands this battering, whatever survives this hostile superimposition, whatever strains through, even if these are largely reverse prototypes, finitypes, pointers that serve by indirection, form the substance of *Don Juan* and *Ulysses*. The present validates the past retroactively because of and despite having destroyed it. To be summarily cumulative, cumulatively critical, and affirmative, is a highly exclusive art.

Byronic-Joycean exegesis sets its creators quite apart from other typologists and other practitioners of cumulative art. It is their unique means for summarizing the past, testing the past, criticizing the past to the point of destruction, and shoring up the resulting (conscientiously abetted) ruins of the past. Summarizing and dispelling their literary inheritance, being yet innovative in relation to it, *Don Juan* and *Ulysses* supersede the books that have preceded them in much the same way as Mahommed's Koran was supposed to supersede the Old and New Testaments.[33]

III

To have such a massively pre-emptive aim necessitates an impression of over-arching paradox, of ambiguity, antinomy, and antithesis. Poet and novelist welcome any and all opportunities to be paradoxical in *Don Juan* and *Ulysses*, to subsume opposites at every turn, to contradict their intents, to make conflicting impressions and disconcert their readers. But for the critic, to reverse the order of Montaigne's '*s'accuser serait s'excuser en ce sujet-là; et se condamner, ce serait s'absoudre*',[34] the subject of paradox is fraught with danger. Speaking of paradox one must also speak in paradoxes and, thus, deftly dig oneself into the quicksands of ambiguity and self-contradiction.

The subject is nonetheless inescapable because Byron and Joyce practice a thoroughly paradoxical art. Paradox is their medium in countless ways, their reason for writing, their excuse in writing, and their ultimate explanation for problems encountered when writing. Every subject in *Don Juan* and *Ulysses*, and every issue raised by their reading, prevails with its counter in mind and turns ultimately on its opposite. Moreover, as with the comprehensiveness of the poem and the novel, their deployment of paradox, while hardly unusual in itself, serves at once to highlight their singularity among other traffickers in paradox and to show them as exemplary of their time.

Joyce was fascinated by the symbolism of The Greek's *moly*, that 'white flower with a black root', and he found Homer's Scylla and Charybdis episode the most splendid of parables. His own preoccupation with antithetical complexes pervades *Ulysses*. As Stephen plies carefully between the rock of dogma and the whirlpool of mysticism, between Aristotle and Plato, Stratford and London, Dublin and Paris, so also does the book wend its way between polarities of every sort, on every level (from Church and State through nature and civilization to cyclic and linear time), to build itself according to a recurring pattern of thesis, antithesis, and synthesis.[35]

The ironic contrast of what occurs between Bloom and Gerty ('still,' as Bloom says at the end of the episode, 'it was a kind of language between us') and what they do, is but one example of the paradoxical tenor of Joyce's work. He shared with Proust the tragic intelligence that all beauty exists in necessary tension with squalor, the perspective that life is a complex contrast, communicable only in paradoxes. The tension between Stephen and Bloom, and Shem and Shaun, are symbols born of the paradoxes in the novelist's life and thought.[36] When he made the funeral of the human race the subject of his last book, he frightened some of his critics with his nihilism. Yet, a legacy of the paradoxes that formed his life and informed his vision of life, *Finnegans Wake* as a book of the Abyss is probably the only book written to ensure that the reader experiences heady, joyous euphoria while falling down and down.

Byron's tendency to communicate in paradoxes also finds its echo in the two-sided nature of the poet's life and its source in his ironic perspective of life. He would prove that a poet could also be a soldier; heroism and farce had each their place in his life as in his poetry; and the flippant yet genuine 'Isles of Greece' remains the best illustration of the poet's ambiguity. Boyd says the history of Byron's intellectual skepticism is the drama of the opposing tendencies in his nature, the drama of one who longs to believe yet shrinks from believing because he sees himself at the center of opposing systems.[37]

For the poet, life was a complex of opposites eternally in tension like the 'best of dark and bright' that meet in the aspect of her who walks in beauty. *Cain* invokes 'the great double mysteries! the *two Principles*' of Light and Dark that rule the world together, and Wilson Knight has demonstrated how these 'two Eternities' represent opposing segments of the poet's vision. It was the poet's talent to live and perceive these antinomies, to preserve the dualities in balance. Hence the pervasive paradoxicality of Byron's later poetry: Cain could be Abel's brother, Lucifer could feel equal to his victor and, in one random example from *Don Juan*, love could be exposed in all its silliness without denying its sweetness.

Since the time when Homer cloaked Athene in various disguises and represented the goddess of Wisdom as implicitly fickle, writers have dealt in paradox and ambiguity. Plato's dialéctics and his Socratic irony, Lucian's dialogues and his use of eulogy for satiric ends, Cicero's *Paradoxa*, Ovid's *Metamorphoses*, Erasmus's *Praise of Folly*, Rabelais's and Montaigne's efforts are few among scores of works whose writers have sought the effects of enigmatic, paradoxical communication. In their employment of paradox in *Don Juan* and *Ulysses*, Byron and Joyce nevertheless distinguish themselves from their antecedents. Their paradoxical art springs from a fundamental division within their minds: it is a product of their divided perspective of man and his world. They differ noticeably in intention from the earlier writers of ambiguity, and in their extensive use of contradictory formations they produce unusual, distinct effects.

Empson's seventh type of poetic paradox, 'the idea of opposite' whose 'total effect is to show a fundamental division in the writer's mind' provides the first handle on distinguishing the kind of ambiguity these writers seek through paradox:

> A contradiction of this kind may be meaningless but can never be blank; it has at least stated the subject which is under discussion, and has given a sort of intensity to it such as one finds in a gridiron pattern in architecture because it gives prominence neither to the horizontals nor to the verticals, and in a check pattern because neither colour is the ground on which the other was placed; it is at

once an indecision and a structure, like the symbol of the Cross.[38]

Poet and novelist perceive the world as an interlocking complex of irreconcilable opposites. Translated into *Don Juan* and *Ulysses*, this perspective takes the form of refusing to choose between two available choices in any given situation and, instead, incorporating both to paradoxical effect.[39] By maintaining a tension between antipoles of theme and situation, by displaying an inconsistency of tone, by giving prominence to no one style, by creating conflicting impressions and being thoroughly undependable, poem and novel give substance to 'the idea of opposite' everywhere.

As in the metaphors of gridiron and checkered-cloth, their kind of ambiguity provides an intensity of texture, a range for inclusion and, most of all, freedom from commitment. Where other writers might list toward one of any two antinomious projections they have set up, or else try to tread a thin line between them, Joyce's and Byron's inclinations are to include both from start to finish and to carry the contradictions to their ultimate extension. They are not so much indecisive as determined not to choose: determined to achieve ultimate complexity by including every possibility, however diverse, in their final impressions.

Paradox for *Don Juan* and *Ulysses* is its own intention, it exists for itself. It is not there to serve the external motives and opinions of the writers but, rather, to further the contradictions and (apparently) mutually-exclusive possibilities it has itself presented. Where other writers have used paradox to accomplish specific intentions, as a device to dispraise, to disconcert readers, to counter prevailing opinion without appearing to do so, to manifest ambiguity on a certain subject, Byron and Joyce are content to have the tension of opposites itself as their first and last intention: as the energy of their work.

Overwrought by the conflicting impressions of *Ulysses*, N. P. Dawson of *The Little Review* (1918–1920) likened Joyce to a cuttlefish emitting inky fluid to conceal its shortcomings. Cuttlefish do not conceal their shortcomings. Moreover Joyce's stance, like the poet's, would be that he has no shortcomings to conceal. Yet, like cuttlefish, he and Byron do use ink to conceal themselves. Knowing that paradox is the verbal equivalent of religious miracle,[40] they blithely surround themselves with paradoxes. Indeed, they use paradox to further deflect any resolution of the ambiguities and to support their refusal to choose between the polarities that they themselves have set up by being paradoxical. They discover, as Wilde, Butler, and Montaigne did also, that paradox screens the writer while giving him freedom and immense manipulatory power. With Butler and Wilde also, they exploit the opportunity paradox provides for polemic expansion: the paradoxes of *Don Juan* and *Ulysses* pose multiple-sided questions and positions which, unresolved, lead to further questions and contrarieties, thus forming an endless, inexhaustible, self-feeding, self-propelling communication.

To recapitulate the involuting, paradoxical patterns of the two works as outlined in earlier chapters: Homeric parallels exist to emphasize the differences between ancient and modern worlds, and these divergences in turn point to deeper connections between past and present forms of the myth. Myths structure and, structuring too much, become farce, which is the best mythic pattern for the modern story. Literary (specifically, epic) tradition, omnipresent, serves best by contributing to its own absence, and provides the best literary examples when it fails to exemplify. Juan and Bloom are unheroic and Odyssean simultaneously, they express their creators' wish to show the significance of trivial things, which makes them most heroic when they are not and, ordinary, extraordinarily Greek. Social organization, so different in each chronological manifestation, heightens the distinctions between old and current worlds while yet assuaging the same human prejudices to imply ultimate, fatal connections between societies. Literature and language, providing the means for their own destruction, secure themselves through self-consciousness only to show that subjectivity is really the highest form of objectivity in the hands of a writer who is, because not, earnest.

We are reminded of the telescoping paradoxes that form one way of looking at Cervantes's *Quixote*. The novel started out as a criticism of courtly ideals, themselves a product of literary fiction, which implied a criticism of literature. It then became, because more real, a critique of literary style, specifically epic and romance. It then evolved into a sympathetic study of its foolish, bookish hero, to express a nostalgic regret for a lost age and, coming full circle, a lost, naive literature.

We are reminded, also, of *Gargantua and Pantagruel*'s paradoxical form of reversed intention and retroactive disintention. Rabelais promises what he does not give and, with what he does write, overturns the effects of what he has given and reverses the intentions of what he has promised. The reader is given, in order, a false successor to the *Grandes Chroniques* which combines satire and enigma to attack a variety of targets; a false successor to *Pantagruel* which is chronologically a predecessor and a quite different book; a false continuation of *Gargantua* which is really a continuation of *Pantagruel*, where nothing happens at all and where the inquiry about marriage turns out to be a pseudo-inquiry; and finally a false continuation of the *Tièrs livre* in which apparent action turns out to be language.[41]

Don Juan and *Ulysses* each present similar ever-reversing effects through a formation that is composed of numerous related paradoxes that telescope inward to point to converses of themselves, and circle outward to include more paradoxical content. Poet and novelist do not employ paradox, they deploy paradox. In the two works it ceases to be merely rhetorical device to become something much larger: a paradoxical art. It is, thus, as much product of the divided Romantic world-view summarized by Shelley's 'Thou knowest how great is man,/Thou knowest his imbecility' – as it is the necessary medium for conveying this vision. Once the Romantics accepted man as that thinking reed, that wretch with immortal longings, infinite in spirit but finite in action, their art became not just a *Mischgedicht*, but necessarily ironic and essentially paradoxical or 'duplicate'.[42] The 'duplicity' of *Don Juan* and *Ulysses*, thus, reflects the split, serio-comic view of man and his world that their creators hold.

Deeply aware of their task as artists, too self-conscious to be serious, Byron and Joyce are forced by their paradoxical art to make significant jokes, treat art as a solemn game, and write a peculiarly grave form of comedy. 'I now mean to be serious,' the poet says in Canto XIII, 'Since laughter now-a-days is deemed too serious'; and he resolves to make his lay 'soar high and solemn' like 'an old temple dwindled to a column'. *Ulysses*, also, obfuscates what is serious and what is humorous, to annul the distinctions between comic and tragic and fulfill *Finnegans Wake*'s paradoxical prayer: 'Loud, heap miseries upon us yet entwine our arts with laughters low'.

Schiller said comedy, not tragedy, was the more difficult and more significant mode, because in it nothing is determined by the substance and everything by the poet. Though tragedy may proceed from a more significant point, comedy proceeds toward a more significant purpose which, were it to attain it, would render tragedy superflous:

Its purpose is uniform with the highest after which man has to struggle, to be free of passion, always clear, to look severely about and within himself, to find everywhere more coincidence than fate, and rather to laugh at absurdity than to rage or weep at malice. [43]

Forced by their world and their ironic perspective of it to a paradoxical task of jesting in earnest, Byron and Joyce write comedy which, bearing similarities to good-humored Pantagruelism and Shandyism, is yet of a special, grim sort, 'comedy with teeth and claws'. [44] Necessity becomes virtue, and the two writers attain Schiller's ideal goal of pre-emptive, significant comedy: they are able to be substantive, tragic, inclusive, and distant, while yet provoking laughter and joy. Out of the most intractable material, pathetic, tragic, horrible, they make true, supportive art.

In the process, they come to discover that their comedy is an end in itself, that (as Schiller had predicted) it renders tragedy at once superfluous and impossible. They perceive absurdity and nullity in their world, and they react with ridicule and savage indignation; but their humor, a vehicle for expressing all this, proves to be as enduringly self-sufficient as it has been paradoxical in its achievements. Like the grin of Carroll's Cheshire cat, it remains for quite some time after all the rest has vanished.

E. M. Forster said art is the only orderly product our muddled race has produced, that it is the only meaning of our world. The human imagination of our time creates art as it creates nature, [45] it sees a universe in impressions of a multiverse, transcendent joy where there is grim drabness, and order where there is none. It bestows value, to bring organic unity as much to the mind as to the world of contradictions. It wills imaginative juncture out of the tension between form and matter:

> Below, the boarhound and the boar
> Pursue their pattern as before
> But reconciled among the stars.   ('Burnt Norton', II)

Transcending the warring opposites it perceives in the world, the modern imagination exerts itself to unify and reconcile. The 'one orderly product', becomes thus the integral order of life: it includes life entire, good and evil, privation and plenitude, in a passing vision of wholeness. [46]

As stillpoint in the turning, teeming, contradictory world of its own creation, thus also functions the paradoxical art of *Don Juan* and

Ulysses. Poem and novel form themselves of irreconcilable opposites and weave their matter out of the polarized world their creators perceive. Then by their very existence, their art, in which opposing entities exist in tension side by side, they provide the image of unity to their chaotic world and exemplify order to it: as Heraclitus said, 'that which is torn in different directions comes into accord with itself — harmony in contrariety, as in the case of the bow and the lyre'.[47] The wheel turns once more and, as they make art the ordered image of the world's disorder, paradox itself (divided in material, unified in creation) becomes the image of Byron's and Joyce's art.

As the self-confidence which Byron and Joyce exhibit is a wilful pose based on nothing around them, so also is the art of *Don Juan* and *Ulysses* an act of will based on nothing outside. It is an act of imaginative ordering, artistic daring flung in the face of the fierce odds of disorder its executors have perceived. Forster said the true artist composes in a condition of love: his art, like love, mediates meaning and, from within itself, confers and apprehends unity.[48] Acknowledging art's premise of order, portraying the process of perceiving a non-existent order, exemplifying order through its existence, and resolved to love, the two writers' art makes its resolute stance, its posture of order — the postulate of life.

But, infected by what Mann calls the modern artist's tendency to view life and see art ('. . . a mythical slant upon life, which makes it look like a farce, like a theatrical performance of a prescribed feast, like a Punch and Judy epic'[49]), poet and novelist display a proclivity for perceiving life as art and for living life as if it were art. If '*Childe Harold* and *Don Juan* are Byron',[50] *A Portrait* and *Ulysses* are Joyce. So essentially, inextricably, are these two authors' works bound with their (albeit very different) lives that we are led back to the question with which Chapter 5 concluded. Were Joyce's and Byron's books, or their worlds, the greater reality: is their art the postulate of ordered life, or is postured life the postulate of art?

Wilson Knight found that Byron's life and work annulled the distinctions between them. The poet lived 'what others write', and gave flesh to the two dominant directions of our poetry ('liberty', and the 'erotic instincts') since Marlowe and Milton:

> Incest, says Shelley, is a very poetical thing: presumably since every act of artistic creation involves a kind of incestuous union with the personality. Byron is suspected of it in actual fact. Next, he dies fighting for the perfect sacrificial cause: the liberty of Greece. He

lives that eternity which is art. He is more than a writer: his virtues
and vices alike are precisely those entwined at the roots of poetry.
He is poetry incarnate. The others are dreamers: he is the thing
itself.[51]

Joyce tried to accomplish much the same thing: he sought wilfully to
be for posterity what the poet only half-artfully was. Consciously,
Joyce tried to live the eternity that was art: to annul the distinctions
between what he did and what he was, what he portrayed and what
he actually executed, what he would represent for posterity and what
his existence tallied so far. His life was an elaborate pose based upon a
composite of the patterns which the lives of the poets from Dante
through Byron suggested. His art grew out of this posturing even as it
pretended (successfully) to represent life at large.

Byron's fighting for Greece, the splendid waste of his sacrifice, was
a Quixotic gesture; inappropriate to his age, it was justified more by
his personality and reputation than by anything else. Painfully self-
conscious, uncharismatic, a physical coward, Joyce was too late and
too removed for sacrificial action. He concentrated instead, with
dogged Joyceanism, on cultivating a heroic stance. Yeats said *Ulysses*
was the work of an heroic mind, and it may well be that, in
internalizing the *Odyssey*'s adventures, Joyce was spurred by a belief
that his own nature was in the heroic mould.[52] Ever concerned for
the artfulness of life, Joyce made his art his life's supreme heroic
gesture. Fighting in the interest of art, fighting for his art's creative
freedom, mirroring the traditional hero in all this, he made his book a
greater reality than life. When later years brought illness and misery
which jeopardized his art, he heroically fought off reality.[53]

No less than Byron, but in a different way and from a very
different starting point, Joyce was the martyr of art: he lived his life as
if it were art, and sacrificed his life to the artful (heroic) gesture of
distinction. He defined the task of the imaginative writer as a
mediation between the world of reality and the world of dreams.[54]
But, mediating between them, he came through his autobiographical
art to annul the distinctions completely: by casting himself as the hero
of the word through his deeds; by making his (largely) postured vices
and virtues the subject of his art; and by ultimately coming to
perceive life as art, more true because it was art. Joyce's success
through art (like that of the poet's) in making life indistinguishably
art, pre-empts all critical attempts to make final distinctions between
them.

IV

As culminative expressions of Western civilization *Don Juan* and *Ulysses* yet give the impression of being endless. The poet sings as if his song could have no ending – as indeed it does not – and Joyce's novel, which Jung found to have neither beginning nor end and just as accessible when read backwards, plunges the reader, with epic vengeance, *in medias res*.[55] Beyond its creator's schematizing, *Ulysses* implies a potential for expansion, sideways in half-hours, through additional episodes, over other 'slightly unusual' days, that is even greater than that suggested by Byron's plans for *Don Juan*.

This impression of endlessness may belong with the overall intention to parody through randomness and inconclusion the completed (and specifically Romantic) quest story. It may also be part of the old rhetorical question on the rogue's incomplete story – 'How can it be finished, my life being not yet ended?' – which found its apotheosis in Tristram Shandy's discovery that he would never overtake himself. Sterne's book brings us closer to home, for his critics argue that he wilfully practiced the art of the 'non-finito' (the term being borrowed from art history as it refers to a particular form of expression – a sketch – which the artist intended to leave unfinished). Indeed, the overall art of eighteenth-century France and England, beyond its formal order, displays a strong disposition toward the 'non-finito' so as to motivate creative cooperation and imaginative expansion in its audience.[56]

Joyce certainly finished *Ulysses*; he even finished, although he did stop in mid-sentence, *Finnegans Wake*. But much as the poet would have us speculate on Juan's successive adventures all the way to hell while reserving the right not to send the boy there, Joyce wants his readers to ponder on the future days of Bloom and Stephen. Although the poem and the novel share the intentions of eighteenth-century open-ended art, for their creators this is not a device to nurture the reader's imagination so much as an inevitable condition, a necessary issue of the art they employ. Imperfect, paradoxical Romantic art is also characteristically, inexhaustibly, 'in a state of becoming'.[57] Hence, as end-products expressing termination and final fiats of their makers, *Don Juan* and *Ulysses* nonetheless fulfill their nature by portraying 'becoming'. Swinburne likened the poem to the ocean, its stanzas to the broad-backed waves, and critics since have noted how the poem's basic action is a rhythm of existence eternally in movement like the sea.[58] Joyce's book also portrays existence in tidal terms, as 'The eternal surge/Of time and tide [which] rolls on, and bears afar/Our bubbles; as the old burst, new emerge' (xv, 99). We are overwhelmed repeatedly by the masses of material that come upon us not only from the fabric of *Don Juan* and *Ulysses* but from behind and beyond their contents. Sequence, an onward rush that does not cease, overturns notions of ending to promise continuity, mutation, evolution.

But if poem and novel face forward and assault us with ongoing motion, it is also true that they write of past time and harken back to static patterns. If they expand time by minutely documenting sequential existence and inconsequential thought much as Sterne did (in Book IV of *Tristram Shandy*) when he promised to make two volumes of one day, they also compress time by reverting back to Homer and compounding myth. As Kermode says of *Ulysses*, the book unites the irreducible *chronos* of Dublin with the irreducible *kairoi* of Homer.[59] The result, in *Don Juan* as in Joyce's work, is near-synonymous with what Eliade calls the abolition of time:[60] eternal repetition: process. Endlessness, expansive potential, and the motion of 'becoming' combine to represent timeless process. Mankind is indeed that 'human pest cycling (pist!) and recycling (past!) about the sledgy streets, [and] here he was (pust!) again!' (*Finnegans Wake*, p. 99).

To the early Greeks, wandering precluded the 'complete integration into an environment, the absolute realization of the self'. The immense emphasis they placed upon the *polis* was derived from their fast-held notions of man's inseparable connection with place, of his need for a source or center to which he could always return.[61] Odysseus could not find integration, self-realization, or the surety that he would prevail, until he came home to Ithaca. For Byron, Joyce, and their protagonists, there can be no integration in this sense, no center of civility to grasp; there is no *polis* worth returning to and, worse, even the realization of self in a self-conscious age proves to be a Pyrrhic victory. In the repeated renewal of cyclic process they nonetheless find the pattern of return and the promise of integration that they need:

> Well – well, the world must turn upon its axis,
> And all mankind turn with it, heads or tails,
> And live and die, make love and pay our taxes,
> And as the veering wind shifts, shift our sails;

The king commands us, and the doctor quacks us,
The priest instructs, and so our life exhales.   (II, 4)

History is that cyclic poem written by Time upon the memories of
man, as Shelley says in his *Defence of Poetry*, and man himself is part of
the cycling motion. Process renews itself, returns, and in its recurring
inevitability man finds the symbol if not the substance of
immortality.

To compensate for what Odysseus and the early Greeks had,
Byron and Joyce saturate their contemporary epics with motifs of
return and motions of homecoming. *Don Juan* and *Ulysses* may
spread out amorphously, wander randomly, and exhibit centrifugal
tendencies at every turn. But a strong centripetal urge is always at
work at several levels. Joyce scatters symbols of tower, omphalos,
egg, and island through his novel, and Byron relies on several homing
images for the Haidée and Norman Abbey episodes. Stephen in
'Proteus' dreams back through cockleshells and afterbirths to his and
the world's origins; Bloom comes home to 7, Eccles Street, back at
the point on the globe at which he began; and Juan, 'though not
approaching *home*' feels reverence for the soil of England and
provides the vicarious means for the poet to return home.

The concept of *nostos* – part of Joyce's metempsychosis – finds
best expression in the stylistic 'homing' and post-patterning through
retrospection of the two works. Byron had the most trouble writing
the early cantos of his poem; later cantos came forth with greater ease,
and the 'English' cantos (Mary Shelley remarked on how fast they
were tossed off, with few erasures) were as effortless as they were
masterful. As Joyce did also, the poet discovered that he wrote best
when his subject was closest to home. *Ulysses* displays a like pattern:
the episodes up to 'Aeolus' reveal a too-careful, 'Flaubertian' effort in
composition reminiscent of *Dubliners* and *A Portrait*; the later episodes
display a polished ease and agility of style. In novel as in poem we
detect a homing of style, a linguistic return. The style of each evolves
unto itself: it wanders through the traditional modes seeking its true
medium, turning on itself and waxing more self-conscious, until it
becomes a style-less manner with its own range and domain.

In their foreshortening of history through exegesis, also, *Don Juan*
and *Ulysses* reiterate the theme of *nostos*. The telling of what is
requires the recollection of what was. Taking that mythic leap
backwards, harkening back to earlier literary traditions, the most

modern of contemporary epics of alienation show their one major preoccupation to be, paradoxically, homecoming.

Spanning three centuries and reflecting yet farther forward and backward, *Don Juan* and *Ulysses* are each an aurora borealis. The brilliant light they shed comes from a glorious literary and historical past behind them, but it is also a reflected light from the phosphorescence[62] of that past's present decay as it lies before them. Much as the picaro's passage flashed critically not only on the distant climes he visited but also, in reflected light, on his starting-place, so also do these two works flash critically not only on the vanity of the centuries they compass but, reflectively, on the whole 'waste and icy clime' of human endeavor.

In *Don Juan* and *Ulysses* the authors may well have each written that book on nothing which Flaubert wished to compose. Works that provide a scathing estimate of literary tradition and human life, that spurn the world for words, they would seem to be anti-books containing only their creators' sense of emptiness, monuments of the Void, tributes to *Rien*. Giovanni Pascoli's *Ultimo Viaggio* (1904) is a disillusioned, pessimistic story of an old Ulysses's futile journeys, his non-adventures — visits to old haunts where nothing happens; it tells of his anonymous death at sea, to conclude with an even more anonymous voice crying, over the body beached on Calypso's isle, that the best fate of man is total annihilation. For some readers, Byron's and Joyce's later work share in the nihilism of Pascoli's miserable poem.

Marchand sees nothing prevailing beyond Byron's skepticism; he sees the poet as a hollow man in this regard, annihilated by his own vision. Trilling identified the later Joyce, growing daily more bitter, inhuman, 'affective will-less', as a paradigm of the nineteenth-century will *in extremis*:

> If from great Nature's or our own abyss
>   Of thought, we could but snatch a certainty,
> Perhaps mankind might find the path they miss —
>
> . . . Pray tell me, can you make fast,
>   After due search, your faith to any question?
>
> For me, I know nought; nothing I deny,
>   Admit, reject, contemn; and what know *you*,
> Except perhaps that you were born to die?   (XIV, 1—3)

says the poet. Joyce's pessimism was at least as extreme. But at the heart of the void which they see is human life, perceived through love, in joy.

'If *Ulysses* isn't fit to read, life isn't fit to live!' Joyce protested to those readers who found his book too profane. The invocation which opens his book '*Introibo ad altare Dei*' is sacrilegious but true, an equivalent of *A Portrait*'s 'Welcome, O life!' Reading *Ulysses*, we go up to the altar of its god. True satirists, Byron and Joyce are half in love with the entity they satirize. Their subject, in *Don Juan* as in the novel, is life, life which exists through (its own) sacrifice.

Boyd has said that love is the most important theme of Byron's poem. The poet says much on love within and without social law, on first love, pure and natural love, impure selfish love, fashionable love, love in marriage, and marriage without love. Though Ellmann says paternity is the primary theme of *Ulysses*, it would be more appropriate to award this place to love, of which paternity is one part. Joyce speaks of paternal love, maternal love, first love, Platonic love, patriotic love, purchased love, love without marriage, and ultimately, adulterous marriage with love. His entire book hinges on the question of whether the principals can love – which is why Bloom comes off better than Stephen, the failed artist who cannot love.

Juan's legend as one who never left women 'Unless compelled by fate, or wave, or wind,/Or near relations' (VIII, 54), is a comical variant on Byron's central endorsement of love as an alternative to war, because it is a higher calling than any conventional type of prowess, and unifies where the latter divides.[63] Yeats remarked that in no one he had met (except William Morris) was the joy of life so keen as in Joyce, an unusual attribute for a nihilist. Like the vivacious Romantic poet, Joyce made love his first act of faith. It is indeed the worst perversion to assume Joyce is identical with his inhuman narrator.[64]

But art also is a process of loving: as we have noted, the Romantic artist perceives in holy joy and composes in a condition of love. Love is the ultimate paradox and contradiction – as Juan says, 'love is only for the free' – the ultimate conciliator and, hence, necessity of life. Because of love poet and novelist are able to contemplate steadily the void that is life in a spirit of joy. Through love they are able to rescue sacrificed life and, true artists, bind and unify its divisions.

'I maintain that [*Don Juan*] is the most moral of poems – but if people won't discover the moral that is their fault not mine.'[65]

Byron's protest is akin to those Joyce made when he discovered shady Dubliners seeing obscenity peeping from behind every comma, dash, and fullstop in *Ulysses* — in a variation of a Rorschach test — while missing the essential symbol of sexual love. The novel and the poem are moral. They are concerned with the distinction between right and wrong: attempts to define goodness, even if this is only accomplished by decrying and denying what is not good. They are interested in teaching true conduct: *Don Juan* is the poetry of action, of helping man to take confidence again in himself; it counsels man to live in his world as best he can;[66] *Ulysses*'s morality is an insistence that man recognize his own limitations and needs, and that he act on these despite his incertitude about higher significance.[67] The one value both assert is charity: a generosity of spirit and ability to perceive kinship that is the basis of living and writing.

'He who doubts all things, nothing can deny,' Byron says (XV, 88). For all its negations *Don Juan* is fundamentally an affirmative poem; its cynicism springs from an ideal of perfection in human nature which the poet sees everywhere betrayed by frailty and ignorance. Remaining a poetry of satiric attack upon the world, it is still, miraculously, 'a poetry of acceptance not rejection'. Joyce 'consciously intended Molly Bloom's ultimate "Yes" as a doctrinal statement', as an assertion made after all the adverse evidence was in.[68] Denying everything everywhere in *Ulysses*, he yet gave Molly his own artistic function of seeing possibility and unifying division.

Through paradox and negation *Don Juan* and *Ulysses* prove themselves moral and affirmative. Too self-conscious to declare for life outright, they affirm the goodness that can exist beyond human vanity, and the process that exists beyond human life. 'Penelope' asserts not human life *per se* but earthly process: the ever-renewed, vulgar, inexhaustible earth, turning mindlessly in the icy void, 'exercising vast magnetic forces, and plucking men like flowers to wear helter-skelter on her indifferent bosom'.[69] When the poet speaks of 'a secret prepossession' just after his most skeptical cantos in *Don Juan* he affirms, even more obliquely, not just the human urge to experience but to continue experience: to plumb the chasm and the whirlpool: the fascination with process.

The full realization of human life, its potential and its limits, leads to its transcendence in *Don Juan* and *Ulysses*. The two epics say 'yes' to process in their closing communications; to ahuman process, a motion that might include human life but which, ultimately, is beyond human life, much greater but also much grimmer. But, as we have said before, process recurs and always returns — to its beginnings, to its parts.

Joyce gazed into nullity for over half a century and found there, as he said, a lovely nothing. Byron pleaded that he not be blamed for his true vision: for holding up the nothingness of life, for showing the show. They each perceived the world and its contents as 'but a show', an *ignis fatuus*, an enormous vacuum of foolish endeavor. Together, they cast a cold light of exposure on the vanity of life, of literature. But however persistent their visions of darkness, however denying their night, however cynical their word, they fail to manifest ultimate nihilism. By their acts of artistic fusion, and by their books' motions which affirm renewal and return, they repudiate their own disavowals. By default and by intention, human folly proves to be yet lovely. Saying 'No!' to everything except process through art, Byron and Joyce send us back to life, and to the sustainer of its fictions, literature,

The generations of all Time
And all the lovely Dead are there.[70]

Notes and References

INTRODUCTION

1. James Joyce, *A Portrait of the Artist as a Young Man* (1916 rprt; New York: Viking Press, 1968) pp. 80–1. In his letters of 1905 Joyce gave superlative praise to two other English Romantics – Wordsworth and Shelley (II, pp. 90–1); since these antedate it, this two-edged comment on Byron is chronologically last.
2. Richard Ellmann, *James Joyce* (New York and London: Oxford University Press, 1959) p. 40.
3. Stuart Gilbert and Richard Ellmann (eds), *Letters of James Joyce*, 3 vols (New York: Viking Press, 1966) I, pp. 165–6.
4. Frank Kermode, *Puzzles and Epiphanies: Essays and Reviews, 1958–1961* (New York: Chilmark Press, 1962) p. 216.
5. Karl Kroeber, *Romantic Narrative Art* (Madison, Wisconsin: University of Wisconsin Press, 1960) pp. 148–9; see also pp. 84, 136–7, 165–7, 189.
6. Meyer H. Abrams, *Natural Supernaturalism: Tradition and Revolution in Romantic Literature* (New York: Norton, 1971) p. 13.
7. Robert M. Durling, *The Figure of the Poet in Renaissance Epic* (Cambridge, Mass.: Harvard University Press, 1965) p. 237. Durling does not anticipate this statement anywhere in his study; since it is part of his concluding declaration, we are left to speculate on precisely what he meant by it.
8. This is Elizabeth French Boyd's phrase for the poem, *Byron's Don Juan: A Critical Study* (New York: Humanities Press, 1958) p. 21.

CHAPTER 1

1. Werner Jaeger, *Paideia: The Ideals of Greek Culture*, 3 vols, 2nd edn, trans. Gilbert Highet (1939 rprt; New York: Oxford University Press, 1945) I, p. xv.
2. See Gilbert Highet, *The Classical Tradition* (1949 rprt; London: Oxford University Press, 1957) p. 355, for an extended version of part of this list.
3. Highet, *Classical Tradition*, p. 360.

4. See also J. A. K. Thompson, 'If the eighteenth century is our Latin, the nineteenth century is our Greek, century', *Classical Backgrounds of English Literature* (1948 rprt; New York: Macmillan, 1962) p. 212.
5. Lionel Trilling, 'James Joyce in His Letters', *Commentary*, 45, no. 2 (1968) 56.
6. Highet, *Classical Tradition*, pp. 92–3.
7. Thompson, *Classical Backgrounds*, p. 38.
8. I use 'himself' strictly for convenience. Homer may have been author or authoress, he, she or it, 'person, collective or corporation' in that marvellous phrase no fewer than Thompson, McKay and Jackson Knight claim as their own.
9. Thompson, *Classical Backgrounds*, p. 32.
10. Brian Wilkie, *Romantic Poets and the Epic Tradition* (Madison and Milwaukee: University of Wisconsin Press, 1965) pp. 3–29.
11. See Thompson (*Classical Backgrounds*, pp. 38–9) on how Homer's art is both mature and traditional, a telling of old stories 'better than they had been told before'.
12. Hermann Fränkel, *Early Greek Poetry and Philosophy*, trans. Moses Hadas and James Willis (New York: Harcourt Brace Jovanovich, 1975) p. 3.
13. In 'Homer's Sticks and Stones', *James Joyce Quarterly*, 6 (Summer 1969) 285–98, and in *The Pound Era* (Berkeley and Los Angeles: University of California Press, 1971, pp. 41–50), Hugh Kenner says each age invents its own Homer, and that Joyce's Homer, as distinct from earlier variations, is the archeologist's Homer. His theory is based on the supposition that, after Schliemann's efforts, moderns like Joyce and Butler had the novel perspective of Homer's world as authentic, tangible, fact, 'real' and 'domestic', no longer a literary construct but something with contemporary equivalents. This may be but Byron, without the benefit of Schliemann's Troy before him and less specifically interested in kitchenware, nevertheless imagines the Homeric world as no less real and counters with his own forms of contemporary domesticity (e.g., Haidée's household). Indeed, Byron offers his own rebuttal to Kenner's proposition: ' 'Tis false — we *do* care about "the authenticity of the tale of Troy". I have stood upon that plain *daily*, for more than a month, in 1810 . . . I still venerate the grand original as the truth of *history* (in the material *facts*) and of place' — Leslie A. Marchand (ed.), *Byron's Letters and Journals*, (Cambridge, Mass.: Harvard University Press, 1978) VIII, pp. 21–2. Far more significant is Kenner's discussion of Joyce's debt to Butler in his mapping of Dublin (à la Trapani), and his remark that as 'Oxen' is a museum of styles, so is the whole of *Ulysses* a museum of Homers — *James Joyce Quarterly*, 248; *Era*, p. 49.

14. Elizabeth Boyd, *Byron's Don Juan: A Critical Study* (New York: Humanities Press, 1958) p. 74.

15. Edward John Trelawny, *Recollections of the Last Days of Shelley and Byron* (London: n.k., 1858) p. 201.

16. Byron, *Don Juan*, I, 41. My quotations from *Don Juan* rely on Truman Guy Steffan's and Willis W. Pratt's revised Variorum Edition (Austin and London: University of Texas Press, 1971).

17. Euphorion, son of Faust and Helen, symbolically combined medieval energy and classical art. Byron, also, was a symbol of Romantic energy and rebellion, of Icarian soaring, and of the Romantic veneration for classical Greece.

18. *c.* 1902. Herbert Gorman, *James Joyce* (New York: Rinehart, 1939) p. 138.

19. Richard Ellmann, *James Joyce* (New York: Oxford University Press, 1959) p. 107; R. Ellmann, *The Consciousness of Joyce* (New York: Oxford University Press, 1977) p. 10.

20. W. B. Stanford quoting Chapman, *The Ulysses Theme: A Study in the Adaptability of a Traditional Hero*, 2nd edn (1963 rprt; Michigan: University of Michigan Press, 1968) p. 184.

21. Charles Lamb, *The Adventures of Ulysses* (1808). Told by an English master to write an essay on 'Your Favourite Hero', Joyce chose Ulysses (Gorman, *Joyce*, p. 45).

22. See Stanford, *The Ulysses Theme*, p. 187.

23. See R. Levin's and C. Shattuck's discussion of the Homeric pattern of *Dubliners*, 'First Flight to Ithaca', in Seon Givens (ed.), *James Joyce: Two Decades of Criticism* (New York: Vanguard Press, 1948) pp. 47–94.

24. Byron was fond of Barthélemy's novel *Le Voyage en Grece de jeune Anarcharsis* of the 4th century BC.

25. 'Georges Borach's Conversations with Joyce', trans. Joseph Prescott, *College English*, XV (March 1954) 325–7.

26. But Joyce, significantly, was led to see the symbolic possibilities in the Homeric poem by Vico's allegorical *Scienza Nuova* (1725).

27. 'An honest gentleman at his return . . . [finds] that *his* Argus bites him by – the breeches.' (*Don Juan*, III, 23). In a letter Byron tells the story of his own dog 'that doted on me at ten years old, and very nearly ate me at twenty. . . . So let Southey blush and Homer too . . .' he concludes. *Byron's Letters and Journals*, IV, pp. 255–6.

28. See Leslie A. Marchand, *Byron: A Portrait* (New York: Knopf, 1970) p. 94.

29. Byron, 'O Weep for Those' and 'Saul', *Hebrew Melodies* (1815).

30. W. F. Jackson Knight speaks of Homer's predilection for sea-raid sagas, as exemplified by his use of them on three different occasions: when Menelaus tells of his visit to Egypt on the way home from Sparta; when Odysseus tells Athene of how he is a refugee from Crete; when

Odysseus tells Eumeus he is a Cretan who fought at Troy, and was captured in a raid on Egypt, *Many-Minded Homer: An Introduction* (London: Allen and Unwin, 1968) pp. 142–3.

31. Coleridge, *Table Talk*, 7 June 1824.
32. Brian Wilkie has noted some of the poem's Homeric parallels, *Romantic Poets*, pp. 204–7.
33. 'The Autumn of the Body', quoted by Ellmann in *The Consciousness of Joyce*, pp. 10–11.
34. Stanford, *The Ulysses Theme*, p. 7.
35. Ibid., p. 7.
36. Gilbert Highet's phrase, in another context, of the symbolist poets, *Classical Tradition*, p. 517.
37. Vivienne Koch, 'An Approach to Homeric Content of Joyce's *Ulysses*', *Briarcliff Quarterly*, I (1944) 129. 'To a remarkable degree, he treated Homeric Greece and 1904 Dublin not as comic contrasts, but as congruent impersonal shapes. Homer may control a particular episode as a whole, but not so decisively the material within it', Robert M. Adams says in *Afterjoyce: Studies in Fiction after Ulysses* (New York: Oxford University Press, 1977) p. 41. His remark reiterates (but from a different angle) the same idea that superficial differences between the plots of *Ulysses* and the *Odyssey* still highlight the basic parallels between them.
38. Koch first noted this connection between Gerty and Nausicaa (p. 122). Compare Byron's verses in *Don Juan* on how 'different' Haidée finds Juan, and on what an object of fascination he is to her.
39. Friedrich von Schiller, *'Naive and Sentimental Poetry' and 'On the Sublime': Two Essays*, trans. Julius A. Elias (New York: Ungar, 1966) p. 88.
40. Koch, 'Homeric Content of Joyce's *Ulysses*', p. 119.
41. M. I. Finley, *The World of Odysseus*, revised edn (1954; New York: Viking Press, 1965) p. xi.
42. Samuel Butler, 'The Humor of Homer', in Henry F. Jones and A. T. Bartholomew (eds), *The Shrewsbury Edition of the Works of Samuel Butler* (New York: Dutton, 1925) II, p. 240.

CHAPTER 2

1. Keats to Leigh Hunt, 'More News of Ulysses', *The Indicator* (1820) I, 65; Douglas Bush, *Mythology and the Romantic Tradition in English Poetry* (1937 rprt; New York: Norton, 1963) p. 118.
2. Brian Wilkie has traced Juan's speech to the drunk sailors, and other elements of the shipwreck scene, to Dante's example, *Romantic Poets and the Epic Tradition* (Madison and Milwaukee: University of Wisconsin

Press 1965) pp. 204—5. Dante's immense influence on *Ulysses* has been well documented by Foster Damon, Ellmann *et al.*

3. Thomas Mann, 'Freud and the Future', *Essays of Thomas Mann*, trans. H. T. Lowe-Porter (New York: Random House, 1957) p. 319.

4. Bush, *Mythology and the Romantic Tradition*, p. 60. Byron's myth-making, as Bush and others have noted, had a perspective distinct from that of Shelley *et al.* Myth in Byron does not undermine the importance he assigned (like other Romantics) to history and the historical (factual) event. As Karl Kroeber discusses in 'Experience as History: Shelley's Venice, Turner's Carthage', *English Literary History*, 41 (1974) 321—39, history mattered to the Romantics: 'the Romantic identifies individual experience with historical process, whereas to the modern "experience" and history are antithetical' (p. 321). Donald H. Reiman, of the Carl Pforzheimer Library (New York), brought this essay to my attention and asked whether the subject of history (as it relates to the individual) did not point to a major difference between Byron and Joyce. One must remember that the Romantics also began the movement of seeing history as spatial (and parallactic, like Homer's wandering rocks). Joyce's notion of history is problematic and not strictly modern. Given his immense debt to Vico's theory of historical process, and *Finnegans Wake*'s attempts to portray how individual experience and historical process coalesce, it would be difficult to say that Joyce saw history and experience as antithetical. History in the *Wake* recalls Byron's overall sense of history as cyclic destruction, which he borrowed from Cuvier (see *Cain*, IX, 37). In *Fiery Dust* (Chicago and London: University of Chicago Press, 1968) Jerome McGann describes Byron's notion of history ('the wretched interchange of wrong for wrong', *Childe Harold*, III, 69) in Joycean terms as 'a blind series of cycles, totally without morality' (p. 249).

5. C. Kerényi and C. G. Jung, *Essays on a Science of Mythology*, trans. R. Hull (1949 rprt; New York: Harper and Row, 1963) pp. 6—7.

6. Mircea Eliade, *The Myth of the Eternal Return*, trans. Willard R. Trask (New York: Pantheon Books, 1954) pp. 34, 112.

7. C. Kerényi, *The Gods of the Greeks* (London: Thames and Hudson, 1951) pp. 3—4.

8. Cedric H. Whitman, *Homer and the Heroic Tradition* (Cambridge, Mass.: Harvard University Press, 1958) p. 297.

9. Kerényi, *Science of Mythology*, p. 2.

10. William York Tindall's words, of Joyce, *Forces in Modern British Literature* (New York: Knopf, 1956) p. 313.

11. M. I. Finley, *The World of Odysseus*, revised edn (1954; New York: Viking Press, 1965) pp. 15—16.

12. Whitman, *Homer and the Heroic Tradition*, p. 13.

13. Cf. Tindall's 'The waking mind of primitive man is the unconscious

mind of modern man, who is at once far more and no less primitive than he dreams', *Forces*, p. 297.

14. Thomas Mann, in a lecture on *Joseph and His Brothers* as translated by A. Geller, *Mythology and Humanism: Letters of T. Mann and K. Kerényi* (Ithaca, N. Y.: Cornell University Press, 1975) p. xi.

15. Mann, 'Freud and the Future', *Essays*, p. 317.

16. Joseph Campbell, *The Masks of God: Creative Mythology* (New York: Viking Press, 1968) pp. 326; 5.

17. Northrop Frye, *A Study of English Romanticism* (New York: Random House, 1968) p. 16.

18. Harry Levin, *James Joyce: A Critical Introduction*, revised edn (New York: New Directions, 1960) p. 220.

19. T. S. Eliot, 'Ulysses, Order and Myth', in Seon Givens (ed.), *James Joyce: Two Decades of Criticism* (New York: Vanguard Press, 1948) p. 201; Ezra Pound, 'James Joyce and Pécuchet', (*Mercure de France*, CLVI) trans. Fred Bornhauser, *Shenandoah*, III (Autumn 1952) 15.

20. Kerényi, *Gods of the Greeks*, pp. 9, 4.

21. Sir John L. Myres, in Dorothea Gray (ed.), *Homer and His Critics*, (London: Routledge and Kegan Paul, 1958) pp. 208–9.

22. Friedrich von Schiller, *'Naive and Sentimental Poetry' and 'On the Sublime': Two Essays*, trans. Julias A. Elias (New York: Ungar, 1966) p. 104. The discussion which follows is based on Schiller.

23. August Wilhelm Schlegel, *A Course of Lectures on Dramatic Art and Literature*, trans. John Black (London: n. k., 1846) pp. 26–7.

24. Byron clearly anticipates Joyce's sense of a connection between the two Homeric nymphs which he expressed in one of his notes ('Circe = Calypso'), Phillip F. Herring (ed.), *Joyce's Ulysses Notesheets in the British Museum*, (Charlottesville, Virginia: University Press of Virginia, 1972) p. 393.

25. T. B. L. Webster, *From Mycenae to Homer* (1958 rprt; New York: Norton, 1964) p. 267; Samuel Eliot Bassett (quoting Milman Parry), *The Poetry of Homer* (Berkeley, California: University of California Press, 1938) pp. 15–16.

26. Hans Eichner, *Friedrich Schlegel* (New York: Twayne Publishers, 1970) p. 27.

27. Julius A. Elias, in his introduction to Schiller's two essays, pp. 12, 31.

28. See *Homer and the Epic* (1893 rprt; New York: AMS Press, 1970) p. 226, where Andrew Lang says these Märchen can be found among the Germanic, Celtic, Finnish, Basque, Slavonic, Asiatic and American peoples. In his *Homer and the Epic* (Cambridge, England: Cambridge University Press, 1965) pp. 77–8, G. S. Kirk distinguishes the theriomorphic cults behind 'owl-faced Athena' and 'cow-faced Hera'. Folktale motifs would include those of the Loyal Wife, the Returning Husband or Hero, the Loyal Dog, and so on. – Denys Page, *The*

Homeric Odyssey (Oxford: Clarendon Press, 1955) chapter 1. Page also notes (pp. 36–7) how the Odyssean catalog is directly indebted to Boeotian models. Webster, in *From Mycenae to Homer* (p. 88), speaks of Sumerian and Egyptian sources. Kirk, Webster, and G. R. Levy, *The Sword from the Rock*, (London: Faber and Faber, 1923) speak of the *Odyssey*'s relation to Near Eastern poetry and myth. Kirk finds attractive suggestions that the Greek epic borrows specific themes from Near Eastern poetry, especially the Gilgamesh story and the Ugaritic tale of Keret (p. 72). Webster finds it credible that 'far behind our *Odyssey* lies a Mycenean borrowing of the Gilgamesh poem' (pp. 83–4) and cites the parallels of: Gilgamesh as 'the man who saw the towns of many men and got to know their way of thinking' and Odysseus who 'saw everything to the ends of the land, who all things experienced, considered all'; Lestrygonians and Gilgamesh's Scorpion man; Circe, and the magic grove where the ale-wife lives; Istar, who can turn men into beasts; Utnapishtim, who gives information like Tiresias; Hades, and the spirit of Enkidu in the underworld. Levy discusses the connection between the *Odyssey*, *Gilgamesh*, and the *Ramayana*: he says it is not a case of imitation or direct borrowing, but of a common, formal, substructure.

29. Kerényi, in *Gods of the Greeks*, says: 'All through our mythology one comes across three goddesses . . . they do not merely form accidental groups of three – usually a group of three sisters – but actually are real trinities, sometimes almost forming a single three-fold goddess' (p. 3).

30. I pass cursorily over the two writers' treatment of Judeo-Christian myth. Numerous studies of Joyce's response to his religious heritage exist. For Byron, who had a lifelong fascination for the Old Testament and had wanted to dramatize it ('What a subject, under his hands, would the Tower of Babel have been!' Goethe said), an adequate discussion of the subject would have to be much more extended than is possible here. See Leslie Marchand's *Byron's Poetry: A Critical Introduction* (Cambridge, Mass.: Harvard University Press, 1968) p. 85; also the studies by George Ridenour and Robert Gleckner.

31. James Joyce, *Ulysses*, 'Scylla and Charybdis' (New York: Random House, 1961), p. 185. All further references to *Ulysses* will use this edition, and appear in parentheses in the text.

32. F. Rabelais, *The Histories of Gargantua and Pantagruel*, trans. J. M. Cohen (United Kingdom: Chaucer Press – Penguin Classics, 1955) Bk 1 (p. 53). All further references to this work will use this translation and appear in parentheses in the text.

33. See 4 above. 'History' here refers to the past as institution – recorded, external, completed tradition. The remarks do not deny the importance Byron placed on historical fact; nor do they deny Joyce's loyalty to Viconian historial process.

34. Pound, 'James Joyce and Pécuchet', p. 11.
35. Levy, *The Sword from the Rock*, p. 15; W. F. Jackson Knight, John D. Christie (ed.), *Many-Minded Homer: An Introduction*, (London: Allen and Unwin, 1968) p. 28.
36. Lawrence Durrell, 'On First Looking into Loeb's Horace', *Selected Poems* (New York: Grove Press, 1956).
37. Wilkie, *Romantic Poets and the Epic Tradition* (Madison and Milwaukee: University of Wisconsin Press, 1965) p. 195; see also Donald Reiman's study of the poem's epic context, '*Don Juan* in Epic Context', *Studies in Romanticism*, 16 (Fall 1977), 587–594.
38. L. Trilling, *The Experience of Literature: A Reader with Commentaries* (New York: Holt, Rinehart and Winston, 1967) pp. 70–1; see also Wilkie, *Romantic Poets*, p. 188.
39. Wilkie, *Romantic Poets*, p. 266.
40. Tindall, *Forces*, p. 313.
41. See Giorgio Melchiori's discussion of the lyricism and verse-rhythms of Joyce's novel in 'James Joyce and the Eighteenth-century Novelists', *English Miscellany*, II (1951), 245; also Boyd's list of Byron's attempts at novel-writing prior to *Don Juan*, pp. 11–12.
42. J. A. K. Thompson, *Classical Influences on English Prose* (1956 rprt; New York: Macmillan, 1962) pp. 100–1, 102–3; *Classical Backgrounds of English Literature* (1948 rprt; New York: Macmillan, 1962) p. 120.
43. See Leslie A. Marchand (ed.), *Byron's Letters and Journals* (Cambridge, Mass.: Harvard University Press, 1973) I, p. 207.
44. Stuart Gilbert and Richard Ellmann (eds), *Letters of James Joyce*, 3 vols (New York: Viking Press, 1966), II, p. 39. See also pp. 44–5 where Joyce says Larbaud is 'beside himself on account of my *Ulysses* which he proclaims the vastest and most human work written in Europe since Rabelais'. We have such circumstantial evidence, but no proof, that Rabelais influenced *Ulysses*.
45. Gilbert Highet, *The Anatomy of Satire* (Princeton: Princeton University Press, 1962). p. 114.
46. Elizabeth Boyd says in *Byron's Don Juan: A Critical Study* (New York: Humanities Press, 1958) the real model of *Don Juan* is the picaresque novel (pp. 34–5); she lists, among its ancestors, *Don Quixote, Gil Blas, Gulliver's Travels, Candide, Tom Jones, Peregrine Pickle*, and *Tristram Shandy*.
47. Arnold Kettle, *An Introduction to the English Novel*, 2 vols (1951 rprt; New York: Harper and Row, 1960) II, p. 136.
48. Adaline Glasheen, *Third Census of Finnegans Wake* (Berkeley, California: University of California Press, 1977) p. 124.
49. See Boyd, *Don Juan: A Critical Study*, p. 55; M. K. Joseph, *Byron the Poet* (London: Gollancz, 1964) pp. 194–5. Byron also knew Diderot's *Jacques le Fataliste* which derives its methods from *Tristram Shandy*.

50. Friedrich Schlegel, 'Lyceums-Fragmente No. 60,' *Dialogue on Poetry and Literary Aphorisms*, trans. Ernst Behler and Roman Struc (University Park: Pennsylvania State University Press, 1968) p. 127.

51. Geoffrey Hartman, *The Unmediated Vision: An Interpretation of Wordsworth, Hopkins, Rilke, and Valéry* (New York: Harcourt, Brace and World, 1966) p. 173. Hugh Kenner's observation that Joyce began *Ulysses* in naturalism and ended it in parody because he knew naturalism could not end anywhere else – discussed at length in *Joyce's Voice's* (Berkeley, California: University of California Press, 1978) – reiterates what Hartman says here, on a point that was first made by Schiller and Schlegel.

52. Barbara C. Bowen, *The Age of Bluff: Paradox and Ambiguity in Rabelais and Montaigne* (Urbana, Illinois: University of Illinois Press, 1972) pp. 99–100.

53. Pound, 'James Joyce and Pécuchet', p. 17; Trilling, *Experience of Literature*, p. 71. Trilling's earlier mention of the other meaning of burlesque (variety show or comedy) brings to mind the influence of the Italian harlequinades or pantomimes on the Don Juan theme upon the poem. The encyclopedic quality of late medieval compendiums like *The Mirror for Magistrates* and Erasmus's satires is also partial precedent for Byron and Joyce.

54. See Cohen's introduction to Rabelais, *Gargantua and Pantagruel*, pp. 17–20.

55. Eric Auerbach, *Mimesis: The Representation of Reality in Western Literature*, trans. Willard R. Trask (Princeton: Princeton University Press, 1953) p. 51.

56. Gerhard Schulz (ed.), *Novalis Werke*, (Munich: Beck, 1969) p. 565 (my translation).

57. Cervantes, *Don Quixote of the Mancha*, registered edn, trans. Thomas Shelton (New York: Collier, 1937) Bk IV, ch. xii, p. 380; Bk IV, ch. xxii, p. 489.

58. Richard Ellmann, *Eminent Domain: Yeats among Wilde, Joyce, Pound, Eliot and Auden* (New York: Oxford University Press, 1967) p. 3.

59. Schiller, 'Naive and Sentimental Poetry', p. 154.

60. G. Highet *Classical Tradition* (1949 rprt; London: Oxford University Press, 1957) p. 337; R. Ellmann, *Consciousness of Joyce* (New York: Oxford University Press, 1977) p. 31.

61. Byron, *Letter and Journals*, VIII, p. 11.

62. Robert Alter, *Rogue's Progress: Studies in the Picaresque Novel* (Cambridge, Mass.: Harvard University Press, 1964) pp. 90–1.

63. Melchiori, 'Joyce and the Eighteenth-Century Novelists' (p. 232) has also discussed parallels between *Ulysses* and Fielding's work.

64. Carl Woodring, *Politics in English Romantic Poetry* (Cambridge, Mass.:

Harvard University Press, 1970) p. 199. See also Peter Quennell, *Byron in Italy* (New York: Viking Press, 1941).

65. Wilkie, *Romantic Poets and the Epic Tradition*, ch. I, especially pp. 10–25. 'The criteria of epic, in other words, are continually emerging. If, at any particular historical moment, one were to hypothesize certain essential norms for epic, a true epic might still emerge which does not meet those norms', Jerome McGann adds, *Don Juan in Context* (Chicago: Chicago University Press, 1976) p. xii. Reiman, in '*Don Juan* in Epic Context', provides a perceptive development on Wilkie's theory as it relates to *Don Juan*. There are, he says, scholarly criteria for maintaining the poem is epic: it fulfills the role for a great epic poem in the sense in which Shelley (in *A Defence of Poetry*) declared Dante's *Commedia* to be an epic; it is a 'bridge thrown over the stream of time' and, joining Homer, Dante and Milton, its author becomes the fourth epic poet by Shelley's criteria. Moreover, Reiman adds, Byron reintroduces aspects of the mode of the 'Primary Epic' as C. S. Lewis defines it in his *Preface to Paradise Lost*. More than any other literary work, he asserts, *Don Juan* 'fulfills the conditions of modern epic'.

66. Byron, *Letters and Journals*, I, p. 13; Thomas Medwin, *Journal of the Conversations of Lord Byron* (New York: Wilder and Campbell, 1824) pp. 111–114.

67. Fritz Senn, in 'Book of Many Turns', Thomas Staley (ed.), *Ulysses: Fifty Years* (Bloomington, Indiana: Indiana University Press, 1974) notes that the *Odyssey* begins with the word 'Andra' in the objective case, that Homer might show clearly that his central subject is Man 'in his most universalized form before the focus narrows to one particular individual' (p. 36); he finds that this particularly agreed with Joyce's purpose in *Ulysses*. It would seem that Joyce is not at all interested initially in Man as an abstract. Like Blake he focuses on particular (minute and mundane) acts of an individual and lets these suggest whatever universalism they might.

68. Butler, in Henry Festing Jones and A. T. Bartholomew (eds), *The Authoress of the Odyssey*, Shrewsbury Edn, (New York: Dutton, 1925) XII, p. 131.

69. Stanford, *The Ulysses Theme: A Study in the Adaptability of a Traditional Hero*, 2nd edn (1963 rprt; Michigan: University of Michigan Press, 1968) p. 39.

70. See Louis D. Rubin, Jr, 'Joyce and Sterne: A Study in Affinity', *The Hopkins Review*, III (1950) 14–22.

71. S. Foster Damon, 'The Odyssey in Dublin', S. Givens (ed.), *James Joyce: Two Decades of Criticism* (New York: Vanguard Press, 1948) p. 207.

72. R. Levin, *James Joyce*, p. 134.

CHAPTER 3

1. Stuart Gilbert and Richard Ellmann (eds), *Letters of James Joyce*, 3 vols (New York: Viking Press, 1966) vol. II pp. 80–1.
2. Carl Woodring, *Politics in English Romantic Poetry* (Cambridge, Mass.: Harvard University Press, 1970) p. 202.
3. See Marilyn French, *The Book as World: James Joyce's Ulysses* (Cambridge, Mass.: Harvard University Press, 1976) p. 236.
4. Bernard Benstock, *Joyce-again's Wake: An Analysis of Finnegans Wake* (Seattle and London: University of Washington Press, 1965) p. 191.
5. Cf. Hermann Fränkel's thesis on how the *Odyssey* represents a departure from the *Iliad*'s values which celebrates 'a new mood', a 'new humanity' and a 'contemporized realist of a new present', and so on in *Early Greek Poetry and Philosophy*, trans. Moses Hadas and James Willis (New York: Harcourt Brace Jovanovich, 1975) pp. 85–6; 93.
6. Joyce, *Letters*, II, p. 81.
7. In *Le Rouge et Le Noir* Stendhal repeatedly invokes the inspiration of Byron's *Don Juan*. If Joyce's Dedalus recalls Julien Sorel, then Byron's treatment of his young Don might well be an important link (and precedent) for these two writers' ironic perspectives of their heroes.
8. W. F. Jackson Knight, *Many-Minded Homer: An Introduction* (London: Allen and Unwin, 1968) p. 126.
9. Fränkel calls this Odysseus's 'sausage simile', an 'extreme example of the decadence of Homeric style in the *Odyssey*', p. 44.
10. Lionel Trilling, *Sincerity and Authenticity* (Cambridge, Mass.: Harvard University Press, 1971) p. 87.
11. W. B. Stanford, *The Ulysses Theme: A Study in the Adaptability of a Traditional Hero*, 2nd edn (1963 rprt; Michigan: University of Michigan Press, 1968) p. 31.
12. Ibid., p. 32.
13. Ibid., p. 33.
14. Werner Jaeger, *Paideia: The Ideals of Greek Culture*, 3 vols, 2nd edn, trans. Gilbert Highet (1939 rprt; New York: Oxford University Press, 1945) pp. xxiii–xxiv.
15. Ulrich Wicks, 'The Nature of Picaresque Narrative: A Modal Approach', *Publications of the Modern Language Association*, 89 (March 1974) 245.
16. Stuart Miller, *The Picaresque Novel* (Cleveland: Case Western Reserve University Press, 1967) p. 70.
17. See Robert Alter, *Rogue's Progress: Studies in the Picaresque Novel* (Cambridge, Mass.: Harvard University Press, 1964) pp. 71–2.
18. 'Deceit and artful tales are dear to you from the bottom of your heart', Athene says to Odysseus (XIII). On roguery in Odysseus, see Finley, *The World of Odysseus*, revised edn (1954; New York: Viking Press, 1965)

pp. 68–9; 123. For comments on Autolycus, and on trickery in the old folktales of the Wily Lad, see Stanford, *Ulysses Theme*, p. 11; C. R. Beye, *The Iliad, the Odyssey and the Epic Tradition* (New York: Doubleday, 1966) p. 163. C. Kerényi, in *The Heroes of the Greeks* trans. H. J. Rose (1959 rprt; New York, Grove Press, 1960) suggests that Odysseus was the son of Sisyphus, the wily contriver (pp. 77–8).

19. Leslie A. Marchand, *Byron: A Portrait* (New York: Knopf, 1970) p. 287.
20. Highet, *The Classical Tradition* (1949 rprt; London: Oxford University Press, 1957) p. 423.
21. Karl Kroeber, *Romantic Narrative Art* (Madison, Wisconsin: University of Wisconsin Press, 1960) p. 150.
22. Juan has 'A most prodigious appetite' and falls upon 'whatever was offer'd, like/A priest, a shark, an alderman, or pike' (II, 157). He agrees with Johnson's argument to go 'to Lunch': 'Besides, I'm hungry, and just now would take, Like Esau, for my birthright a beef-steak' (v, 44). Byron, recalling Homer's example, has Haidée prepare 'the best dish that e'er was cook'd since Homer's/Achilles order'd dinner for newcomers' (II, 123). Food, as most observe, is ever-present in Bloom's consciousness. For Odysseus's food fixation, see Samuel Bassett, *The Poetry of Homer* (Berkeley, California: University of California Press, 1938) p. 46; Stanford, *Ulysses Theme*, p. 70.
23. S. T. Coleridge, *Biographia Literaria*, ch. XXIII, 'Critique of Bertram' (2nd edn; London: Pickering, 1847) II, pp. 262–73.
24. Auerbach, *Mimesis: The Representation of Reality in Western Literature*, trans. Willard R. Trask (Princeton: Princeton University Press, 1953) p. 276.
25. F. von Schiller, *'Naive and Sentimental Poetry' and 'On the Sublime'*: *Two Essays*, trans. Julius A. Elias (New York: Ungar, 1966) p. 93.
26. Alter, *Rogue's Progress*, p. 34. Kerényi speaks of the myth of the primordial child, of Pan, Zeus, *et al.*, in *Science of Myth* (p. 28): they 'show us two things: the solitariness of the child-god, and the fact that he is nevertheless *at home* in the primeval world — an equivocal situation, at once that of orphan-child and a cherished son of the god'. Like the uncertain parentage of modern heroes like Jay Gatsby and Hyacinth Robinson, some mystery, in the form of harsh gossip, clouds the parentage of Juan and Bloom.
27. Finley, *World of Odysseus*, p. 25.
28. Butler, in Henry Festing Jones and A. T. Bartholomew (eds), *The Authoress of the Odyssey*, Shrewsbury Edn, (New York: Dutton, 1925) XII, p. 110
29. Carl Woodring, *Politics in English Romantic Poetry* (Cambridge, Mass.: Harvard University Press, 1970) p. 202. Donald Reiman has pointed out to me another Romantic pacifist with direct connections to Bloom — Shelley's Wandering Jew, Ahasuerus.

30. For this strategem, Joyce credited Odysseus as the inventor of the tank: an armored car concealing men.
31. C. R. Beye, *The Iliad, the Odyssey, and the Epic Tradition* (New York: Doubleday, 1966) p. 163.
32. Woodring, *Politics*, p. 202.
33. Kroeber, *Romantic Narrative Art*, pp. 102–3; Lionel Trilling, *The Opposing Self* (New York: Viking, 1955) was first to note parallels between Wordsworthian affirmation, Quietism, and Bloom's non-militancy (pp. 149–150); it is significant that Joyce decided Wordsworth, of all English men of letters, best deserved the title 'genius' (Joyce, *Letters*, II, pp. 90–1
34. Stanford, *Ulysses Theme*, p. 43.
35. Jaeger, *Paideia*, p. 419n.
36. Whitman says Odysseus's beggar's disguise is 'symbolic of a condition of the self', *Homer and the Heroic Tradition* (Cambridge, Mass.: Harvard University Press, 1958) pp. 300–1.
37. Miller, *Picaresque Novel*, p. 16.
38. See Alter, *Rogue's Progress*, p. 5.
39. The *Iliad* tells of the Wrath of one man that brings disaster upon a people. The *Odyssey*, too, hinges in part upon Anger – the anger of Poseidon, and of Helios. See W. J. Woodhouse, *The Composition of Homer's Odyssey* (Oxford: Clarendon Press, 1969) pp. 32–7.
40. Jaeger, *Paideia*, p. 13; see also Fränkel, *Early Greek Poetry*, p. 532.
41. Fränkel, *Early Greek Poetry*, p. 532; cf. Jaeger's discussion, pp. 5–14.
42. Elizabeth Boyd, *Byron's Don Juan: A Critical Study* (New York: Humanities Press, 1958) pp. 37–8.
43. Jaeger, *Paideia*, p. 418n.
44. The depiction of the human ideal in our times never turns panegyric. The same authorial retrospection that perceives essential parallels also provides sincerity of vision. Juan's popularity in Russia is owed to his youth, valor, and blood – 'but most . . . to an old woman and his post' (X, 29); like his environment (Catherine's court), the boy turns unhealthy. Insightful Bloom also manifests the salesman's eye for the main chance. To counter his mental agility, especially when it settles on platitudes like 'Love' as universal panacea, comes (four lines later) mocking denunciation of the partiality and silliness of love: 'Love loves to love love. . . . Constable 14A loves Mary Kelly. . . . Li Chi Han lovey up kissy Cha Pu Chow. Jumbo, the elephant, loves Alice, the elephant. . . . You love a certain person. And this person loves that other person because everybody loves somebody but God loves everybody' (p. 333).
45. E. M. Forster, 'What I Believe', *Two Cheers for Democracy* (New York: Harcourt Brace and World, 1938) p. 73.
46. Cf. Whitman, *Homer and the Heroic Tradition*, p. 175.

47. French, *The Book as World*, p. 42.
48. See Trilling, *The Opposing Self* ('The Poet as Hero: Keats in his Letters'), pp. 3−49.
49. Frank Budgen, *James Joyce and the Making of Ulysses* (London: Grayson and Grayson, 1934) p. 19.
50. Woodring, *Politics*, pp. 2−3; Trilling, *Sincerity and Authenticity*, p. 90, speaking of Quixote and Bloom.
51. Joyce, *Letters*, I, p. 160.

CHAPTER 4

1. W. Jaeger, *Paideia: The Ideals of Greek Culture*, 3 vols, 2nd edn, trans. Gilbert Highet (1939 rprt; New York: Oxford University Press, 1945) I, p. xxviii.
2. Ibid., pp. xxiii−xxiv.
3. Ernst Cassirer's terms for culture, *An Essay on Man: An Introduction to a Philosophy of Human Culture* (New York: Doubleday, 1953) p. 286.
4. Crane Brinton's word, *The Temper of Western Europe* (Cambridge, Mass.: Harvard University Press, 1953) p. 74.
5. Alfred North Whitehead remarks that the western world's direction lacks vision, *Science and the Modern World* (1925 rprt; New York: Macmillan, 1967) pp. 196−7.
6. A. N. Whitehead, *Process and Reality: An Essay in Cosmology* (1929 rprt; New York: Macmillan, 1969) p. 399.
7. Raymond Williams, *Keywords: A Vocabulary of Culture and Society* (New York: Oxford University Press, 1976) pp. 243−6; R. Williams, *The English Novel from Dickens to Lawrence* (New York: Oxford University Press, 1970) p. 13.
8. Henri (Stendhal) Beyle, in Henri Martineau (ed.), *Le Rouge et le Noir: Chronique de XIXᵉ Siècle* (Bourges, France: Editions Garnier Freres, 1960) p. 76.
9. Leslie A. Marchand, *Byron: A Portrait* (New York: Knopf, 1970) p. 122; Stuart Gilbert and Richard Ellmann (eds), *Letters of James Joyce*, 3 vols (New York: Viking Press, 1966) I, p. 64.
10. Leslie A. Marchand (ed.), *Byron's Letters and Journals* (Cambridge, Mass.: Harvard University Press, 1973) I, p. 13; V, p. 35. Rumors at this time in England ('Anti-Byron' had just been published) claimed the poet had formed a conspiracy to overthrow, through rhyme, all forms of government and religion.
11. Lionel Trilling, *The Liberal Imagination* (London: Secker and Warburg, 1964) p. 212.
12. R. Williams, *Culture and Society: 1780−1950* (New York: Doubleday, 1959) pp. 33−6; Frank Kermode quoting M. Beguin on Lichtenberg,

Romantic Image (New York: Random House, 1957) p. 4; Crane Brinton, *A History of Civilization* (Englewood Cliffs, New Jersey: Prentice-Hall, 1955) ii, pp. 345–6. The last named distinguishes the perspectives of writers in the nineteenth and twentieth centuries from those of earlier writers who felt their times to be out of joint. He says the period is distinct not only from those periods which show intellectuals as conformists (for example, the period from Livy to Virgil, or of Louis XIV), but also from those periods (for example, the Enlightenment) when intellectuals, bitterly against things as they are, yet write with hope of what is to come.

13. Harry Levin, *James Joyce: A Critical Introduction*, revised edn (New York: New Directions, 1960) pp. 134–5.

14. Byron, *Letters and Journals*, iii, p. 179.

15. See E. F. Boyd, *Byron's Don Juan: A Critical Study* (New York: Humanities Press, 1958) p. 73; Byron, *Letters and Journals*, viii, p. 78.

16. See Robert Alter's comment on the picaro's critical interest in society in *Rogue's Progress: Studies in the Picaresque Novel* (Cambridge, Mass.: Harvard University Press, 1964) p. 17. It is true that Byron often gives Juan an insider's place (as court-favorite or as house-guest) similar to the poet's own before he left England. But we must remember that Juan is only an apparent insider (he is a foreign catalyst in the system) and further distinguish his situation from the overall perspective of the poet, writing in exile.

17. Alick West, *Crisis and Criticism* (London: Lawrence and Wishart, 1937); R. Ellmann, *The Consciousness of Joyce* (New York: Oxford University Press, 1977) p. 89.

18. See Williams, *The English Novel*, p. 23, and his discussion of Coleridge's differentiation between the cultivation of certain intellectual and artistic values (positive), and the process of civilization (largely negative); also his comments on how the Romantics distinguished between social acts (positive) and society (negative), *Keywords*, p. 246.

19. See Trilling, *The Liberal Imagination*, p. xii.

20. Frank Budgen, *James Joyce and the Making of Ulysses* (London: Grayson and Grayson, 1934) p. 16. See Andrew Lang, *The World of Homer* (London: Longman, Green, 1910): 'Though Homer describes a military aristocracy he is remarkable for his love of peace and hatred of war' (p. 28); C. R. Beye, *The Iliad, the Odyssey, and the Epic Tradition* (New York: Doubleday, 1966) p. 154: 'Those who would like to believe that Homer glorifies death are sentimental. Over and over he contrasts the wastage and the sorrow of war with the beauty and humanity of peace. . . . Nowhere is this better demonstrated than during the extremely emotional description of Hektor's mad, sad flight to his death.'

21. Lang, *World of Homer*, p. 28.

22. Ellmann, Introduction, *Letters of James Joyce*, II, p. lii.

23. I borrow Ernst Cassirer's rhetorical term, *Essay on Man: Philosophy of Human Culture*, pp. 95–6.

24. Hardly inviolate, Stephen comes to assume some of his society's tartuffery: he wears mourning but could not kiss his mother on her deathbed, nor obey her last wish; he denies his religion yet retains disdainful Jesuitic perspectives. Clive Hart has noted how 'Wandering Rocks', a chapter full of traps for reader and character alike, presents a city that is continually deceitful and evasive. Clive Hart and David Hayman (eds), *James Joyce's Ulysses: Critical Essays* (Berkeley, California: University of California Press, 1974) p. 188.

25. Lionel Trilling, *The Opposing Self* (New York: Viking Press, 1955) p. 59.

26. See Jaeger, *Paideia*, pp. 22–3: 'woman is not only the goal and ideal of erotic admiration . . . she also has a constant social and legal status as mistress of the household, and as such her virtues are sober morality and domestic prudence. . . . In the *Odyssey* [Helen] is the pattern of all great ladies, the model of social elegance. . . . The Homeric nobility honours woman as the repository of high morality and old tradition.'

27. Byron, *Letters and Journals*, VIII, p. 148.

28. Ellmann, *Consciousness of Joyce*, p. 83.

29. Boyd, *Byron's Don Juan: A Critical Study*, p. 64.

30. Joyce, *Letters*, I, p. 170.

31. Joyce, *Letters*, II, p. 99.

32. K. Kroeber, *Romantic Narrative Art* (Madison, Wisconsin: University of Wisconsin Press, 1960) p. 159.

33. See William York Tindall, *A Reader's Guide to James Joyce* (New York: Farrar, Straus and Giroux, 1959) p. 76.

34. B. Wilkie, *Romantic Poets and Epic Tradition* (Madison and Milwaukee: University of Wisconsin Press, 1965) pp. 207–8.

35. H. E. Rollins (ed.), *The Keats Circle: Letters and Papers, 1816–1878*, (Cambridge, Mass.: Harvard University Press, 1948) II, p. 134; E. M. Forster, *Aspects of the Novel* (New York: Harcourt Brace, 1927) p. 121.

36. I adapt Kroeber's words for Byron, *Romantic Narrative Art*, p. 138.

37. See Raymond Williams, *Culture and Society*, p. 30, and R. Williams, *Keywords*, pp. 48–9; Lionel Trilling, *Freud and the Crisis of our Culture* (Boston, Mass.: Beacon Press, 1955) especially pp. ix–x, 39; Richard Poirier, *The Performing Self: Compositions and Decompositions in the Languages of Contemporary Life* (New York: Oxford University Press, 1971) p. xiii.

38. Hayden White, *Metahistory: The Historical Imagination in Nineteenth-Century Europe* (Baltimore and London: Johns Hopkins University Press, 1973) p. 234. Burckhardt felt the modern age was a period of loss, that culture was misplaced sometime between 1600 and 1815. He

explained culture as an eternal moment which flourished when the compulsive and restrictive powers (Church and State) were weak.

39. I rely on Williams's terms for my formulation, *Keywords*, pp. 48–50. He says the term 'civilization' first referred to a process; it became, in the eighteenth century, a term combining 'the idea of process and an achieved condition'; in the nineteenth century it took on negative connotations, often referred to bourgeois life, and led to the development of alternate terms like 'culture' and 'cultivate'. I use the terms culture and cultural nearly synonymously with civilization in my discussion; I avoid any sense of their being antithetical terms (as in the opposition of cultivation and civilization, which Williams correctly traces to Coleridge) for the simple reason that Byron (the skeptical man of action) and Joyce (who sometimes aspired to 'socialist' art) would abhor notions of cultivation and taste, and specifically criticized 'culture' in their abuse of learning and the arts (as I discuss in Chapter 5). I acknowledge the inherent irony of all this: Byron and Joyce were unusually cultured, cultivated men in their age.

40. See Jacques Barzun on Jarry, *The Energies of Art* (New York: Harper, 1956) p. 19.

41. Joyce, *Letters*, II, p. 48.

42. Byron, *Letters and Journals*, VI, 142; letter to Scrope Davies, 7 Dec. 1818, printed in part in *The Byron Journal* (London: Byron Society, 1977) no. 5. One might well question whether the Romantic Byron could have been as nihilistic as Joyce. The latter is more consistently extreme, but it is also true that only a question of degree (and the poet's lighter but nastier touch) separate them in their massive alienation.

43. David Daiches, *The Novel and the Modern World*, revised edn (Chicago: University of Chicago Press, 1960) p. 103.

44. Michel Foucault, *Madness and Civilization: A History of Insanity in the Age of Reason*, trans. Richard Howard (New York: Random House, 1965) p. 40; p. 63.

45. Trilling, *The Opposing Self*, pp. x–xi.

46. Williams, *English Novel*, p. 26.

47. Joyce to Georges Borach in Richard Kain and Marvin Magalaner, *Joyce: The Man, the Work, the Reputation* (New York: New York University Press, 1956) p. 274.

48. M. French, *The Book as World: James Joyce's Ulysses* (Cambridge, Mass.: Harvard University Press, 1976) p. 32.

CHAPTER 5

1. 'We are all wind'. Donald M. Frame (ed.), *Montaigne's Essays and Selected Writings* (New York: St Martin's Press, 1963) p. 432.

2. On the island of Ruach, the people live on wind; the primary law under which they function is tied mysteriously to an obscene story of how a little rain lays a large wind. F. Rabelais, *The Histories of Gargantua and Pantagruel*, trans. J. M. Cohen (United Kingdom: Chaucer Press—Penguin Classics, 1955) Book IV, ch. v.

3. R. Poirier, *The Performing Self: Compositions and Decompositions in the Languages of Contemporary Life* (New York: Oxford University Press, 1971) p. 45.

4. L. Trilling, *The Liberal Imagination* (London: Secker and Warburg, 1964) p. 278.

5. Poirier, *Performing Self*, pp. xii, 27–8.

6. Stuart Gilbert and Richard Ellmann (eds), *Letters of James Joyce*, 3 vols (New York: Viking Press, 1966) I, p. 140.

7. Alvin B. Kernan, *The Plot of Satire* (New Haven: Yale University Press, 1965) p. 174.

8. Joyce, *Letters*, I, p. 129. Laurence Sterne, before Joyce, attempted to write down musical sound. In Bk v, ch. xv of *Tristram Shandy*, a violin solo interrupts the dialogue between the Shandys and Uncle Toby: 'Ptr . . r . . r . . ing – twing – twang – prut – trut – 'tis a cursed bad fiddle. – Do you know whether my fiddle's in tune or no? – trut . . prut – They should be *fifths*. – 'Tis wickedly strung – tr. .a.e.i.o.u.'

9. See George M. Ridenour on Byron, *The Style of Don Juan* (New Haven: Yale University Press, 1960).

10. I adapt Poirier's words on Joyce, *Performing Self*, p. 39.

11. 'Mad at mass' and 'pliant in the buttock', Rabelais, *Gargantua and Pantagruel*, Bk II, ch. xvi, p. 224; Bk II, ch. i, p. 172.

12. D. W. Jefferson, '*Tristram Shandy* and the Tradition of Learned Wit', *Essays in Criticism*, I (July 1951) 225–48.

13. Joyce's debt to Smollett in *Finnegans Wake* would seem to be even greater than he admitted. More than the effects of punning 'importunity' for 'opportunity' and 'asterisks' for 'hysterics', Joyce learned to use the unusual spelling for more subtle suggestions, concentration, and layering. I offer a passage from the Welsh maid Winnifred Jenkins's eighth letter in *Humphry Clinker*:

> Who would have thought that mistriss, after all the pains taken for the good of her prusias sole, would go for to throw away her poor body? that she would cast the heys of infection upon such a carrying crow as Lashmyhago! as old as Mathewsullin, as dry as a red herring and as poor as a starving veezel – . . . The young squire called him Dunquickset; but he looked for all the world like Cradoc-ap-Morgan, the ould tinker that suffered at Abergany for steeling a kettle.

14. Gogarty remarked that 'No man had more erudition at so early an age'. Atherton adds: '[Joyce] became a literary antiquarian whose knowledge, conspicuous because of its strangeness, bore more weight per given quantity. He delved into medieval tracts, studied learned discussion of conscience (*Agenbite of Inwit*) by forgotten monks, and memorized quaint old ballads. . . .', James S. Atherton, *The Books at the Wake* (New York: Viking Press, 1960) pp. 19–20.

15. I rely on Ridenour's argument in *The Style of Don Juan*.

16. Alexander Pope, *Peri Bathous: The Art of Sinking in Poetry*, ch. I; IV.

17. Jacques Barzun, *The Energies of Art* (New York: Harper, 1956) p. 72.

18. W. Y. Tindall, *A Reader's Guide to James Joyce* (New York: Farrar, Straus and Giroux, 1959) pp. 65–6, speaks of these examples as parodies of 'romantic ecstasy'. Joyce was certainly criticizing decadent romanticism embodied in the young Dedalus, but one must remember that bad poetry, or sentimental and bathetic expression, existed long before the period of decadent romanticism.

19. See Seon Givens's Introduction to *James Joyce: Two Decades of Criticism*, (New York: Vanguard Press, 1948) p. 13.

20. Byron's detractors have used his wife's words to support their claim that he is not a serious poet. See Auden's 'The Life of a That-There Poet', *The New Yorker* (26 April 1958) pp. 135–42.

21. It would be difficult to question Joyce's moral earnestness. Woodring, in *Politics in English Romantic Poetry* (Cambridge, Mass.: Harvard University Press, 1970) makes a distinct case for the poet's earnestness: 'Byron would make clear in "The Vision of Judgement" and *Don Juan* what is implied in his squibs against Thurlow: any writer not in earnest is a serious menace to literature and to society' (p. 171). Like Pope, Byron felt a moral fervor against dullness, as manifest in the Laureate Southey. Southey did not 'write in earnest', his existence was a threat to poetry, the word, moral life; his dullness 'came from indifference to things that matter' (p. 196).

22. M. K. Joseph, *Byron the Poet* (London: Victor Gollancz, 1964) pp. 194–202.

23. Ibid., pp. 201–2.

24. Percy Lubbock, *The Craft of Fiction* (New York: Viking Press, 1957) p. 147.

25. Alick West, *Crisis and Criticism* (London: Lawrence and Wishart, 1937) p. 165.

26. See Louis D. Rubin, 'Joyce and Sterne: A Study in Affinity', *The Johns Hopkins Review*, III (1950) 14–22; also Giorgio Melchiori 'James Joyce and the Eighteenth-Century Novelists', *English Miscellany*, II (1951) 236–8.

27. Joseph, *Byron the Poet*, p. 202.

28. Leslie A. Marchand (ed.), *Byron's Letters and Journals* (Cambridge, Mass.:

Harvard University Press, 1976) VI, p. 207; Jerome McGann, in *Don Juan in Context* (Chicago: Chicago University Press, 1976) marks the poem's habit of 'picking up whatever it may have happened to lose' and turning this into poetic material: 'Prose reports from history books and newspapers suddenly find themselves transformed, sometimes verbatim, into poetry, like Southey's bad verse. Nothing escapes the possibility of finding its poetic existence, not even the flash language of the day' (pp. 133–4).

29. Joyce, *Letters*, I, pp. 178–9; McGann's observation that *Don Juan* is not a poem that develops but one that is added to (*Don Juan in Context*, p. 60) supports my point on multiple-directioned growth.

30. Byron, *Letters and Journals*, VI, p. 208.

31. Joyce, *Letters*, I, p. 194.

32. Hugh Kenner, 'How the Trick Was Done', review of the *Facsimile*, *New York Times' Book Review*, 11 Jan. 1976, 7–8. Michael Groden, *Ulysses in Progress* (Princeton, New Jersey: Princeton University Press, 1977) provides detailed study of three stages of the book's accretive composition.

33. Hans Eichner, *Friedrich Schlegel* (New York: Twayne Publishers, 1970) p. 64.

34. Woodring, *Politics*, p. 200.

35. *Montaigne's Essays and Selected Writings* ('Of Democritus and Heraclitus'), p. 133.

36. Ibid., pp. 375, 21, 313, 377. Cf. Tristram Shandy's 'I have a strong propensity in me to begin this chapter very nonsensically, and I will not balk my fancy' (Bk I, ch. 23).

37. Robert Martin Adams, *Surface and Symbol* (New York: Oxford University Press, 1967) p. 253.

38. *Montaigne's Essays and Selected Writings*, pp. 191, 275.

39. E. Auerbach, *Mimesis: The Representation of Reality in Western Literature*, trans. W. R. Trask (Princeton: Princeton University Press, 1953) p. 303; G. Highet, *The Classical Tradition* (1949 rprt; London: Oxford University Press, 1957) p. 192.

40. L. Trilling, *The Experience of Literature: A Reader with Commentaries* (New York: Holt, Rinehart and Winston, 1967) p. 70.

41. See R. Ellmann, *James Joyce* (New York and London: Oxford University Press, 1959) p. 368; also Richard Kain on Joyce's tendency to interpose himself between work and reader: 'The Significance of Stephen's meeting Bloom', Staley (ed.), *Ulysses: Fifty Years*, p. 152.

42. Joseph, *Byron the Poet*, p. 201; Mary Colum, 'The Confessions of James Joyce', *Freeman*, V, 19 July 1922, 450–2.

43. Auerbach, *Mimesis*, p. 303.

44. W. Jaeger, *Paideia: The Ideals of Greek Culture*, 3 vols, 2nd edn, trans. G. Highet (1939 rprt; New York: Oxford University Press, 1945) p. xxiii.

45. F. von Schiller, *'Naive and Sentimental'* and *'On the Sublime'*: *Two Essays*, trans. Julias A. Elias (New York: Ungar, 1966) pp. 110–11; 115–16; 158; 179–80.

46. There is not an absolute square between Schiller's *'naiv'* and *'sentimentalisch'* and Schlegel's *'objectiv'* and *'interessant'* (Schlegel did not like the term 'subjective'). For our purposes, the terms essentially correspond.

47. Some critics have based their theories of modern fiction on the tenets set forth by Schiller and Schlegel. Notable among these would be Georg Lukács who, in his Preface to *The Theory of the Novel* (1920; trans. Anna Bostock, Cambridge, Mass.: M.I.T. Press, 1971) freely acknowledges his debt to these two Romantic philosophers.

48. Northrop Frye, *A Study of English Romanticism* (New York: Random House, 1968) pp. 17–18.

49. S. L. Goldberg, *Joyce* (1962 rprt; New York: Capricorn Books, 1972) p. 70.

50. Joseph, *Byron the Poet*, p. 195.

51. Walter Silz, *Early German Romanticism* (Cambridge, Mass.: Harvard University Press, 1929) pp. 7, 9.

52. Cf. Byron's 'but really it is a relief to the fever of my mind to write — and as at present I am what they call popular as an author — it enables me to serve one or two people without embarrassing anything but my brains' (Byron, *Letters and Journals*, IV, p. 35).

53. Elizabeth Boyd, *Byron's Don Juan: A Critical Study* (New York: Humanities Press, 1958) p. 30.

54. Byron, *Letters and Journals*, VI, p. 207. Boyd called the poet of *Don Juan* a ventriloquist. James Maddox, in *Joyce's Ulysses and the Assault Upon Character* (New Brunswick, New Jersey: Rutgers University Press, 1978) supports my contention when he makes a point on the artist of *Ulysses* as ventriloquist 'projecting his voice at various pitches' (p. 167).

55. Woodring, *Politics*, p. 199.

56. Auerbach speaks of the Christian era's disruption of the classical rule for a separate *sermo sublimus* and *sermo humilis*. His example is Dante, whose 'conception of the sublime differs essentially from that of his models, in respect to subject matter no less than to stylistic form. The themes which the *Comedy* introduces represent a mixture of sublimity and triviality which, measured by the standards of antiquity, is monstrous'. Dante's 'elevated style consists precisely in integrating what is characteristically individual and at times horrible, ugly, grotesque, and vulgar with the dignity of God's judgement.' However low they sink, Dante's content and style are always directly connected with the sublime. *Mimesis*, pp. 184, 194.

57. Take the Frenchman's tongue-in-cheek essay 'Of Vanity': he begins on a mock-solemn note, quoting Scripture, but the first two sentences

contradict each other. The second says that we should meditate on what Ecclesiastes has to say 'about vanity, the first says that the worst kind of vanity is to write about it. See Barbara Bowen, *The Age of Bluff: Paradox and Ambiguity in Rabelais and Montaigne* (Urbana, Illinois: University of Illinois Press, 1972) p. 119.

58. For example, in Canto I (50–9) of *Orlando Furioso*, Sacripant recites an eulogy on the 'virginal flower' he has lost. At this point, Angelica shows herself. 'She told him all that had befallen her . . . and how her virginal flower was still as intact as the day she had borne it from her mother's womb.' Ariosto adds, without pause, 'This may have been true, but scarcely plausible to anyone in his right mind'. Canto IX opens with an inspired tract on 'Cruel, treacherous love' only to lapse into the author's voice condoning treachery and vice in others and himself. Canto X describes Ruggiero who, on seeing the naked Angelica on the desolate shore, 'dismounted, but could scarcely restrain himself from climbing onto a different mount'. At this point, the narrator coyly retreats, past objectivity, to a new canto. Ariosto, *Orlando Furioso*, trans. Guido Waldman (London: Oxford University Press, 1974).

59. S. T. Coleridge, *Table Talk*, 15 June 1830.

60. Cyril Connolly, *The New Statesman and Nation*, XXI (18 Jan. 1941) p. 59.

61. Friedrich Schlegel, *Dialogue on Poetry & Literary Aphorisms*, trans. Ernst Behler and Roman Struc (University Park, Pa.: Pennsylvania State University Press, 1968) p. 126.

62. Silz, *Early German Romanticism*, p. 178.

63. Alfred E. Lussky, *Tieck's Romantic Irony* (Chapel Hill, N. Carolina: University of N. Carolina Press, 1932) pp. 67–9.

64. Ibid., pp. 81, 23. In *Consciousness of Joyce* (p. 22), Ellmann discusses Joyce's '*deeply ingrained*' connections with Goethe.

65. Schlegel, *Dialogue on Poetry and Literary Aphorisms*, p. 155; H. Eichner, *Friedrich Schlegel* (New York: Twayne Publishers, 1970) p. 72.

66. Jacques Barzun, *Berlioz and the Romantic Century* (New York: Columbia University Press, 1950) p. 388.

67. Some may wish to protest that ottavo rima *is* Byron's style in *Don Juan*. Certainly, no one would react to the poem as Jung did to the stylelessness of *Ulysses* when he said: 'If worms were gifted with literary powers they would write with the sympathetic nervous system for lack of a brain. . . . something of this kind has happened to Joyce. . . .' 'Ulysses – A Monologue', 1932 rprt, *Nimbus*, 2 (1953) 7–20. I would suggest that ottavo rima for Byron is more a convenient, flexible, neutral tool for essential stylelessness in the poem.

68. 'Satire' comes from the word 'saturate', meaning ' "a medley" full of different things', G. Highet, *The Anatomy of Satire* (Princeton: Princeton University Press, 1962) pp. 303, 18. Fritz Senn's remark that *Ulysses* is Joyce's *Metamorphoses*, albeit made in another context, and his

note that English is a most Odyssean language, would seem to support my point on fluidity of style, 'Book of Many Turns', in Thomas Staley (ed.), *Ulysses: Fifty Years* (Bloomington, Indiana: Indiana University Press, 1974) pp. 32, 43).

69. Kernan on *Don Juan, Plot of Satire*, pp. 174–5.
70. Arnold Goldman, *The Joyce Paradox: Form and Freedom in his Fiction* (Evanston, Illinois: Northwestern University Press, 1966) p. 100.
71. Byron, *Letters and Journals*, VI, p. 232.
72. A. Walton Litz, 'Ithaca', in Clive Hart and David Hayman (eds), *James Joyce's Ulysses: Critical Essays* (Berkeley, California: University of California Press, 1974) p. 386.
73. See Robert Durling, *The Figure of the Poet in Renaissance Epic* (Cambridge, Mass.: Harvard University Press, 1965) p. 176. Durling echoes Schlegel when he comments on Ariosto's godlike control over his material, his shifts in tone, his reconciliation of antinomies, the total subjection of poem to poet, and so on.
74. Kenner's point on how all the major scenes in Joyce happen off-stage (see *Joyce's Voices*, pp. 42–3) supports my suggestion. McGann also appears to support it when he says *Don Juan* aims to explore the interfaces between different things, events, moods, that the poem is always in transition, and that transitions between styles, stanzas, and tones are the loci of all opportunities (*Don Juan in Context*, p. 95). A pertinent aside to my point is Robert M. Adams's remark in *Afterjoyce* (New York: Oxford University Press, 1977) p. 77 that Woolf's *Between the Acts* is her most essentially Joycean book.
75. Poirier, *Performing Self*, p. 38.
76. Barzun, *Energies of Art*, p. 76.
77. R. Williams speaking of Joyce in *The English Novel from Dickens to Lawrence* (New York: Oxford University Press, 1970) pp. 167–8.
78. Donald A. Low, 'Review of J. J. McGann's *Don Juan in Context*', *The Byron Journal* (London: Byron Society, 1977) no. 5, 106–7.
79. Montaigne, *Essays* ('Of Giving the Lie') p. 287.
80. Ellmann, *Consciousness of Joyce*, pp. 91, 93.
81. Cf. Montaigne's 'I have no more made my book than my book has made me – a book consubstantial with its author. . . .' *Essays*, p. 281.
82. Byron, *Letters and Journals*, VIII, p. 104.
83. Frank Kermode, *Puzzles and Epiphanies: Essays and Reviews* (New York: Chilmark Press, 1962) p. 87.

CHAPTER 6

1. George Bornstein's metaphor, *Transformation of Romanticism in Yeats, Eliot, and Stevens* (Chicago: University of Chicago Press, 1976) p. 15.

2. Leslie A. Marchand (ed.), *Byron's Letters and Journals* (Cambridge, Mass.: Harvard University Press, 1973) VI, p. 10.

3. Thomas Hardy, *Journal*, November 1880; Florence Emily Hardy, *The Early Life of Thomas Hardy*, (London and New York: Macmillan, 1928) p. 189.

4. Wilde, in infamy, began to hope his career would serve as an archetype of the victimized artist as Byron's did; Woolf acclaimed the 'elastic shape' of *Don Juan*; Auden found the poem 'sympatisch', and liked his muse ('because she's gay and witty') enough to try and match the effects (unsuccessfully) in his 'Letter to Lord Byron'.

   Jacques Barzun was perhaps the first to observe the fallacies inherent in the prevailing opinion of Romanticism, and to demonstrate how it had sounded all the themes of the nineteenth and twentieth centuries in its first movement (*Romanticism and the Modern Ego*, 1943, reprinted as *Classic, Romantic, and Modern*, 1961). Since then, among those who have argued for Modernism as a continuation of Romanticism list: Northrop Frye, who (in *A Study of English Romanticism*, 1968) marked the Romantics' establishment of a mythological construction which is still in operation today and noted that many aspects of Romanticism could best be comprehended in their development in writers like Joyce, Eliot, Proust, Yeats and Lawrence; Frank Kermode, who (in *Romantic Image*, 1957) demonstrated that the symbol of the French is the Romantic image writ large and given metaphysical support and remarked that modern literature is still working out the revolutionary theses of the Romantics, developing some to the point of mania; Stephen Spender, who (in *The Struggle of the Modern*, 1965) said the modern revolution in technique carries a Romantic emphasis on imagination at its thematic core; Lionel Trilling, who (in *The Liberal Imagination*, 1964) perceived that Eliot's notion of 'pastness' in 'Tradition and the Individual Talent' belonged with Nietzsche's concept of historical sense as a 'sixth sense'; Morse Peckham, who sees literature as *The Triumph of Romanticism* (1970); Harold Bloom, who has argued that Yeats and others are easily accommodated within Romantic tradition; and Monroe Spears, who discusses the 'Dionysiac' element in modern literature.

5. F. Kermode, *Puzzles and Epiphanies: Essays and Reviews, 1958–1961* (New York: Chilmark Press, 1962) p. 88.

6. L. Trilling, 'James Joyce in His Letters', *Commentary*, 45, no. 2 (1968) p. 58. Trilling's point is that in their grandiosity as chieftains of art, in temperament, and in energy, all the major figures of the first quarter of the twentieth century show 'a closer affinity with their nineteenth-century predecessors than with their successors'. Among them, Joyce is unusual in the extent to which he naively assumed the role and personality of cultural titan: 'None so cherished the purpose of

imposing himself upon the world, of being a king and riding in triumph through Persepolis'.

7. M. H. Abrams, *Natural Supernaturalism: Tradition and Revolution in Romantic Literature* (New York: Norton, 1971) pp. 419–21, 13.

8. See Trilling, *Liberal Imagination*, pp. 35, 41.

9. See Bornstein on Yeats, Eliot, and Stevens, *Transformation of Romanticism*, p. xii. Silz's discussion of the Romantic enthusiasm for *Bildung* is pertinent to Joyce's painstaking attempt to record his vocation, *Early German Romanticism* (Cambridge, Mass.: Harvard University Press, 1929) pp. 40–1.

10. Kenner has stated in *Joyce's Voices* (Berkeley, California: University of California Press, 1978) p. 49 that 'Romanticism skipped Ireland'; it would appear that the egotistical Joyce pre-empted the slight by not permitting Romanticism to skip him.

11. W. Y. Tindall, *A Reader's Guide to James Joyce* (New York: Farrar, Straus and Giroux, 1959) p. 76 notes that Stephen, when weighing the choice between poetry and piety, exile and nation, world and church in *A Portrait*, walks back and forth, symbolically, between Byron's Pub and Clontarf Chapel: 'Defending Byron, Stephen becomes one with a heretic, a romantic outlaw, and, as poet, creator of *Cain*'.

12. Cf. Joyce's letters to Grant Richards, and Byron's letters to Murray and Kinnaird, Byron, *Letters and Journals*, VI, pp. 109, 105–6.

13. The poet's declaration of world citizenship echoed an Enlightenment tradition; Joyce's was a specific rejection of extreme nationalism (provincialism).

14. Carl Woodring, 'Nature and Art in the Nineteenth Century', *Publications of the Modern Language Association*, 92 (1977) 196.

15. Byron, *Letters and Journal*, III, p. 109.

16. Edward E. Bostetter, 'Introduction', *Twentieth Century Interpretations of Don Juan: A Collection of Critical Essays* (Englewood Cliffs, New Jersey: Prentice-Hall, 1969) p. 11; Barzun, also, suggests the parallel between Byron's generation and the post-Great War generation, *Energies of Art*, p. 17. Marchand says it is Byron's honesty in the poem that is his final appeal to a disillusioned world, see *Byron: A Critical Introduction* (Cambridge, Mass.: Harvard University Press, 1968) p. 244; Ernest J. Lovell, Jr., *Byron: The Record of a Quest* (Austin, Texas: University of Texas Press, 1949) writes an excellent postscript chapter on 'The Contemporaneousness of Byron'; Donald H. Reiman and Doucet D. Fischer, *Byron on the Continent* (New York: New York Public Library, 1974) pp. 49–50, discuss the areas where *Don Juan* anticipates future generations to incorporate all the central themes of later Western literature 'more pertinently than does any other work written by one author under a single title'.

17. T. S. Eliot wrote an imitation of *Don Juan* (in ottavo rima) at age 16.

Called 'A Fable for Feasters', the poem told of a group of monks in a monastery living as epicures until a ghost at Christmas destroys their idyll by abducting the abbot up a chimney: the Church designates the abbot a saint, and the monks return to abstinence. Presumably, Eliot thought this cured him of the disease of Byronism.

18. W. H. Auden, 'The LIfe of a That-There Poet', *The New Yorker* (26 April 1958) p. 135.

19. K. Kroeber, *Romantic Narrative Art* (Madison, Wisconsin: University of Wisconsin Press, 1960) p. 148.

20. Barzun, *The Energies of Art* (New York: Harper, 1956) p. 70.

21. G. Melchiori, 'James Joyce and the Eighteenth-Century Novelists', *English Miscellany*, II (1951) p. 244.

22. F. R. Leavis, *Revaluation* (New York: Norton, 1936) p. 153.

23. Barzun, *Classic, Romantic and Modern*, pp. xx, 14.

24. Elizabeth Boyd, *Byron's Don Juan: A Critical Study* (New York: Humanities Press, 1958) p. 45; Alvin Kernan, *The Plot of Satire* (New Haven: Yale University Press 1965) pp. 173–74.

25. Byron, *Letters and Journals*, VI, pp. 114, 68. Joyce called *Finnegans Wake* his great 'tour of Bibel'.

26. E. Auerbach, *Mimesis: The Representation of Reality in Western Literature*, trans. W. R. Trask (Princeton: Princeton University Press, 1953) pp. 544, 547.

27. Joyce found he could best prepare himself for writing *Finnegans Wake* by memorizing a page of 'Sirens': 'It is a bewildering business. I want to do as much as I can before the execution. Complications to right of me, complications to left of me, complex on the page before me, perplex in the pen beside me, duplex in the meandering eyes of me, stuplex on the face that reads me. And from time to time I lie back and listen to my hair growing white', in Stuart Gilbert and Richard Ellmann, (eds), *Letters of James Joyce*, 3 vols (New York; Viking Press, 1966) I, p. 222.

28. See H. Eichner, *Friedrich Schlegel* (New York: Twayne Publishers, 1970) pp. 57, 59; Silz, *Early German Romanticism*, p. 211.

29. The term 'encyclopedia' derives from the *pseudo* Greek *egkuklopaideia*, which in turn derives from the Greek *egkuklios paideia* (an encyclical education: the circle of arts and sciences vital to liberal life). From Joyce's parodic use of W. H. Roscher's encyclopedia of Greek myth and Richmal Mangnall's text-book of nineteenth-century knowledge, and from Byron's crack on the encyclopedists who would mix flesh and fowl (XV, 68), both writers seem richly aware that all encyclopedias known to man are pseudomorphs which must undermine their own purpose.

30. The subject of the democratization of art is a perennial one: Walter Savage Landor said a rib of Shakespeare would have made a Milton, a rib of Milton all poets since; Macaulay's essay on Milton (1825) had as its

central premise the notion that as civilization advances, poetry necessarily declines; Peacock, of course, wrote his *Four Ages of Poetry* (1820) which suggested poetry was a cultural mental rattle to be put aside by mature contemporary man. Walter Jackson Bate, *The Burden of the Past and the English Poet* (Cambridge, Mass.: Harvard University Press, 1970) discusses the possibility of art in modern times.

31. G. Highet on Homer, *The Classical Tradition* (1949 rprt; London: Oxford University Press, 1957) p. 482. Reiman ('*Don Juan* in Epic Context', p. 594) says that as Homer was to 5th century Greece, and *Paradise Lost* to the Enlightenment, so too does *Don Juan* serve as 'the clearest articulation of the stage of Western civilization in which we live and the roots from which it sprang'.

32. An article in *Strand Magazine* describes this experiment. I am indebted to James Atherton for this fact, which he applies to the plot of *Finnegans Wake*. *The Books at the Wake* (New York: Viking, 1960) p. 23.

33. Joyce's thinking on the function of *Finnegans Wake*, as a universal bible, would support this notion.

34. 'To accuse oneself would be to excuse oneself in that subject, and to condemn oneself would be to absolve oneself'. Donald M. Frame (ed.), *Montaigne's Essays and Selected Writings* (New York: St Martin's Press, 1963) p. 272.

35. See Richard Ellmann, *Ulysses on the Liffey* (New York: Oxford University Press, 1972).

36. For example, the cold, egotistical, morose artist of the early years was nicknamed 'Sunny Jim' and wanted to be a songster. The man who chose exile to avoid 'the stink' of Dublin, was to acknowledge that he had never left Dublin — a sentiment that compares well with Byron's stanzas in 'Beppo', beginning 'England! with all thy faults I love thee still'. Joyce's sense of sin and his fear of thunder-storms were sufficiently at odds with his attacks on Catholicism to lead Patrick Kavanagh to wonder whether the outbursts did not constitute 'the horrible howl of the believer'.

37. Boyd, *A Critical Study*, p. 162.

38. William Empson, *Seven Types of Ambiguity* (New York: New Directions, 1947) p. 192. I quote Empson here with innumerable reservations, not the least of these being that his technique for reading literature lends itself better to poetry than to prose; that his sense of 'ambiguity' does not really compass the extensive nature of the quality in these two books; and that he considers Byron (with the exception of the 'first cantos' of *Don Juan*) to have had nothing to say beyond his 'infantile incest-fixation upon his sister' (p. 20).

39. In an essay on 'Ithaca' in Clive Hart and David Hayman (eds), *James Joyce's Ulysses: Critical Essays* (Berkeley, California: University of

California Press, 1974) p. 391, A. Walton Litz points out the futility of 'either/or' arguments on *Ulysses's* effects.

40. Leo Knuth, 'Joyce's Verbal Acupuncture', Thomas Staley (ed.), *Ulysses: Fifty Years* (Bloomington, Indiana: Indiana University Press, 1974) p. 70.
41. Barbara Bowen, *The Age of Bluff: Paradox and Ambiguity in Rabelais and Montaigne* (Urbana, Illinois: University of Illinois Press, 1972) p. 99.
42. Schlegel said that the products of minds which perceived the paradoxical position of mankind had to exhibit a strong element of irony; and 'Irony is the form of paradox' or the paradoxical, in Eichner, *Friedrich Schlegel*, p. 74; Friedrich Schlegel, *Dialogue on Poetry and Literary Aphorisms*, trans. Ernst Behler and Roman Struc (University Park: Pennsylvania State University Press, 1968) p. 126. Eichner says Schlegel never tired of defining and redefining the paradoxical nature and function of romantic art. It was the dialectic fusion not of one pair of opposites, but of many pairs, all of which, shading off into each other in subtle nuances, were the periphery of the same mysterious center that was the heart of the paradox. The essential 'duplicity' of art, reflected the 'duplicity' of man and the duplicity of the world (p. 70).
43. F. von Schiller, *'Naive and Sentimental Poetry' and 'On the Sublime': Two Essays*, trans. J. A. Elias (New York: Ungar, 1966) pp. 120–22; Cassirer's comments on comic art apply as well to *Don Juan* and *Ulysses*: 'Comic art possesses in the highest degree that faculty shared by all art, sympathetic vision. . . . Great comic art has always been a sort of *encomium moriae*, a praise of folly', *Essay on Man: Philosophy of Culture* (New York: Doubleday, 1953) p. 192. Echoing Schiller's definition Joyce came to call his youthful ideal of 'the perfect manner in art' (which he achieved in *Ulysses*) 'comedy'. He called it comedy because it embraced the whole of life, even its tragedy, and contemplated it steadily in a 'spirit of joy'. See S. L. Goldberg, *Joyce* (1962 rprt; New York: Capricorn Books, 1972) p. 69 on Joyce's critical theory; also Ellmann *Ulysses on the Liffey*, p. xi, on comedy.
44. R. Ellmann's phrase for Joyce, *The Consciousness of Joyce* (New York: Oxford University Press, 1977) p. 79.
45. E. M. Forster, 'Art for Art's Sake', *Two Cheers for Democracy* (New York: Harcourt, Brace and World, 1951) p. 92; Woodring, 'Nature and Art in the Nineteenth Century', p. 195.
46. Kermode, *Puzzles and Epiphanies*, p. 84.
47. Heraclitus, 'Fragment no. 51', trans. Charles M. Bakewell, *Source Book in Ancient Philosophy* (New York: Scribners, 1907), p. 31.
48. See E. M. Forster, 'The *Raison d'Etre* of Criticism in the Arts', *Two Cheers*, pp. 107–23. My terms are borrowed from Kermode's discussion of Forster, *Puzzles and Epiphanies*, p. 79.

49. Thomas Mann, 'Freud and the Future', *Essays*, p. 321.

50. N. Frye, *Romanticism Reconsidered: Selected Papers From the English Institute* (New York; Columbia University Press, 1963) p. 16.

51. G. Wilson Knight, 'The Two Eternities', in Paul West (ed.), *Byron: A Collection of Critical Essays* (Englewood Cliffs, New Jersey: Prentice-Hall, 1963), p. 16.

52. Ellmann, *Consciousness of Joyce*, p. 11.

53. Kermode, *Puzzles and Epiphanies*, p. 90.

54. Joyce in his essay on James Clarence Mangan (1902), Ellsworth Mason and Richard Ellmann (eds), *James Joyce: The Critical Writings* (1959 rprt; New York; Viking Press, 1964).

55. Harry Levin, *James Joyce: A Critical Introduction*, revised edn (New York: New Directions, 1960) p. 95.

56. See Marcia Allentuck, 'In Defence of an Unfinished *Tristram Shandy*: Laurence Sterne and the Non-Finito', in *The Winged Skull: Papers from the Laurence Sterne Bicentenary Conference*, Arthur H. Cash and John M. Stedmond (eds), (Kent, Ohio: Kent State University Press, 1971), pp. 147, 150. See also Eric Rothstein, '"Ideal Presence" and the "Non-Finito" in Eighteenth-Century Aesthetics', *Eighteenth-Century Studies* (Spring 1976) 317–32.

57. Eichner, *Friedrich Schlegel*, pp. 57–8. Schlegel's aphorisms and Goethe's *Faust* are two examples of the relation between 'incompletion', infinite suggestiveness, and 'becoming' in Romantic art.

58. See Alvin Kernan, *The Plot of Satire*, p. 88.

59. Frank Kermode, *The Sense of An Ending: Studies in the Theory of Fiction* (New York: Oxford University Press, 1967) p. 58.

60. M. Eliade, *Cosmos and History: The Myth of the Eternal Return*, trans. Willard R. Trask (New York: Pantheon Books, 1954) p.153.

61. C. R. Beye, *The Iliad, The Odyssey, and the Epic Tradition* (New York: Doubleday, 1966) p. 189.

62. My image is conjured from Byron's description of shallow thinking as 'A sort of *Ignis Fatuus* to the mind' (XI, 27).

63. B. Wilkie, *Romantic Poets and Epic Tradition* (Madison and Milwaukee: University of Wisconsin Press, 1965) pp. 214–15. Wilkie makes an interesting point that behind Juan's legend of never leaving women is a memory of Aeneas's abandonment of Dido, and Hector's farewell to Andromache. He sees all this as part of the poet's attempt to reverse the anti-feminism, implied in one form or another, by almost every traditional epic.

64. M. French, *The Book as World: James Joyce's Ulysses* (Cambridge, Mass.: Harvard University Press, 1976) p. 265.

65. Byron, *Letters and Journals*, VI, p. 99.

66. Ernest J. Lovell, Jr., 'Irony and Image in *Don Juan*', in Clarence D. Thorpe, Carlos Baker and Bennett Weaver (eds), *The Major English*

Romantic Poets, (Carbondale, Illinois: Southern Illinois University Press, 1957) p. 148.

67. French, *Book as World*, p. 265.
68. Boyd, *A Critical Study*, p. 161; Lovell, 'Irony and Image', p. 148; L. Trilling, 'James Joyce in His Letters', *Commentary*, 45, no. 2, p. 53.
69. Robert M. Adams, *Nil: Episodes in the Literary Conquest of Void During the Nineteenth Century* (New York: Oxford University Press, 1966) p. 188.
70. Oliver St John Gogarty, 'Tot Milia Formosarum'; as Mulligan, he is the Denying Spirit of *Ulysses*.

Index

Works cited, except Byron's and Joyce's own, will be found under the author's name.